# SPENSER STUDIES
# VI

# SPENSER
# STUDIES
## A Renaissance
## Poetry Annual
# VI

EDITED BY

*Patrick Cullen* AND *Thomas P. Roche, Jr.*

**AMS PRESS, INC.**
NEW YORK, N.Y.

# SPENSER STUDIES:
## A RENAISSANCE POETRY ANNUAL

*edited by Patrick Cullen and Thomas P. Roche, Jr.*

is published annually by AMS Press, Inc. as a forum for Spenser scholarship and criticism and related Renaissance subjects. Manuscripts must be submitted *in duplicate* and be double-spaced, including notes, which should be grouped at the end and should be prepared according to the format used in this journal. All essay-length manuscripts should enclose an abstract of 100-175 words. They will be returned only if sufficint postage is enclosed (overseas contributors should enclose international reply coupons). One copy of each manuscript should be sent to Thomas P. Roche, Jr., Department of English, Princeton University, Princeton, N. J. 08544 and one copy to Patrick Cullen, 300 West 108th Street, Apt. 8 D, New York, N. Y. 10025.

ISSN 0195-9468
Volume VI, ISBN 0-404-19206-8

For

Hugh Maclean

upon his retirement

> . . . *beloued ouer all,*
> *In whom it seemes, that gentlenesse of spright*
> *And manners mylde were planted naturall.*
>                                   *(FQ, VI.i.2)*

# Contents

Preface
*xiii*

## Was Spenser a Puritan?

JOHN N. KING

*1*

It is inaccurate and anachronistic to label the ecclesiastical eclogues of *The Shepheardes Calender* ("May," "July," and "September") as a manifestation of Puritan zeal. Language that in modern times may seem to have an unorthodox tinge often fell into the broad area of consensus shared by moderate Puritans and English Protestants loyal to the Elizabethan Settlement. Spenser's thought was in alignment with that of the progressive faction led by the Earl of Leicester and Sir Francis Walsingham, and to ignore that Protestant commitment to continuation of church reform both in England and on the Continent flattens the dialectical interplay of the eclogues to one-dimensional tractarian argument. Protestant ideology governs Spenser's use of the language of biblical pastoral, his imitation of the "Chaucerian" tradition of native bucolic satire, the introduction of anagrams and nicknames identifying a circle of reform-minded bishops close to Edmund Grindal, the recently suspended Archbishop of Canterbury, and the narration of fables concerned with religious issues facing the mid-Elizabethan church.

## The Thirsty Deer and the Lord of Life: Some Contexts for *Amoretti* 67–70

ANNE LAKE PRESCOTT

*33*

Spenser's love sonnets, now widely believed to refer to the church calendar, can be shown to have additional ties to the Christian liturgy. The hind of *Amoretti* 67 has many relatives in scripture and in biblical commentary, deer which appear also in the liturgy at the end of Lent, especially in the Sarum rite;

one commentary on Psalm 42 even anticipates Spenser's wording. Spenser was not the first to show a deer giving itself up just before Easter or to follow this immediately with a poem in some way associating the Resurrection with erotic love. Marguerite de Navarre had done the same in a sequence of lyrics with striking parallels to *Amoretti* 67–70. Finally, there may be an indirect liturgical allusion in the number of Spenser's sonnets, for the 1559 prayerbook also has 89 "days" in its set of communion readings.

## 'Beside the shore of siluer streaming Thamesis': Spenser's *Ruiness of Time*

### DEBORAH CARTMELL

### 77

Instead of Du Bellay's *Antiquitez*, it is suggested that Spenser models his *Ruines of Time* on 'Super Flumina,' Psalm 137, the song of the exiles who refuse to sing in Babylonian captivity. Spenser's persona's refusal to sing the lament which Verlame asks of him equates him with the speaker of the 137th Psalm; however, unlike the Psalmist, Spenser's persona ultimately sings in his own voice and the final visions concluding *The Ruines of Time* suggest that he has overcome Verlame's domination and is able to produce an alternative lament to Sir Philip Sidney. Like his much missed patron, Spenser begins his own translation of the Psalms, but the 137th is translated into a contemporary context: *The Ruines of Time* re-enacts the movement from Babylon to Sion or from Marian to Elizabethan England and rather than a poem lamenting the fall of Roman England in the manner of Du Bellay's *Antiquitez*, Spenser's poem ultimately celebrates the English *break* with Rome as foretold by the Psalmist:

> And Babilon, that did'st us waste,
> Thy self shalt one daie wasted be.

## Florimell at Sea: The Action of Grace in *Faerie Queene*, Book III

### PAMELA J. BENSON

### 83

The fisherman's sexual assault on Florimell in *Faerie Queene* III.7 and 8 and her rescue by the lecherous Proteus are presented by Spenser as the result of the direct intervention of Providence and Grace respectively. In both cases God's action is problematic because it puts her in a dangerous situation; however, Florimell is able to withstand Proteus' challenge to her virtue, whereas she clearly would have been defeated by the fisher had Proteus not appeared. The difference in Florimell's response to the sexual challenge of her assailants is due to the action of grace. Just before Florimell enters the fisher's boat, she is determined to commit suicide to escape the witch's rapacious beast. Providence rescues her from this desperate spiritual and physical situation and removes her from her social context only to confront her with male sexuality in its roughest form. This time she abandons self-reliance and calls on God for aid; as a result, grace intervenes and, like an Ovidian god, transforms her. But the metamorphosis is spiritual, not physical, and is due to Florimell's recognition that she is not capable of achieving virtue on her own. Forced to suffer with no way out, not even suicide, Florimell finally asks for help. The outer sign of the efficacy of this prayer is the arrival of Proteus, the inner sign is her ability to withstand his spiritual attacks without fear; she has been changed from a terrified female fleeing male passion to a steadfast lady confidently resisting attack. The spiritual content of this episode explains the strangely tranquil, even humorous, tone of the narrator when describing the fisher's attempt at rape. Protected by Providence, Florimell can be initiated into male sexuality and fecundity without being in any real danger. The intervention of grace in this episode demonstrates that chastity depends on the gift of grace and not on the will of the individual, just as the intervention of grace in the eighth canto of each other book of *The Faerie Queene* indicates the dependence of each other virtue on grace.

## *AXIOCHUS* and the Bower of Bliss: Some Fresh Light on Sources and Authorship

### HAROLD L. WEATHERBY

#### 95

Whether, as Frederick Padelford believed, Spenser translated the 1592 (Pseudo-Platonic) *Axiochus* (attributed by Cuthbert Burbie to "Edw. Spenser") is a question still to be answered. After Padelford published the long missing book and presented his case for Spenser's authorship (in 1934), Bernard Freyd, Marshall Swan, and Celeste Turner Wright argued from strong external evidence that Padelford was mistaken, that the translator was in fact Anthony Munday, and the ascription to Spenser either Burbie's error or Munday's fraudulent attempt to profit from Spenser's popularity. In the *Variorum*, Rudolf Gottfried countered in defense of Padelford with internal evidence—a long list of parallels between the language of *Axiochus* and Spenser's poetry. Gottfried overlooked, however, the most striking resemblance in phrasing—between a description of the climate in Elysium (in *Axiochus*) and the weather in Acrasia's bower in *FQ* II, xii, 51. The similarities both in language and syntax are sufficiently exact as virtually to prove: (1) that if Spenser did not translate the 1592 *Axiochus* he was influenced by it; (2) that the translator of *Axiochus* (if not Spenser presumably Munday) was influenced by *The Faerie Queene*; or (3) that Spenser wrote the translation as well as the poem. Since we cannot date the translation (only its publication), neither of the first two possibilities can be eliminated from consideration. The third, however, seems the most probable, not only because of the traditional ascription but also because in the Bower of Bliss Spenser demonstrates knowledge not only of the 1592 English *Axiochus* but also of the Latin version of the dialogue by Rayanus Welsdalius, on which the English version was based. Spenser's combining peculiarities of both Latin and English phrasing in his poem argues strongly for his having an intimate acquaintance with both—precisely the sort of knowledge of two texts which a translation from one to the other would have afforded him. That the climate of the Bower also seems to echo the original Greek of the passage whereas the 1592 translation manifests no acquaintance with the Greek need not be taken as disproving Spenser's authorship. Padelford argued convincingly for a very early date for the translation, in the 1570s; Spenser could have learned Greek later and compared the original with the Latin and English versions. The stanza in *The Faerie Queene* is best explained as a composite of Welsdalius's Latin, Spenser's (perhaps school-boy English), his mature knowledge of Greek, and of course his equally mature poetic English.

## The Union of Florimell and Marinell: The Triumph of Hearing

### DAVID O. FRANTZ

*115*

The ending of Book IV of *The Faerie Queene* can best be understood in terms of the neoplatonic debate over which sense is more elevated in apprehending beauty, the sense of hearing or the sense of sight. What Spenser gives us at the end of Book IV is a muted, momentary victory for the sense of hearing, for Florimell wins Marinell's love not when he sees her but when he overhears her complaint in Proteus's cave. This victory is fittingly ironic in Florimell's case, since she is one of the females so persistently pursued and assailed for the physical beauty that males see. Florimell and Marinell become exemplars for other lovers, most notably Britomart and Amoret, and their union embodies the three loves of Book IV, love of kindred, lover, and friend. The episode also prepares the reader for further investigation of seeing and hearing in Books V and VI, culminating in Calidore's encounter with Colin Clout on Mt. Acidale, a moment that is both auditory and visionary, enabling us to gain access to the worlds of love, cognition, and art.

## Spenser and Sidney on the *Vaticinium*

### LOUISE SCHLEINER

*129*

Both Spenser and Sidney included the *vaticinium* concept in their thinking about the importance of inspiration in poetic creation. In the *Apology for Poetry* and in *The Shepheardes Calender*'s "October" eclogue, Sidney and

Spenser's glossarist "E. K." both follow Scaliger in fencing off a region of 'higher' from one of 'lower' genres. And both designate as corresponding kinds of poet the *vates* or poet of lofty divine inspiration and the "maker" or "right" poet. But "E. K." and Sidney differ markedly in the number of genres they consider vaticinally inspired (fewer for Sidney) and in their ways of reimporting inspiration into the lower region. "E. K."—and Spenser in the eclogue—follow Scaliger still farther in declaring the "maker" to be inspired by Bacchic power, so that for him as for the *vates* poetic matter is through "enthousiasmus . . . powred into the witte" and "adorned . . . with labour and learning." Sidney, by contrast, pays inspiration a more grudging but therefore notable tribute, imaging it not as a liquid but as a necessary airy force puffing Icarus the "maker" into flight, where he must then rely on skill and rules as he creates a poem.

## 'Some Quirk, Some Subtle Evasion': Legal Subversion in Spencer's *A View of the Present State of Ireland*

DAVID J. BAKER

*147*

Contrary to a recent claim, Spenser's *A View of the Present State of Ireland* was not suppressed by the Privy Council because it revealed the terrorism of official policy in the colony. Instead, official readers suspected this treatise because it exposed the vulnerability of English law to internal manipulation and subversion. Even within the precincts of the courts, the covertly rebellious Irish could exploit the indeterminacies inherent in common law procedure to indetectably evade or reconstrue the "truth" as officials saw it. For Spenser, no solution was possible but the immediate and definitive re-establishment of English law on the ground of absolute royal prerogative. Though later, under James, official hegemony could seem plausible, Spenser's proposal was a desperate denial of the conditions he faced in Ireland, and he offered the *View* to Elizabeth as a last plea for the direct imposition of her transcendent authority.

## Unpublished Letters by Mary Sidney, Countess of Pembroke

MARGARET P. HANNAY

*165*

Four holograph letters by Mary Sidney, Countess of Pembroke, have recently come to light. Overlooked by Frances Young in her 1912 listing of Mary Sidney's correspondence, the basis for subsequent references to her letters, they have never been published. The first is an undated letter written to Robert Devereux, Earl of Essex, on behalf of her husband, Earl of Pembroke, which sheds some light on the tortuous relationship between the two great Welsh lords. It was probably written just prior to Essex's Cadiz expedition in 1596 and may indicate that young William Lord Herbert accompanied Essex on that voyage.

The other three unpublished letters, written in 1603 and 1604, evidence the increasing frustration Mary Sidney felt in her attempts to obtain justice against her former employee Edmund Mathew, who had defied her authority in Cardiff, stolen her jewels, planned the murder of her trusted servant—and yet succeeded in convincing the new king that she was merely an hysterical woman. For recourse, she wrote first to Sir Julius Caesar, Knight of His Majesty's Requests, and then to her son's prospective father-in-law, the Earl of Shrewsbury. These letters clearly establish Mary Sidney's administrative duties in Cardiff, and the difficulties of the widow caught in the town's struggle to abolish the seigneurial hold of the Earls of Pembroke.

Although she was eulogised primarily as "Sidney's sister, Pembroke's mother," those roles were more than they might appear. We have long known that as Sidney's sister, she edited his work, completed his Psalm translation, and encouraged the hagiography which established him as a Protestant martyr. We now know that as Pembroke's mother, she held the castle and borough of Cardiff until his majority, a position which involved this literary woman in struggles with determined advocates of self-rule, and with vandals, pirates, and murderers.

# Index

*191*


# Contents of Previous Volumes

*203*

# Preface

Since its inception, *Spenser Studies* has benefited from the suggestions of its readers and reviewers. In response to these suggestions, we are making the following changes in our editorial policy, effective Volume VII.

1. *Elimination of a maximum length for essays.* Current edititorial policy specifies a 10,000–word cut-off. That policy has already been set aside tacitly since we have published one essay at least three times the stated maximum length. Although we do not intend to publish work of monographic length (that is, work sufficiently long to be published separately), we recognize that there is no reason or magic to justify a commitment to a 10,000–word maximum; and we suspect that a number of prospective authors have material not fitting the customary length of either an essay or a book that they would prefer not cutting up and publishing in different journals and years. We now welcome their submissions.

2. *Gleanings.* This new section in effect also eliminates the minimum cut-off for submission. We are establishing the section at the suggestion of a number of readers, but especially Anne Prescott, who has given it its English name from the "glanes" of French journals. We prefer this name to the more traditional "Notes" because we do not wish to limit ourselves to the format of *English Language Notes* or *Notes and Queries*. Over the years most readers have doubtless made little discoveries or speculations that do not warrant the space of a brief article or even a "note": some

have been left with paragraphs after they had reached the word limit of the *Spenser Encyclopedia*: others have brief addenda or corrigenda to work (theirs or others') published with us or elsewhere; and surely all Spenserians have their marginalia— apercus on obscurities or puzzles in the text, intertextual echoes and foreshadowings, notes on wordplay, and such—that deserve an audience larger than the classroom. These are instances of what we mean by your "gleanings," and we would appreciate your permitting us to see them.

3. *Form*. This new section takes *PMLA*'s *Forum* as a model. We solicit your responses to the essays we publish. Our authors will of course have the right to respond.

These editorial changes are designed to provide structures to encourage openness and play of mind. We hope they will also encourage you to submit to us your reflections on Spenser and sixteenth-century poetry.

JOHN N. KING

# Was Spenser a Puritan?[1]

*A*N ATTEMPT has been mounted recently to revive the notion that
Spenser was a spokesman for Puritan zeal, yet little more is offered
in proof than the circumstantial evidence that the Protestant
pastors in the ecclesiastical satires of *The Shepheardes Calender*
("May," "July," and "September") speak in the "idiom . . . of
Elizabethan Puritan propaganda" that was familiar from the 1560s
vestiarian dispute and the 1570s Admonition controversy. The
"tryfles," "bells," and "babes" cited in Piers' attack on the papist
Fox, which are interpreted by E. K. as the "reliques and ragges of
popish superstition" ("May," ll. 238–240 and gloss), are thus taken
to be well-worn catchwords and clichés from Puritan pamphlets.[2]
Even though Puritans did use such language, it falls nevertheless
into the area of consensus among progressive Protestants who
thought of themselves as "godly" and obedient Christians. When
John Foxe employed similar language and style reflective of biblical ideals and imagery, he was speaking as an establishmentarian
Protestant whose *Book of Martyrs* was available by law in English
cathedrals as a text that supported the Elizabethan Settlement. To
ignore Spenser's zeal as a progressive Protestant in an effort to align
him with a Puritan camp,[3] or Catholic,[4] or Anglican[5] groupings,
imposes upon *The Shepheardes Calender* anachronistic assumptions about the state of Elizabethan religion at the same time that it

flattens the rich dialectical interplay of his eclogues to one-dimensional tractarian argument.

I

There can be little doubt that Spenser's *Shepheardes Calender* articulates many of the "godly" concerns that were matters of deep conviction to his patrons—John Young, Bishop of Rochester; Robert Dudley, Earl of Leicester; and Sir Philip Sidney—during the "Grindalian" era of the late 1570s. For religious leadership they looked to Edmund Grindal, a zealous Protestant who was appointed to the see of Canterbury in early 1576 with the backing of William Cecil, Lord Burghley, and whose religious earnestness represented a throwback to the heyday of reform under Edward VI. Grindal's accession as primate seemed to hold out the possibility of resolving divisions that had emerged among presbyterians, other Puritans, and the religious establishment. Although Grindal shared the commitment of the Puritans to continuing reform of the church, to increased emphasis on preaching, and to the ideal of a learned and humble clergy, he attacked nonconformity; he tried instead "to make presbyterianism unnecessary by reforming the church."[6] Grindal's refusal to execute Queen Elizabeth's order to suppress the "prophesyings" (gatherings of zealous clergy and laity for Bible study and disputation) led to his sequestration by May 1577.

By alluding in the "July" eclogue to the archbishop's disgrace, Spenser reflects the concern of like-minded Protestants that a period of church reform had come to a close. Although his commitment to clerical reform here and in the other ecclesiastical eclogues does address issues of concern to religious purists, the *Calender* offers little if any support for the seventeenth-century tradition that Spenser articulates a Puritan attack on the Elizabethan church settlement. Although the Grindal allusion is daring, pastoral dialogue and disguise furnish Spenser with a means of self-protection and of treating religious and ethical problems without taking sides in factional argument.

A major deficiency in received interpretations of the religious eclogues is the failure to recognize the integration of such ideas into poems that function as literary fictions rather than theological arguments. Because Spenser structures each eclogue as a genuine

dialogue or debate rather than a one-sided ideological formulation, reduction of his artistry to mere argumentation loses sight
of the dramatic interplay and dialectical tension within the various months of the *Calender*.[7] The satirical eclogues attack
"papist" vestiges, but they also call into question forms of extreme Protestant piety and devotion that alienate some of the
rigorist shepherd-pastors from more moderate and humane
forms of conduct and belief. Although the satirical eclogues
possess lively topical interest, their main concern is with broad
issues and programs of public policy rather than with extended
historical allegory concerning individual persons and contemporary events.[8] Political events and motivations remain veiled and
enigmatic in even the most topical sections of the *Calender*,
those stories alluding to Grindal's destruction despite his humility ("July," ll. 215–228) and the Bishop Young's exposure of a
secret papist who was preying on the "flock" of devout Christian
"sheep" ("September," ll. 180–225).

Tudor readers could recognize contemporary religious issues
in the satirical eclogues; yet their topical readings would have applied a frequently used set of types—the shepherds, sheep,
wolves, and foxes of biblical pastoral—to broad Reformation
problems of faith, spiritual regeneration, and salvation. The
moral eclogues call for sincere worship based upon the scriptures, and they attack clerical laxness based upon pride, avarice,
and ignorance. Puritan issues involving ecclesiastical polity and
discipline, clerical vestments, the use of candles, kneeling during
communion, and the playing of music during services are absent
from the text. Spenser himself goes no farther than applying the
gospel model of the primitive church to the broadly progressive
yearning both to eradicate any residual traces of Romanism and
to bring devotional life in line with the predestinarian theology
of grace that was fundamental to the English Reformation.

How should we label this opinion if, indeed, it is justifiable to
label it at all? Anthea Hume speaks as the descendent of a long
line of critics when she calls Spenser a "Puritan." Virgil Whitaker instead finds an "Anglican" mentality. "Protestant" is the
term that Spenser and like-minded Christians would themselves
have used, as does Hume in her book title, although she insists
that he was a "Puritan" at the time of the *Calender*. E. K., for
example, consistently opposes "protestant" to "Catholic,"
"popish," or "papist" in his glosses and notes. If the former term

encompasses the zealously progressive quality of the Protestantism implied in Spenser's religious eclogues, *i.e.*, that it is a
movement devoted to reform in the church establishment, in
society, and in individual devotion, then Spenser and E. K. were
pious Protestants whose thought was in alignment with the Leicester-Walsingham faction and the progressive bishops who were led
by Grindal until the controversy over the prophesyings.

Understanding of Elizabethan Protestantism has undergone
considerable revision since the appearance of the landmark histor-
ies by M. M. Knappen and A. G. Dickens.[9] During Spenser's life-
time a consensus existed among members of the religio-political
establishment on the doctrine and discipline hammered out in the
Elizabethan Compromise. A recent historian demonstrates that
merely "to refer to this strain as 'Calvinism' can be misleading," for
the predestinarian theology of grace of Zwinglian and Rhineland
reformers like Martin Bucer, Pietro Martire Vermigli (Peter
Martyr), and Heinrich Bullinger is at the core of the English Reformation.[10] The Elizabethan Settlement was consistent with almost
any aspect of the Genevan church except ministry and discipline,
but in essence it reaffirms the largely Zwinglian settlement in religion imposed during the reign of the zealously Protestant Edward
VI (1547–1553).[11] The encyclopedic *Common Places* of Peter
Martyr, who had been appointed Regius Professor of Divinity at
Oxford University by King Edward, comes closer to defining the
position of the Elizabethan church than Calvin's *Institutes*.[12]

Recognition of the existence of a formal consensus on the
predestinarian theology of grace does not deny the presence of a
militantly reformist Protestant movement during the first half of
Queen Elizabeth's reign, when sharp lines of contention were
drawn that were to soften by the 1610s. Recent studies show that
a deep cleavage existed during the 1560s and 1570s between a
self-proclaimed "godly" minority and the multitude of the "ungodly," rather than between "Puritan" and "Anglican"
factions.[13] It is inappropriate, moreover, to apply the second pair
of terms to factional religious divisions during the sixteenth and
seventeenth centuries because "Anglicanism" came into being
during the nineteenth century with the High Church Oxford
Movement and Anglo-Catholicism of John Henry Newman.

Because of the extraordinary fluidity and flexibility of the
word "Puritan" and its almost exclusive application during Elizabeth's reign as a stigmatizing term, that epithet tells more

about the social and political dynamics of religious conflict than the beliefs of those under attack. Puritans, for example, could regard as orthodox what Arminians termed Puritan. Tudor Protestantism was an all-embracing body of thought and belief that included conformists and nonconformists, "godly" and "ungodly."[14] The progressive Protestants of the mid-1570s identified themselves with Grindal and placed predestination, election, and religious assurance at the center of daily life and piety. Those having a more formalistic faith tended, on the other hand, to follow the line associated with Grindal's successor, John Whitgift; despite conformity to the Protestant consensus, they failed to make zealous observance a prerequisite for preaching or daily life. In arguing that "'moderate puritan'" best describes the "predominant style current in the Elizabethan church," Peter Lake rejects as a false dichotomy the choice of "*either* a rigidly defined, party-based conflict or opposition, *or* a conflict-free consensus." Inhering in neither criticism of the liturgy and church polity nor in formal consensus, this moderate Puritan position rested in the yearning of zealous believers to separate "the community of the godly . . . from the profane and the ungodly." Vestiges of Roman belief were clearly "ungodly."[15]

This religious schism cut across class lines, drawing together members of the social elite and more humble citizens into a "godly" inner circle that often stood in a special relationship to zealous preachers. Distinctively Protestant belief was never popular, as such, because the great majority conformed to the religious forms established by the prayer book while remaining ignorant or unobservant of the tenets of Protestant faith, Bible teachings, and the everyday practices of piety and devotion. The "godly" comprised an educated elite well versed in Protestant theology, who differed from the many people who were ignorant of or rejected Protestant predestinarianism "for what might be termed popular Pelagianism."[16] Widespread ungodliness and ignorance were encouraged by the absenteeism of non-resident and non-preaching clergy and widespread ministerial ignorance, avarice, and idleness that had survived the Reformation. A large residue of conforming "church papists" survived among both the people and the clergy. The Tudor "Puritan" movement was therefore directed against widespread irreligious behavior and "papistry" that thrived among citizens who were in formal conformity to the Church of England.[17]

II

From their initial publication, Spenser's "moral" eclogues were interpreted as generalized Protestant satire against Roman Catholic abuses. E. K. assumes this in his repeated references to "protestant" and "Catholique" speakers (*e.g.*, the argument of "May"); his comments must have helped to channel early readings of the text. According to William Webbe's *Discourse of English Poetrie* (1586), the "Morall lessons" of the *Calender* include "the commendation of good Pastors, and shame and disprayse of idle and ambitiouse Goteheardes, in the seauenth: the loose and retchlesse lyuing of Popish Prelates, in the ninth. . . ."[18]

Spenser deploys the Foxes and Wolves in the ecclesiastical eclogues as allegorical types for Roman Catholic priests and crypto-Catholic clergy within the Church of England who prey upon an innocent "flock." Thomalin's application of the Parable of the Good Shepherd is no more than an *exemplum* that remains closely aligned with the biblical text (John 10:1–16):

> O blessed sheepe, O shepheard great,
>     that bought his flocke so deare,
> And them did saue with bloudy sweat
>     from Wolues that would them teare.
>                 ("July," ll. 53–56)

Such scriptures are expanded and fictionalized, however, into extended tales that are fully moralized by E. K.'s glosses in "May," where the imagery of biblical pastoral is infused into the Aesopic fable of the Fox and the Kid (originally the Wolf and the Kid), and "September," where Diggon Davie's account of Roffy's watchfulness applies Christ's admonition against "false prophetes, which come to you in shepes clothing, but inwardely they are rauening wolues" (Matt. 7:15).

Spenser's conversion of the Wolf into a Fox in "May" alludes to William Turner's satirical conceit that the Wolves who could prey openly during a Roman Catholic regime conceal themselves as covert Foxes under Protestant monarchs. Elizabethan Puritans employed the same symbolism, which was widely known through the Protestant animal fables of Turner and John Bale. This imagery was adapted to the 1560s vestiarian controversy when Anthony Gilby gave a Puritan twist to one of

Turner's dialogues by adding an attack on "popish" vestments as
a preface. A contemporary dialogue "of square caps and certain
abundant vestures" has the identical thrust (Bodleian Library,
MS Tanner 79, fol. 16). Nevertheless Gilby's adaptation is the
sole Elizabethan edition of these evangelical allegories out of the
total of six that appeared in print.[19] The imagery of Romish
Wolves and Foxes in the satirical hunting-dialogues of Turner
and Bale was applied to the broad outlines of Reformation controversy during the reigns of Henry VIII, Edward VI, and Mary
Tudor; these works predate by ten to twenty years the first stir-
rings of a Puritan movement.[20]

The appearance of the Fox in *Mother Hubberds Tale* should
come as no surprise because Spenser evidently thinks of the beast
fable as a satirical genre. His description of that work as "hauing
long sithens [been] composed in the raw conceipt of my youth"
in his 1591 preface and the prominence in it of ecclesiastical allegory underscore its close connection to the *Calender*. The variety of disguises assumed by the hypocritical Fox of *The Tale*
(clerk, courtier, minister, lawyer, broker, farmer) makes it difficult, however, to reduce that role to a stock Puritan type for a
crypto-papist cleric. On the contrary, the Priest's recommenda-
tion that the Fox "fashion eke a godly zeale" in order to curry
favor with a noble patron of "a zealous disposition" (ll. 491–493)
sounds very much like a slap against hypocritical Puritans. It
makes little sense to claim further that E. K., probably from cau-
tion, veils Puritan hostility to semi-papists by referring instead
to conflict between "two formes of pastoures or Ministers, or
the protestant and the Catholique" in the argument of "May."
Peter Lake reminds us that hatred of "popery" was not a Puritan
monopoly;[21] this was an axiomatic position of the Elizabethan
church.

Puritans could have attempted to impose their own cryptic
readings on Spenser's Wolves and Foxes, but those types are applied with greater ease and fidelity to the literal text as references
to the manifold varieties of error discovered through the Reformation conflict between "true" and "false" churches. One must
remember that E. K. explicitly guides the reader to interpret the
text in terms of the fundamental Reformation division between
England and Rome when he identifies the Fox with "the false
and faithlesse Papistes" (gloss on l. 174) and explains "May" as a
warning that "the protestaunt beware, howe he geueth credit to

the vnfaythfull Catholique" (gloss on l. 304). The recent organization of the Jesuit Mission to England made Catholic priests and laity controversial subjects for Protestant satirical attack during the year of the *Calendar*'s publication.

Topical interpretations of "May" in particular have given great weight to the immediate political context of the *Calender*. One cannot deny that the text appeared about one decade after the emergence of a Puritan faction during the vestiarian controversy and only a few years following the continuation of that dispute by the radical Admonitors. Nevertheless E. K.'s condemnation of the "tryfles" and "merchandise" carried by the false Fox in his peddler's pack and E. K.'s association of them with the "reliques and ragges of popish superstition"—bells, idols, and paxes—allude to commonplace Reformation attacks on Roman superstition ("May," ll. 238–240 and gloss, l. 298). Thomas Cranmer, for example, enumerates the following "Papisticall supersticions and abuses" in the third part of his "Homilie or sermon, of good workes annexed unto faithe":

> . . .as of Beades, of Lady Psalters and Rosaries, of .xv. Oos [fifteen oes], of sainct Bernardes Verses, of sainct Agathes letters, of Purgatory, of Masses satisfactory, of Stacions and Jubilies, of feined Reliques, of halowed Beades, Belles, Breade, Water, Palmes, Candelles, Fire and suche other: of Supersticious fastynges, of Fraternities, of Pardons, with suche lyke marchaundise, whiche were so estemed and abused to the great prejudice of Gods glory and commaundementes. . . . Yea also, vaine invencions, unfruictfull Ceremonies, and ungodly Lawes, Decrees and Counsailes of Rome.

As part of the first *Book of Homilies* (1547) originally issued under Edward VI (1547–53),[22] this sermon was preached under orders from the Crown throughout Queen Elizabeth's reign.

John Foxe, in taking an overview of the entire course of the English Reformation through the first decade of Elizabeth's reign, attributes to the "Romish Church" the "trinkets," "images," and "paultrye" that were suppressed by the iconoclastic statutes promulgated under Edward VI.[23] As a loyal adherent to the royal supremacy in church and state, Foxe sees the Elizabethan Settlement as a return to and fulfillment of the radically Protestant reforms implemented by the queen's late brother. The thoroughly Protestant religious practices embodied in the

*Book of Homilies*, *Book of Common Prayer*, and Forty-two Articles (1553) drawn up by Cranmer as Edward VI's Archbishop of Canterbury remained the same in almost every respect in the prayer book, the official homilies (a second "tome" was added in 1563), and the Thirty-nine Articles mandated by law during the reign of Elizabeth. The Elizabethan prayer book of 1559, for example, as a modification of the second *Book of Common Prayer* (1552), returns to the religious practices in place during the "fifth and sixth year of the reign of King Edward the Sixth."[24]

The negative position taken by Piers on Maying customs reflects the contemporary origins of English Sabbatarianism; yet even this movement to observe Sunday strictly as a day of worship, Bible reading, and rest is broadly Protestant rather than distinctively Puritan in nature. A contemporary petition of Justices of the Peace attacks "enormities of the Saboothe" such as "wakes, fayres, marketts, barebaits, Bulbaits, Ales, maye-games, resortinge to Alehouses in tyme of divyne service, pypinge and dauncinge, huntinge, and all manner of unlawfull gamminge" as vestiges of Roman Catholic practice rather than Protestant abuses.[25] Control of Sunday sports and entertainments would not become the focus of violent controversy until James I promulgated the *Book of Sports* authorizing Sunday recreations considered by many to be sacrilegious.[26] The issue was not firmly identified with the Crown during Spenser's time, because Elizabeth held herself aloof from the argument. The Privy Council did exert control during Sunday services, but it tended to take a lenient position on traditional festivities during the rest of the day so long as a modicum of public order and piety was maintained. Strict Puritans did prefer a twenty-four hour observance, but until very late in Elizabeth's reign Protestant Sabbatarians accepted the government position.[27]

Although sharp factional divisions on Sabbath observances had not yet coalesced by 1579, rigorous Sabbatarians did believe that Sunday entertainment characterized Roman Catholic rather than English Protestant belief. Piers's opponent, Palinode, is associated with the proliferation of holidays and veneration of the saints in the sacred calendar of the Roman church ("May," 11. 15, 310). Elizabethan Sabbatarians emphasized the keeping of the Fourth Commandment rather than the prohibition of Maying, play-going, and other pastimes. Their overwhelming goal was to prevent profanation of Sunday. Rather than being a distinctively Puritan issue, this concern goes back to the origins of the English Reformation; it was shared by many devout Protestants who opposed the secular pastimes and festivities that dominated traditional saints' festivals. (Zealous reformers forgot that works like Robert Mannyng of Brunne's *Handlyng Synne* documented medieval efforts to impose restraints on Sunday celebrations.) Cranmer's original simplification of the church calendar to include only those saints' days substantiated by scriptural testimony was extended by some extremist Puritans, however, into a denial of the validity of all holidays except Sunday. It was in this way that radical Sabbatarians and seventeenth-century New England Puritans justified even the exclusion of Christmas among traditional "Catholic" celebrations. Although Piers echoes the Puritan attack on May games, he is not a Sabbatarian. Instead he cites Algrind as his authority for imposing a higher moral standard on clergy than laity: "But shepheards (as Algrind vsed to say,) / Mought not liue ylike, as men of the laye" ("May," ll. 75–76).[28] Piers's views, like those of Diggon Davie, conform to the Protestant consensus of Elizabethan England.

Opponents of May Day and the drama did fear that public entertainments might encourage idleness and immorality, but even when the opening of the first public theater in 1576 crystallized the attack on the stage, it was grounded not in religious principle or opposition to drama as such, but in allegations concerning the corrupting social effects of the commercial theater.[29] Thus during the reign of Edward VI, Hugh Latimer opposed the failure of parishioners at a rural church to attend his preaching on Robin Hood's Day (May 1) when, according to custom, people had gone out to welcome the Lord and Lady of May, bring in green boughs, and erect Maypoles as the focus for dancing and festivity.[30] Shortly before the *Calender* appeared, John Northbrooke attacked as a papist vestige the avoidance of Sunday services and sermons in order to hunt, play games, and attend plays.[31] John Stockwood preached at Paul's Cross on 24 August 1578 against Sunday performances of plays, bear baiting, and bull baiting,[32] and Thomas Lovell attacked the same pastimes in the *Dialogue between Custom and Veritie concerning the use and abuse of Dauncing and Minstrelsie* (1581). Philip Stubbes's *Anatomie of Abuses* (1583) attacked May games and the governance of a Lord of Misrule as invitations to idolatry and sexual license (sigs. M3ᵛ-4ʳ).

In his railing attack on Maying customs, Piers raises fundamental Protestant questions concerning clerical ignorance and
avarice, and spiritual failures due to hireling shepherds who
"playen, while their flockes be vnfedde":

> Perdie so farre am I from enuie,
> That their fondnesse inly I pitie.
> Those faytours little regarden their charge,
> While they letting their sheepe runne at large. . . .
> (ll. 37–40, 44)

For half a century similar attacks on non-preaching clergy and
the holding of multiple benefices had fueled reformist appeals in
writings like Robert Crowley's apocalyptic satires and Hugh
Latimer's "Sermon on the Plowers." Similarly Roffy's portrait
in "September" as an ever-watchful shepherd who protects his
flock from the depredations of the papist Wolf accords with the
traditional Protestant yearning for a learned and humble clergy
devoted to pastoral care.

Spenser's scripturalism and E. K.'s biases might seem to
weight "May" in favor of Piers's strident attack. Nevertheless
the poet himself takes no explicit stand. Palinode's call for tolerance is not altogether lacking in sympathy, and his position
approaches that of Hobbinol, the idealized shepherd in "September," whose stoical counsel of acceptance and contentment is opposed to the unbending rigorism of Diggon Davie, a visionary
cousin of Piers:

> Ah fon, now by thy losse art taught,
> That seeldome chaunge the better brought.
> Content who liues with tryed state,
> Neede feare no chaunge of frowning fate:
> But who will seeke for vnknowne gayne,
> Oft liues by losse, and leaues with payne.
> (ll. 68–73)

Furthermore Piers's attack on Maying customs is at this time associated with attacks on drama and fiction because they "lie" or

exert a morally corrupting influence. Spenser's evident approval of fiction as it is embodied in the complex interplay of narrative and dramatic structures in the *Calender* is articulated explicitly in the same shepherd's defense of poetic fiction in the October eclogue. The dedication of the *Calender* honors the Protestant progressive Sir Philip Sidney who, soon after its publication, wrote *An Apologie for Poetrie* (composed *ca.* 1583). The open-endedness and ambiguity of "February" suggest that Spenser is willing to frame a complex dialectic in which both speakers and their arguments may contain a mixture of wisdom and folly. His pastoral dialogues are genuine discussions in which speakers disagree and valid arguments may be brought forward on both sides. We need to take seriously E. K.'s interpretation of the May eclogue in Piers's favor, but clearly the shepherd is neither flawless nor a simple mouthpiece for Spenser's religious opinions. The issues that Piers raises are nevertheless standard Protestant concerns of the time.


## III


Spenser adopts a distinctively Protestant stance when he pays homage to the longstanding native tradition of bucolic satire by conflating medieval English devices of characterization and language associated with the simple plowman who implicitly or explicitly represents Christian social ideals—poverty, hard work, piety, and humility—and the shepherd conventions of pastoral satire. Long before the Elizabethan age, the *persona* of the plain-speaking plowman or roaming countryman had evolved into a device for religious and social protest. A distinct sub-genre of Reformation satire emerged during the mid-Tudor period in a prolific series of conventional debates between a bluntly honest Protestant peasant and a Catholic cleric whose ignorant attempts at sophisticated eloquence cannot mask his spiritual ignorance.[33]

Chaucer and the *Piers Plowman* poet (known during the sixteenth century as Robert or William Langland) held out special appeal as models for Protestant authors because of the association of their rustic figures with a relentless search for spiritual truth. Although neither author was a Wyclifite, both were reinterpreted during the mid-Tudor Reformation and Elizabethan age as proto-Protestant reformers who had anticipated later attacks on the Roman church establishment. The mute honesty of Chaucer's Plowman (*General Prologue*, ll. 529–541) represents an extension of the simple gospel ethic of his brother, the Parson, in potent contrast to the unsavory greed of the Monk, Summoner, and Pardoner, who are standard types from medieval anticlerical satire.[34]

*Piers Plowman*, in particular, amalgamated simple colloquial speech and subjective inward piety that was thought compatible with the Protestant assault on formalistic religion. During the sixteenth century, Protestant authors continued in the earlier Lollard tradition of articulating appeals for reform in the voice of a blunt, truth-telling character named Piers Plowman.[35] The extraordinary power of the plowman conceit during this age of religious renewal and reform is manifest in the very popular sermons of Hugh Latimer, who adopts a homely and archaic manner in order to imitate the plain Englishman of the *Piers Plowman* tradition. His 1548 "Sermon on the Plowers," for example, modulates Christ's Parable of the Sower beginning at Luke 8:5 ("He that soweth, the husbandman, the plowman, went forth to sow his seed") into English bucolic tradition as a figure for the fulfillment of clerical vocation. In this analysis of the Protestant ministry, the simple gospel conceit for the divine Word of the Bible as seed, the preacher as plowman, and the people as the sown fields of the Lord unites clergy with laity as common laborers in the Reformation plowland.[36]

Spenser's infusion of the type figure of the bluntly honest peasant into pastoral shepherds such as Thomalin, Piers, and Diggon Davie evokes the primitive Protestant heritage of the Church of England. Spenser aligns the May eclogue, in particular, with the apocryphal Chaucer-Langland tradition through his heavy alliteration and choice of Piers as the narrator for the imbedded fable of the Fox and the Kid, which imitates "Chaucerian" prototypes such as the debate between the Pelican and the Griffin in *The Plowman's Tale*.[37] Piers's attack on worldly clerics exemplifies this nativist voice:

> Some gan to gape for greedie gouernaunce,
> And match them selfe with mighty potentates,
> Louers of Lordship and troublers of states.
>
> (ll. 121–123)

That Renaissance readers recognized a "Chaucerian" tradition of anticlerical satire is suggested by the marginalia of an edition of *The Plowman's Tale* published in 1606 soon after Spenser's death, in which the anonymous editor expands the work's title with an explanatory note: "Shewing by the doctrine and lives of the Romish Clergie, that the Pope is Antichrist and they his Ministers." The tale proper is presented as a "complaint against the pride and covetousnesse of the Cleargie: made no doubt by *Chawcer*, with the rest of the Tales." A marginal gloss interprets the work explicitly as a subtext for Spenser's ecclesiastical eclogues by explaining that "of such shepheards speakes maister *Spencer* in his Kalender" (sig. A3$^v$–4$^r$).

The presence in the *Calender* of the pose of the plain-spoken truth-teller serves, almost in itself, to establish the religious eclogues as Protestant rather than Puritan satire. The "honest" peasant is just about to disappear, totally, from popular religious propaganda, to be replaced by a view of the unlettered country-man as an obstinate opponent of true religion whom the preacher must, if he can, convert. Thomas Nashe transforms Piers Plow-man into a malcontent rogue who rails against vices of which he is himself guilty in *Pierce Penilesse His Supplication to the Divell* (1592). The religion of the common people would in the future be seen as ungodly and anticlerical (*i.e.*, anti-Puritan), in contrast to views of "godly" laity who side with the clergy.

The *locus classicus* for this harsh view of the obdurate laity is *The Countrie Divinitie* (1581)[38] by George Gifford, Sidney's chaplain and deathbed confessor. In this dialogue, the Puritan preacher Zelotes aims to refute the attitudes of Atheos, who is not an atheist in the modern sense of the word, but rather an un-learned believer in witchcraft and other "ungodly" superstitions who nevertheless conforms to the Elizabethan Settlement. Gif-ford's *Sermon upon the Parable of the Sower* (1582) loses touch with the sympathy extended to the common people and vernac-ular speech in Latimer's exposition of the same parable in his "Sermon on the Plowers." Another "exposition of the parable of the Sowers" that is markedly anti-popular in its tendency is *The Difference of Hearers* (1614) by William Harrison, one of the royal preachers in Lancashire. Arthur Dent's often-published *Plaine Mans Path-way to Heaven. Wherein every man may clearly see, whether he shall be saved or damned* (1601) echoes and even quotes Gifford's *Countrie Divinitie* without acknowledgment. Although Dent sets it "forth Dialogue-wise, for the better understanding of the simple," this work also attacks popular lay religion. The unlearned layman Asunetus (α + συνετός. "not intelligent") inverts the values of Spenser's zealous shepherds, for he loathes sermons and remains ignorant of the scriptures. The lines of argument in all of these texts parallel the godly "protestant" beliefs that E. K. attributes, on the other hand, to speakers like Piers and Diggon Davie.

## IV

Most of the personal allusions in *The Shepheardes Calender* refer to "godly" Protestants active in the religious disputes of the 1570s. Accordingly Spenser includes prominent praise of his patrons, the Earl of Leicester and his nephew, Sir Philip Sidney, whose respective names are mentioned in the gloss for "October" (l. 47) and the dedication.[39] The pen name used by Spenser throughout his career, Colin, appears here for the first time, and E. K. identifies Colin's friend Hobbinol as Master Gabriel Harvey ("September," gloss on l. 176). (A decade later Harvey signed the name Hobynoll to a commendatory poem in *The Faerie Queene*.)

Anagrams or nicknames are used, on the other hand, to provide a thin veil for the identities of high-ranking clerics including Edmund Grindal, whose exclusion from royal favor is identified with the destruction of the idealized pastor, Algrind. E. K. insists upon the presence of such private meanings when he mentions sections of the *Calender* with "secret meaning in them" and others "whose speciall purpose and meaning I am not priuie to" (pp. 11–12). It is altogether likely that Spenser wrote most if not all of *The Shepheardes Calender* during his period of service as secretary to Grindal's protégé, John Young, whose recent elevation to the bishopric of Rochester is commemorated in the good shepherd Roffy (or Roffynn), a name derived from *episcopus Roffensis*.[40] Hobbinol's praise of "meeke, wise, and merciable" Roffy identifies him as Colin's patron: "Colin clout I wene be his selfe boye" (September," ll. 174–176). Probable cases can be made for for identifying Thomalin and Diggon Davie with Thomas Cooper, Bishop of Lincoln, and Richard Davies, Bishop of St. David's, both of whom signed a letter to the queen in support of Grindal at the time of his fall. The name of Thomalin's debating opponent in "July," Morrell, is very likely an anagram for John Aylmer, Bishop of London, whose name was spelled variously as Elmer and Elmore. It is unlikely, however, that the name Piers alludes to John Piers, Bishop of Salisbury, because he, like Aylmer, was a religious conservative, and he advanced under John Whitgift's patronage.[41] Surely the most likely allusion is to *Piers Plowman* and the apocryphal texts associated with it.

The daring reference in "July" to Grindal's 1577 suspension from his duties as Archbishop of Canterbury and sequestration by Queen Elizabeth furnishes a powerful reason for the veiling of the names of both author and commentator under the guise of Immerito and E. K. This allusion takes the form of an application of the legendary account of the death of Aeschylus in the tale of the braining of Algrind with a shellfish flung down by a soaring Eagle, evidently the queen. It is important to recognize, however, that neither explanation nor blame is attached to the queen's decision, and Spenser tactfully backs away from open criticism in an acknowledgment of royal fiat. This awareness of both the queen's power and potential ruthlessness complements the epideictic praise of the April eclogue, where Protestant biblical rhetoric is invoked in a more one-sided celebration of Elizabeth and the Tudor dynastic succession.[42]

In line with his character as an idealized shepherd-pastor, Thomalin confers a homiletic coloring on his account of the tragic fall of Algrind, which exemplifies the clerical ideals of humility exemplified by Christ, the Good Shepherd, and the Old Testament types for priesthood, Moses and Aaron. Although the name of Algrind, the lamented shepherd, obviously alludes to Grindal, Thomalin's tale articulates broadly Protestant moral principles rather than anti-government satire. Thomalin himself interprets Algrind's destruction as an *exemplum* concerning the conventional danger of rising high on Fortune's Wheel:

> He is a shepheard great in gree,
>   but hath bene long ypent.
> One daye he sat vpon a hyll,
>   (as now thou wouldest me:
> But I am taught by *Algrins* ill,

to loue the lowe degree.)
(ll. 215–220)

This *de casibus* tragedy recapitulates the biblical archetypes of sin and fall enacted in all of the religious eclogues, and despite its obvious sympathy with Algrind as an individual, he is presented as an example of the general danger of "height."

The queen's original appointment of Grindal through William Cecil's patronage stirred up expectations of continued reform of the ministry and church discipline at a time when a considerable body of zealous Protestants within the Privy Council, at court, and among the bishops favored eradication of continuing vestiges of papistry and widespread Pelagianism, and preachers and pamphleteers were displaying a new awareness of "sin" as it is manifested in theater, dance, maying, dicing, and like activities. The progressive faction associated with Grindal included all of the public figures mentioned in *The Shepheardes Calender* except Aylmer, whose opposition to further reform is apparently mirrored in the unflattering association of Morrell with "proude and ambitious Pastours" ("July," argument). Zealous Protestants fervently supported gospel preaching, cooperation between gentry and clergy, and an evangelical episcopacy devoted to pastoral care rather than prelatic prerogative. Grindal's thinking on these matters was greatly influenced by Martin Bucer, under whom he probably studied when the immigrant reformer received appointment as Regius Professor of Divinity at Cambridge University through the patronage of Edward VI. (Cecil himself began to advance in his public career by virtue of the patronage of Edward's stepmother, Catherine Parr, and the royal uncle and Protector of the Realm, the Duke of Somerset).

Grindal's most able and recent biographer concludes that "it would be inappropriate to label, still less to dismiss, as 'puritan'" continuing Protestant reforms backed by Grindal and the progressives, because their goals "enjoyed solid governmental support." The crisis came in 1576–77 over the "prophesyings," which were gatherings of zealous clergy to expound biblical texts outside the context of the authorized homilies and licensed sermons permitted in Sunday services. They constituted a kind of "'continuing education'" for clergy with deficient training. Although Grindal's commitment to Bible preaching and devoted pastoral care led him, on grounds of conscience, to refuse to transmit the queen's command to suppress the prophesyings, he had also protected those gatherings from "puritan abuse."[43]

This affair blew up at a time when opponents of evangelical Protestantism like Lord Hunsdon and crypto-Catholics such as Sir James Croft opposed powerful progressives like Leicester, Walsingham, and Sidney, who were backing the Protestant cause in the Netherlands against the perceived international peril posed by the Spanish Hapsburgs and other Catholic powers. Soon after Grindal's fall, the Leicester faction opposed the possibility of the queen's marriage to a foreigner, the Duc d'Alençon.[44] Although the progressive Protestant laity who supported further reform evidently sympathized with Grindal, it is equally clear that he had become a "liability" for their cause. The stand that he took embodies not "political puritanism but that sturdy strain in reformed protestantism which rediscovered the difference between religion and politics and for which 'policy' was almost a term of abuse." He lacked the prudent obedience to the royal supremacy that marks the careers of Leicester and Walsingham, and the circle of reform-minded bishops identified in the *Calender*.[45]


V


The major external evidence cited in support of reading the *Calender* as a Puritan text rests upon the assumption that Spenser shared the religious views of 1) the Earl of Leicester; 2) Jan van der Noot, in whose *Theatre for Worldlings* (1569) Spenser's first verse appeared; and 3) Hugh Singleton, the printer of the first edition of *The Shepheardes Calender*.[46] We have already noted why it is over-simple to define the progressive faction led by Leicester as a Puritan clique. Furthermore, while authors certainly aim to please prospective patrons, patrons do not necessarily determine the positions taken by their protégés.[47]

The case of van der Noot is more complex, but surely it is inappropriate to call him a Puritan. He was a zealously Protestant Brabantine, native to Antwerp, who wrote in Flemish and emigrated to London after the invasion of the Netherlands by the Duke of Alva. It seems likely that Spenser prepared his verse translations from Petrarch and du Bellay under commission from van der Noot, who supplied a commentary drawn largely from the scriptures and Protestant commentators. The description of the Whore of Babylon in the "Sonets" drawn from Revelation is charged with the generalized hatred of the the Church of Rome shared by all Protestants rather than a Puritan critique of English religion:

> She seemde with glorie of the scarlet faire,
> And with fine perle and golde puft vp in heart.
> The wine of hooredome in a cup she bare.
> The name of Mysterie writ in hir face.
> The bloud of Martyrs dere were hir delite.
>                               (ll. 20–24)

Despite his antipapal stance, van der Noot's own quietism and pacifism runs against the grain of English Puritanism and the progressive Protestant movement. The millennial prophecies that he gathers out of Bale's *Image of Both Churches* and Bullinger's *In Apocalypsim Iesu Christi* (Basel, 1557) (published in 1561 in a translation entitled *A Hundred Sermons upon the Apocalips*) are characterized instead by an amalgamation of medieval, Lutheran, and Swiss reformed scriptural commentary.[48]

According to long-standing tradition, the man who printed *The Shepheardes Calender*, Hugh Singleton, made his career by printing and publishing work by Puritans,[49] notably a controversial text that appeared in August 1579, less that one year prior to the *Calender*: John Stubbs's *Discoverie of a Gaping Gulf Whereinto England Is Like To Be Swallowed by an other French mariage*.[50] Nevertheless examination of all extant books imprinted by Singleton during his career of forty-five years fails to substantiate this claim.[51] Although he was an appropriate printer for both the *Gaping Gulf* and the *Calender*, his career was not marked by the Puritan partisanship of Robert Waldegrave or Richard Schilders.[52] The available evidence suggests further that although Singleton was chosen as publisher for the *Gulf* and the *Calender*, he exercised no influence over the ideology, poetic content, or organization of the editions. There is, however, every reason to believe that he was probably the "instrument of the Leicester-Walsingham faction."[53]

The activities of Singleton are too diverse to be labelled simply as those of a "Puritan" member of the book trade. In 1548 Singleton began his career as a printer and publisher with translations of Lutheran writings and works written in support of the magisterial reforms implemented under Edward VI. His Edwardian output included John Foxe's first publication, *De Non Plectendis morte adulteris Consultatio*, a treatise opposing capital punishment for adultery that was written under the patronage of the zealously Protestant Duchess of Richmond, as well as translations by Foxe of works by Luther and two Rhineland reformers, Joannes Oecolampadius and Urbanus Regius (*STC* 16983, 18787, and 20847). Going underground during Mary Tudor's effort at counter-reformation, Singleton continued to publish Protestant tracts and translations including writings by Calvin, Bale, Knox, and both English and German Lutheran reformers. Some of these fugitive publications may have been printed for him on the Continent, and their imprints include some satirical colophons including "Rome, before the castel of s. Aungel at the signe of sainct Peter" (*STC* 4392, 1307, 15059.5, 13208, and 13457). Under Queen Elizabeth he continued to publish translations by Continental reformers and non-controversial works of Protestant devotion, including Theodore Beza's *Little Catechism* and some of the frequently published writings of Otto Werdmueller, the German Lutheran, in translations by Miles Coverdale (*STC* 2022–2023.5, 24219, 25250–25250.5, 25253, 25258–25258.5). The Werdmueller translations were first published during the reign of Queen Mary, except for the text of *A Spyrytuall and Moost Precyouse Pearle* that Edward Seymour edited soon after his deposition as Edward VI's Lord Protector. Singleton's output also included a funeral elegy, a tract against enclosures, a translation of a medieval contemplative manual, a handbook of accounting, and regulations that he printed for the City of London.

Circular reasoning lies behind extrapolation from Singleton's "Puritanism" to that attributed to Spenser, because the originator of that view of the publisher's career cites Spenser's alleged Puritanism as one proof of Singleton's views.[54] Singleton, like many other "printers," often functions as a publisher for books printed by one or many undesignated hands. The word "printer" is used loosely at this time to describe the person undertaking to have books printed, and colophons often credit booksellers with books that they only publish. Complicated business arrangements frequently lie behind apparently simple imprints, and it is these circumstances rather than ideological intention that often explain the publication of works like the *Calender* and Stubbs's *Gaping Gulf*.[55] Singleton specialized in publication of texts compatible with the broad consensus of the Elizabethan church. Thus it should come as no surprise to find that hostility to the Roman Church permeates most of his publications, but taken as a group they fail to outline a "Puritan" program of reform.

Although some great printer-publishers like John Day and Richard Tottel commissioned works and collaborated with their authors, many other members of the book trade accepted whatever work came their way in order to make a living. Singleton was notoriously unsuccessful in his career. Because his printing of Stubbs's *Gaping Gulf* was commissioned by William Page, a gentleman who was implicated in the prosecution for that edition, it seems unlikely that the printer had any influence over the content of the text. The Stubbs affair ruined Singleton, who, after giving up his press in 1581–82, continued to publish after his appointment as Printer to the City of London in 1584.[56]

The most recent and thorough bibliographical studies of the *Calender* conclude that Singleton failed even to control decisions concerning the layout and typography, and that Spenser determined the organization of the volume and program for the illustrations, which are integral to the text. Because Singleton had never before produced an illustrated book, he lacked both experience with woodcuts and regular access to the woodcutters who prepared the blocks.[57] It seems unlikely that so impoverished a publisher would volunteer suddenly to undertake the major investment of capital required to produce an extraordinarily well-illustrated text. The woodcuts seem not to have been part of his printing stock, and they went as a unit to John Harrison the Younger, the publisher who commissioned the printing of the four editions of the *Calender* that were the work of four different printers between 1581 and 1597.

## VI

Not until the eve of the English Civil War were Spenser's ecclesiastical eclogues reinterpreted as Puritan anti-prelatical propaganda when Milton argued that it is the prelates of the Church of England against whom "our admired *Spencer* inveighs against, not without some presage of these reforming

times."[58] Milton evidently uses the *Calender* as a model for ecclesiastical satire in his own pastoral elegy, *Lycidas* (1638),
which "by occasion foretells the ruin of our corrupted Clergy
then in their height."[59] Milton's approval of Spenser's satires
suggests that Piers's defense of poetry in "October," ll. 19–20
("*Cuddie*, the prayse is better, then the price, / The glory eke
much greater then the gayne"), may be one exemplar for the first
consolation in *Lycidas*:

> "But not the praise,"
> *Phoebus* repli'd, and touch'd my trembling ears;
> "*Fame* is no plant that grows on mortal soil,
> Nor in the glistering foil
> Set off to th'world, nor in broad rumor lies. . . ."
> (ll. 76–80)

During the Restoration, Henry More reverted to the Tudor
reading of the *Calender* by interpreting "February" not as a Puritan attack, but as a prophecy of how Puritans would suffer in
consequence of their attack on the episcopacy.[60] The modern interpretation of *The Shepheardes Calender* as a Puritan text has
no authority prior to Milton's time, and even he sees it as
*prophetic of* seventeenth-century ideology rather than distinctively Puritan in its own right.

Few have argued that Spenser's mature work in *The Faerie
Queene* is marked by Puritan sentiment, indeed opinion dating
back to his own age identifies him with the conservative attack
on late Elizabethan radicals. Ben Jonson supported this interpretation in conversation with Drummond, when he stated: "that jn
that paper S. W. Raughly had of the Allegories of his Fayrie
Queen by the Blating beast the Puritans were understood by the
false Duessa the Q of Scots."[61] A version of the episode of the
Giant with the Scales (V.ii.29–54) that was issued separately during the Civil War sees Spenser as a royalist opponent of Puritanism.[62]   This view was firmly in place a century later when
Thomas Warton discovered in *The Mutabilitie Cantos* "a satirical stroke against the Puritans, who were a prevailing party in
the age of Queen Elizabeth; and, indeed, our author, from his
profession, had some reason to declare himself their enemy, as
poetry was what they particularly stigmatiz'd, and bitterly in-
veigh'd against."[63]

The recent effort to distinguish between the alleged Puritanism of *The Shepheardes Calender* and the Protestantism of *The Faerie Queene*[64] fails to acknowledge that the latter work was well under way in 1580 when Spenser collaborated with Harvey on *Three Letters*. Harvey's comment on the poetic excellence of Revelation, the model for Spenser's most distinctively Protestant composition, "The Legend of Holiness," suggests that he may well have seen a version of that work within one year of the publication of the *Calender*.[65] Piers's appeal to Cuddie to "abandon then the base and viler clowne" and devote himself to epic verse ("October," ll. 37–42) indicates that Spenser was concerned with *The Faerie Queene* as he wrote his pastoral eclogues. Christopher Marlowe and Abraham Fraunce quoted from a manuscript containing the first two books of the epic that was circulating in London by 1587 or 1588.[66] The chronological break between *The Shepheardes Calender* and *The Faerie Queene* is not as great as it has been made to seem.[67]

All available circumstances identify Spenser, during the period of the late 1570s through the 1590s, as a zealous Protestant. Attempts to align him with a Puritan camp, or Anglican, or Catholic groupings, impose overly reductive or anachronistic assumptions on his work. The work of *The Faerie Queene* is at one with the satirical eclogues of *The Shepheardes Calender* in articulating the progressive Protestantism of his age.

*Bates College*

## NOTES

1. A Huntington Library-NEH Fellowship and an ACLS Grant-in-Aid supported the preparation of the present essay. It is indebted throughout to conversations with James P. Bednarz and Patrick Collinson. Quotations from *The Shepheardes Calender* follow the text in Edmund Spenser, *Works: A Variorum Edition*, ed. E. A. Greenlaw, C. G. Osgood, F. M. Padelford, *et al.*, 10 vols. (Baltimore, Md.: Johns Hopkins University Press, 1932–57), VII, Pt. 1; hereafter cited as *Variorum*. Scriptural texts are from *The Geneva Bible*, facsimile of the 1560 edition intro. Lloyd E. Berry (Madison: University of Wisconsin Press, 1969). Abbreviations and contractions are expanded.

2. Anthea Hume, *Edmund Spenser: Protestant Poet* (Cambridge: Cambridge University Press, 1984), pp. 13–40, esp. pp. 14, 21–23. David Norbrook notes in *Poetry and Politics in the English Renaissance* (London: Routledge and Kegan Paul, 1984), on the other hand, that superficial similarities between Spenser's rhetoric and that of religious radicals "led many later

Puritans to claim him as one of their own" (p. 60). Alan Sinfield's *Literature in Protestant England 1560–1660* (London: Croom Helm, 1983) treats Spenser as a "puritan" in the sense that "puritanism" is a harshly punitive creed denying benevolence, tolerance, and humanity. He does not consider questions of church discipline and polity that are commonly identified with the Elizabethan Puritan movement.

3. Hume adds her voice to the long line of critics who, for more than one century, have read the satirical eclogues as polemical allegory articulating a radical or moderate Puritan position on the religious issues facing mid-Elizabethan England. See the summary in *Variorum*, VII, Pt. 1, 600–609, which cites the following adherents to this tradition: G. L. Craik (1863), J. R. Lowell (1875), C. H. Herford (1895), L. Winstanley (1900), R. E. N. Dodge (1908), E. A. Greenlaw (1911), J. J. Higginson (1912), A. H. Tolman (1918), and W. A. Renwick (1930). See also F. M. Padelford, "Spenser and the Puritan Propaganda," *Modern Philology*, 11 (1913–14), 85–106. R. W. Church's 1879 judgment that Spenser's thought is "very far removed from the iconoclastic temper of the Puritans" issues the solitary dissent during this period. Higginson has been the chief proponent of this view, and his conjectural reading of the text as a Puritan roman à clef in *Spenser's Shepherd's Calender in Relation to Contemporary Affairs* (New York: Columbia University Press, 1912) was a major cause for the reaction against topical interpretation of Spenser's verse in the decades since the *Variorum*. Greenlaw follows in the Higginson tradition of discovering intricate topical allusions to persons and historical events in *Studies in Spenser's Historical Allegory* (Baltimore, Md.: Johns Hopkins University Press, 1932), pp. 104–132.

4. Despite Higginson's excesses, sometimes he is right and his views have remained influential. Paul McLane, for example, follows him in supplying detailed identifications of persons and political events in support of the view that the *Calender* protests Queen Elizabeth's alleged intention of marrying the Catholic Duc d'Alençon, a religio-political problem that did draw lively public interest in the year that Spenser's collection of pastoral eclogues appeared in print. McLane inverts the Puritan interpretation, alleging instead that Spenser has High-Church "Catholic" sympathies in *Spenser's "Shepheardes Calender": A Study in Elizabethan Allegory* (Notre Dame, Ind.: University of Notre Dame Press, 1961), pp. 117—118, *et seq*. See also his argument that "Spenser sometimes adopted Catholic points of view" in "Spenser's Political and Religious Position in the *Shepheardes Calender*," *Journal of English and Germanic Philology*, 49 (1950), 332; and "Spenser and the Primitive Church," *English Language Notes*, 1 (1963), 6–11. For a critique of McLane's position, see Norbrook, *Poetry and Politics*, p. 297, nn. 10–11.

5. The consideration of the doctrine, ritual, and discipline of the Elizabethan Church of England in Virgil Whitaker's *The Religious Basis of Spenser's Thought* (Stanford, Calif.: Stanford University Press, 1950) is the major reassessment of received opinions concerning the "Puritan" Spenser (pp. 7–10, 19–21). Defining Elizabethan Puritans as individuals "who desired an approximation to the Geneva discipline and polity" and "preferred a more rigorous personal piety than the church enjoined" (p. 10), Whitaker finds that the concern with church ritual and ceremonial in Spenser's eclogues represents

objections to the Church of Rome shared in common by Elizabethan Puritans and conservative Anglicans. He argues that the *Calender* reflects the doctrine and ritual promulgated in the Elizabethan Settlement of Religion in 1559 ("The Elizabethan Compromise").

6. Norbrook, *Poetry and Politics*, p. 68.

7. William Nelson comments on the reductivism implicit in an over-simple "identification of the speakers with Protestanism and Catholicism" in *The Poetry of Edmund Spenser: A Study* (New York: Columbia University Press, 1963), p. 46. Patrick Cullen similarly observes that a dialectical pattern is at work within the eclogues in *Spenser, Marvell, and Renaissance Pastoral* (Cambridge, Mass.: Harvard University Press, 1970), pp. 29–32, 54.

8. See David Bevington's correction of uncritical approaches to topical interpretation in *Tudor Drama and Politics: A Critical Approach to Topical Meaning* (Cambridge, Mass.:Harvard University Press, 1968), pp. 5–6, 13, 25–26.

9. *Tudor Puritanism: A Chapter in the History of Idealism* (Chicago, Ill. University of Chicago Press, 1939); *The English Reformation* (London: B. T. Batsford, Ltd., 1964).

10. Dewey D. Wallace, Jr., *Puritans and Predestination: Grace in English Protestant Theology, 1525–1695* (Chapel Hill: University of North Carolina Press, 1982), pp. viii, x–xi, *et seq.* In *Protestant Poetics and the Seventeenth-Century Religious Lyric* (Princeton, N.J.: Princeton University Press, 1979), Barbara K. Lewalski demonstrates the extension of this formal Protestant agreement on theology and devotional life into later poetic theory and practice in a manner that overrides conventional opinion concerning an "Anglican-Puritan divide" (pp. ix, 7–27, and *passim*). For alternative views on the "Calvinism" of the Elizabethan church, see Whitaker, *Religious Basis of Spenser's Thought*, pp. 8–9; and Sinfield, *Literature in Protestant England*, pp.12–13.

11. At that time Cranmer Anglicized most elements of the reformed theology affirmed by the Swiss churches during the 1540s, which was codified by Zwingli's successor, Heinrich Bullinger, in the *Consensus Tigurinus* (1549) and published as *Consensio mutua in re sacramentaria Ministrorum Tigurinae Ecclesiae* (Zurich, 1552; London, 1552). This prepared the way for the definitive consensus on sixteenth-century Protestant belief, Bullinger's Second Helvetic Confession (1566), which was issued in England as *A Confession of Fayth, made by common consent of divers reformed Churches beyonde the Seas* (*ca.* 1568). Andrew Weiner demonstrates the usefulness of this confession in defining the religious views of Sidney, Leicester, and contemporary Protestant progressives in *Sir Philip Sidney and the Poetics of Protestantism: A Study of Contexts* (Minneapolis: University of Minnesota Press, 1978), pp. 8–18, and 192, nn. 24–25.

12. Patrick Collinson observes in "England and International Calvinism, to 1640," forthcoming in *International Calvinism*, ed. Menna Prestwich (Oxford: Clarendon Press, 1985), that "English theologians were as likely to lean on Bullinger of Zurich, Musculus of Bern or Peter Martyr as on Calvin or Beza . . . [and] if we were to identify one author and one book at the centre of theological gravity of the Elizabethan Church it would not be Calvin's *Institutes* but the *Common Places* of Peter Martyr." On the patronage ties of

Continental reformers to the English royal court, see John N. King, *English Reformation Literature: The Tudor Origins of the Protestant Tradition* (Princeton, N.J.: Princeton University Press, 1982), pp. 107, 168, 275, 457, 460. Martyr's closeness to the English establishment is suggested by the initial publication of the posthumous edition of his *Loci Communes* (1576) in London by John Kingston, in what constituted a reversal of the prevailing practice of importing Continental editions of Latin texts or republishing works that had already appeared abroad. Martyr's *Common Places* was closely associated with royal circles when it was "translated and partlie gathered by Anthonie Marten, one of the Sewers of hir Majesties most Honourable Chamber," dedicated to the queen at her "Majesties Court in Greenewich the eight of Maie. 1583," and "allowed according to hir Majesties Injunctions."

13. Patrick Collinson, *The Religion of Protestants: The Church in English Society 1559–1625* (Oxford: Clarendon Press, 1982), p. 194 and chapter 5, *passim*. Peter Lake shares this terminology in *Moderate Puritans and the Elizabethan Church*, (Cambridge: Cambridge University Press, 1982).

14. Patrick Collinson, "A Comment: Concerning the Name Puritan," *Journal of Ecclesiastical History*, 31 (1980), 483–488. Nonetheless Richard Greaves joins many others in continuing to employ the dichotomy of Puritan versus Anglican in *Society and Religion in Elizabethan England* (Minneapolis: University of Minnesota Press, 1981).

15. *Moderate Puritans and the Elizabethan Church*, pp. 279–280, and 281–292, *passim*.

16. Peter Lake, "Calvinism in the English Church, 1570–1635," forthcoming; he agrees with the argument of Collinson's *Religion of Protestants*.

17. Patrick Collinson, "The Church: Religion and Its Manifestations," in *William Shakespeare: His World, His Work, His Influence*, ed. John F. Andrews, 3 vols. (New York: Charles Scribner's Sons, 1985), I, 30–35.

18. G. G. Smith, ed., *Elizabethan Critical Essays*, 2 vols. (Oxford: Clarendon Press, 1904), I, 264.

19. These works are directed specifically against Stephen Gardiner, the conservative Bishop of Winchester much vilified by Protestants, who during the reign of Henry VIII is said to have thwarted religious reform by concealing himself cunningly as a Fox or secret papist only to reveal himself openly as a Roman Wolf during the reign of the Catholic queen, Mary Tudor. When Bale's *Yet a Course at the Romyshe Foxe* (Zurich [*i.e.*, Antwerp], 10 December 1543) appeared under the pseudonym of James Harrison, it imitated Turner's *Huntyng and Fyndyng Out of the Romishe Fox* (Basel [*i.e.*, Bonn], 14 September 1543), which was issued as the work of William Wraghton. Turner later wrote sequels entitled *The Rescuynge of the Romishe Foxe Other Wyse Called the Examination of the Hunter Deuised by Steuen Gardiner* (Winchester [*i.e.*, Bonn], 1545) and *The Huntyng of the Romyshe Vuolfe* (Emden, *ca.* 1555). The second Turner work attacks a reply by the Bishop of Winchester, which is now extant only in the form in which Turner quotes it for purposes of refutation; it was reissued with a new preface by Anthony Gilby under the title, *The Hunting of the Fox and the Wolfe* (London, *ca.* 1565).

20. Anthea Hume's interpretation of these texts as "Puritan" tracts (pp. 21–23) fails to dismiss Harold Stein's observation in "Spenser and William Turner," *Modern Language Notes,* 51 (1936), 350, that it is "misleading" to equate "foxes with High Church Anglicans and wolves with Roman Catholics . . . because Protestants varied greatly in their definitions of essentially Protestant and Romanist practice." For alternative views see Rainer Pineas, "William Turner's Polemical Use of Ecclesiastical History and His Controversy with Stephen Gardiner," *Renaissance Quarterly,* 33 (1980), 599–608; King, *English Reformation Literature,* p. 446; and Norbrook, *Poetry and Politics,* pp. 60–61.

21. *Moderate Puritans,* p. 280.

22. Sig. K1$^r$. Hugh MacLachlan argues in "The Death of Guyon and the *Elizabethan Book of Homilies,*" *(Spenser Studies* 4, Patrick Cullen and Thomas P. Roche, Jr., eds. [New York: AMS Press, 1983], 93–114) that the hero's faint dramatizes the distinction in this sermon between a true, living faith and a dead faith. John N. Wall, Jr., locates the Protestant vision of *The Faerie Queene* in the reformist program of popular religious education that Cranmer incorporated into the church service during Edward VI's reign in "The English Reformation and the Recovery of Christian Community in Spenser's *The Faerie Queen,*" *Studies in Philology,* 80 (1983), 150–156. See also King, *English Reformation Literature,* pp. 122–138.

23. *Actes and Monuments,* 2nd ed., rev. and enlarged, 2 vols. (1570), II, 1483, *et seq.*

24. *The Book of Common Prayer 1559,* ed. John E. Booty (Charlottesville: University Press of Virginia for the Folger Shakespeare Library, 1976), p. 6. See also John N. Wall, Jr., "The 'Book of Homilies' of 1547 and the Continuity of English Humanism in the Sixteenth Century," *Anglican Theological Review,* 58 (1976), 75–87; and John E. Booty, ed., David Siegenthaler, and John N. Wall, Jr., *The Godly Kingdom of Tudor England: Great Books of the English Reformation* (Wilton, Conn.: Morehouse-Barlow, 1981), pp. 13–14, and *passim.*

25. Duke of Sutherland, Ellesmere MS 6299 (*ca.* 1582–89); punctuation added.

26. Kenneth Parker, "The Sabbath in England, 1580–1640," Ph.D. Diss., Cambridge University, 1984.

27. See Peter Milward, *Religious Controversies of the Jacobean Age: A Survey of Printed Sources* (London: Scolar Press, 1978), p. 44.

28. See Norbrook, *Poetry and Politics,* p. 72.

29. William A. Ringler, Jr., "The First Phase of the Elizabethan Attack on the Stage, 1558-1579," *Huntington Library Quarterly,* 5 (1942), 391–418. See also Collinson, *Religion of Protestants,* pp. 146–147, 199–200.

30. *Selected Sermons,* ed. A. G. Chester (Charlottesville: University Press of Virginia for the Folger Shakespeare Library, 1968), p. 105.

31. *Spiritus est vicarius Christi in terra. A Treatise Wherein Dicing, Daunc-*

ing, Vaine Playes or Enterlud[e]s with other idle pastimes etc. commonly used on the Sabboth day, are reproved . . . (ca. 1577), sigs. C4ᵛ, D4ʳ, I2ʳ–4ᵛ

32. E. K. Chambers, *The Elizabethan Stage*, 4 vols. (Oxford: Clarendon Press, 1923), IV, 199–200; see also IV, 231–233, 311.

33. This outburst includes homely works such as *A Godly Dyalogue and Dysputacion betwene Pyers Plowman, and a Popysh Preest* (anonymous, ca.1550) and Luke Shepherd's *John Bon and Mast[er] Person* (1547). Anthony Gilby's *A Pleasaunt Dialogue, betweene a souldior of Barwicke and an English Chaplaine* (1581) is perhaps the latest example of this sub-genre. See King, *English Reformation Literature*, pp. 258–260, 286–287. Norbrook places the *Calender* in the Protestant satiric tradition that looks back to Edwardian prophetic poets like Robert Crowley in *Poetry and Politics*, pp. 59 and 76.

34. Chaucer *Works*, ed. F. N. Robinson, 2nd ed. (Boston: Houghton Mifflin, 1957). Roger S. Loomis concludes in his 1940 essay, "Was Chaucer a Laodicean?" that, despite Chaucer's doctrinal orthodoxy, the clerical portraits in *The Canterbury Tales* align him with reformist views held in common with the Wyclifites; republished in *Chaucer Criticism*, ed. Richard Schoeck and Jerome Taylor, 2 vols. (Notre Dame, Ind.: University of Notre Dame Press, 1960–61), I, 291–310.

35. See King, *English Reformation Literature*, pp. 50–52, 319–339.

36. *Selected Sermons*, pp. 28–31. Robert Kelly argues that Latimer uses Langland as a stylistic model in "Hugh Latimer as Piers Plowman," *Studies in English Literature, 1500–1900*, 17 (1977), 14–15.

37. On the reformist coloration of Spenser's imitation of Chaucer and Langland, see John N. King, "Spenser's *Shepheardes Calender* and Protestant Pastoral Satire," forthcoming in *Harvard English Studies*.

38. The complete title is *A Briefe Discourse of Certaine Points of the Religion, which is among the common sort of Christians, which may be termed the Countrie Divinitie.* See Dewey D. Wallace, Jr., "George Gifford, Puritan Propaganda and Popular Religion in Elizabethan England, "*Sixteenth Century Journal*, 9, No. 1 (1978), 28–38.

39. In "Spenser, Shakespeare, Honor, and Worship, " *Renaissance News*, 14 (1961), 159–161, William A. Ringler, Jr., demonstrates that the recipient of the dedication was changed at the last minute from Leicester to Sidney and, at the same time, that Spenser altered E. K.'s preface prior to publication.

40. 10 April 1579, the date of E. K.'s preface, is the likely *terminus ad quem* for the composition of the *Calender*. Spenser's 1578 appointment by Young first became known with the discovery of an inscription in which Gabriel Harvey noted his receipt of a gift copy of *The Traveiler of Jerome Turler* (1575) from his friend: "Ex dono Edmundi Spenseri, Episcopi Roffensis Secretarii, 1578." Noted by Israel Gollancz in "Spenseriana," *Proceedings of the British Academy*, [3] (1907–08), 103. See also Alexander C. Judson, *A Biographical Sketch of John Young, Bishop of Rochester, with Emphasis on his Relations with Edmund Spenser*, Indiana University Studies, 21, No. 103 (Bloomington, 1934), pp. 17, *et seq.*, and his *Life of Edmund Spenser* in *Variorum*, VIII, 48–53.

41. James P. Bednarz substantiates these identifications in forthcoming articles on Young and Algrind in *The Spenser Encyclopedia*, ed. A. C. Hamilton, *et al.* (Toronto, Ont.: University of Toronto Press). Viola Hulbert observes in "Diggon Davie," *Journal of English and Germanic Philology*, 41 (1942), 349–367, that the use of Welsh dialect in the opening lines of "September" points strongly toward Davies. Hugh McLane's *Spenser's "Shepheardes Calender": A Study in Elizabethan Allegory* supplies a detailed context for the identification of topical allusions, including the suggestion that Thomalin is derived from Cooper's episcopal signature: Thom Lincoln (p. 207; see also pp. 176–187, 190, 207, 216–234). McLane's case for the following identifications is conjectural: Leicester (the Oak), the Earl of Oxford (the Briar), Duc d'Aubigny (the Fox in "May"), James VI of Scotland (the Kid), Edward Dyer (Cuddie), and Fulke Greville (E. K.).

42. L. Staley Johnson comments on the use of Canticles imagery in distinctively Protestant praise of Elizabeth during the 1560s and 1570s in "Elizabeth, Bride and Queen: A Study of Spenser's April Eclogue and the Metaphors of English Protestantism," *Spenser Studies* 2, Patrick Cullen and Thomas P. Roche, Jr., eds. (Pittsburgh, Pa.: University of Pittsburgh Press, 1981), 75–91.

43. Patrick Collinson, "The Downfall of Archbishop Grindal and Its Place in Elizabethan Political and Ecclesiastical History," in his collected papers, *Godly People: Essays on English Protestantism and Puritanism* (London: Hambledon Press, 1983), pp. 375–376, *et seq.* See also his *Elizabethan Puritan Movement* (Berkeley and Los Angeles: University of California Press, 1967), pp. 166–176, 186–188; and *Archbishop Grindal 1519–1583: The Struggle for a Reformed Church* (Berkeley and Los Angeles: University of California Press, 1979), pp. 167–183, 219–252, *passim.*

44. See Weiner, *Sidney and the Poetics of Protestantism*, pp. 18–28.

45. Collinson, "Downfall of Archbishop Grindal," pp. 388–389.

46. Hume, *Protestant Poet*, pp. 6–8.

47. In *Sidney and the Poetics of Protestantism*, Weiner notes of Leicester's patronage of extreme Puritans and Presbyterians that "one could support Puritans fervently in the 1570s without accepting their definition of discipline" (p. 6).

48. *Variorum*, VII, Pt. 2, p. 23. Jan van Dorsten agrees that the *Theatre* "is not a Puritan tract" even though it does "fiercely attack the abuses of the papacy" in *The Radical Arts: First Decade of an Elizabethan Renaissance* (London and Leiden: Sir Thomas Browne Institute, 1970), p. 77. Carl J. Rasmussen argues that van der Noot's prose text furnishes an intrinsically Protestant commentary on Spenser's verse translations in "'Quietnesse of Minde': A *Theatre for Worldlings* as a Protestant Poetics," *Spenser Studies* I, Patrick Cullen and Thomas P. Roche, Jr., eds. (Pittsburgh, Pa.: University of Pittsburgh Press, 1980), pp. 3–27. See also King, *English Reformation Literature*, pp. 445, 448; and Collinson, "England and International Calvinism," forthcoming.

49. *The Shepherd's Calender*, ed. W. L. Renwick (London: Scholartis Press, 1930), p. 168; H. J. Byrom, "Edmund Spenser's First Printer, Hugh Singleton," *Library*, 4th Ser., 14 (1933), 121–156. See also A. F. Scott Pearson,

*Thomas Cartwright and Elizabethan Puritanism, 1535–1603* (Cambridge: Cambridge University Press, 1925), pp. 188–189.

50. Soon after publication in late August or early September 1579, *The Discoverie of a Gaping Gulf* was suppressed by a proclamation dated 27 September. See *Tudor Royal Proclamations*, ed. Paul L. Hughes and James F. Larkin, 3 vols. (New Haven, Conn.: Yale University Press, 1964–69), No. 642. Stubbs was convicted at Westminster on 30 October 1579 and suffered the loss of his right hand on 3 November; he was imprisoned for more than one year. Singleton and his publisher, William Page, were prosecuted at the same time and sentenced to lose their hands; Singleton's penalty was never executed. Shortly after this affair he was appointed as official printer of the City of London. See also *John Stubbs's "Gaping Gulf" with Letters and Other Relevant Documents*, ed. Lloyd E. Berry (Charlottesville: University Press of Virginia for the Folger Shakespeare Library, 1968), pp. xxvi–xxxl; E. Gordon Duff, *A Century of the English Book Trade* (London: Bibliographical Society, 1905), p. 148; and Byrom, "Singleton," pp. 140–141. Ringler demonstrates in "Honor, and Worship" that Spenser revised the preface for *The Shepheardes Calender* after E. K. dated it from London on 10 April 1579 (p. 160). It was published at some point between its entry into the Stationers' Register on 5 December 1579 and the end of the legal year, 24 March 1579/80.

51. These conclusions concerning Singleton's career are derived from *A Short-Title Catalogue of Books Printed in England, Scotland, & Ireland, and of English Books Printed Abroad, 1475–1640*, compiled by A. W. Pollard and G. R. Redgrave, 2nd ed., rev. and enlarged, begun by W. A. Jackson and F. S. Ferguson, completed by Katharine F. Pantzer, Vol. 2 (I–Z) (London: Bibliographical Society, 1976). Miss Pantzer has kindly given access to the proofsheets for vol. 1 (A–H) of the revision and to the reference cards for vol. 3, which will contain chronological and printers' indexes. Hereafter referred to as *STC*.

52. J. Dover Wilson comments in "Richard Schilders and the English Puritans," *Library*, 3rd Ser., 11 (1909–11), 69, that "when the Puritans wished to publish anything dangerous they turned, and turned with confidence, to one or other of these two men." See also Collinson, *English Puritan Movement*, pp. 273–275.

53. Byrom, "First Printer," p. 142.

54. *Ibid*, p. 147. This article follows Edwin A. Greenlaw, "'The Shepheards Calender,'" *PMLA*, 26 (1911), 436–438.

55. See W. W. Greg, *Some Aspects and Problems of London Publishing between 1550 and 1650* (Oxford: Clarendon Press, 1956), p. 83.

56. Byrom, "First Printer," pp. 131–132; see also Stubbs, "*Gaping Gulf*," ed. Berry, pp. xxvi–xxxvi. Singleton was "one of the poorest of London stationers" (Byrom, p. 121).

57. Ruth S. Luborsky, "The Allusive Presentation of *The Shepheardes Calender*," *Spenser Studies* I, Patrick Cullen and Thomas P. Roche, Jr., eds. (Pittsburgh, Pa.: University of Pittsburgh Press, 1980), p. 41; and "The Illustrations to *The Shepheardes Calender*," *Spenser Studies* II, Patrick Cullen and Thomas P. Roche, Jr., eds. (Pittsburgh, Pa. University of Pittsburgh Press,

1981), p. 18 and n. 21. This two-part study digests exhaustive analyses of the printing practices of both Singleton and contemporary publishers of illustrated editions.

58. *Animadversions against Smectymnuus* (1641), in *Complete Prose Works*, ed. Don M. Wolfe, *et al.*, 8 vols. in 10 (New Haven, Conn.: Yale University Press, 1953–82), I, 722.

59. Quoted from *Complete Poems and Major Prose*, ed. Merritt Y. Hughes (New York: Odyssey Press, 1957). See the treatment of the *Calender* as a "general context for *Lycidas*" by Joseph A. Wittreich, Jr., in *Visionary Poetics: Milton's Tradition and His Legacy* (San Marino, Calif.: Huntington Library, 1979), pp. 105–116.

60. *A Modest Enquiry into the Mystery of Iniquity* (1664), pp. 514–515.

61. *Works*, ed. C. H. Herford, Percy Simpson, and Evelyn Simpson, 11 vols. (Oxford: Clarendon Press, 1925–52), I, 137. On the 1617 folio edition of the collected works of Spenser in which Raleigh's wife annotated similar topical allusions for her son, see Walter Oakeshott, "Carew Ralegh's Copy of Spenser," *Library*, 5th Ser., 26 (1971), 1–21. For contemporary identifications of Duessa with Mary Stuart in I.xii.26 and V.ix.38–50, see respectively John Dixon, *The First Commentary on "The Faerie Queene"*, ed. Graham Hough (Stansted, 1964), p. 10; and *Variorum*, V, 244.

62. *The Faerie Leveller: Or King Charles his Leveller descried and deciphered in Queene Elizabeths dayes* (1648).

63. Commentary on *FQ*, VII.vii.35.9, in *Observations on the "Faerie Queene"* (1754), p. 291.

64. Hume, *Protestant Poet*, p. 9.

65. *Variorum*, IX, 471–472.

66. Fraunce quotes *FQ*, II.iv.35, in *The Arcadian Rhetorike* (1588); see William Wells, ed., "Spenser Allusions in the Sixteenth and Seventeenth Centuries," *Studies in Philology*, 68, No. 5 (1971), p. 10. On Marlowe's imitation of I.vii.32 in Part 2 of *Tamburlaine the Great* (1587–88), see Stephen Greenblatt, *Renaissance Self-Fashioning: From More to Shakespeare* (Chicago, Ill.: University of Chicago Press, 1980), pp. 223–224.

67. On Spenser's reduplication in both works of the Protestant royalist iconography that emerged during the reigns of Henry VIII and Edward VI, see John N. King, "The Godly Woman in Elizabethan Iconography," *Renaissance Quarterly*, 38 (1985), 81–83.

ANNE LAKE PRESCOTT

# The Thirsty Deer and the Lord of Life: Some Contexts for *Amoretti* 67–70

*A*S THE HUNTSMAN of *Amoretti* 67 sits resting in the shade, he may think he is alone with his hounds and the approaching hind. Readers of the poem, however, know that he is accompanied by the ghosts of many deer and hunters past. Two of the most famous hunters, of course, are Petrarch and Wyatt. Less often noted but probably around somewhere is Tasso's "fera gentil," and recently a little attention has gone to the panting hart of Psalm 42. I would like to examine the relevance of these and other deer, particularly some biblical ones, to the significance of *Amoretti* 67, and also to suggest a hitherto unremarked source or analogue for the lover's unusual situation in this sonnet and for several sonnets that follow it. Finally, I will try to tie these sonnets even more closely than they have been linked so far to the liturgy, both to that of the relatively deer-poor Book of Common Prayer and to the older Sarum rite.

As the notes to the Variorum edition of Spenser demonstrate, it is hard to read *Am.* 67 without recalling Petrarch, so much so that one may well suspect an almost mischievous invitation to compare the successful courtship of Elizabeth Boyle to the disasters and losses in the *Rime*. Petrarch is left weltering in a weatherbeaten galley charged with forgetfulness (*Rime* 189), but Spenser's lover can with some confidence "descry the happy shore" after "long stormes and tempests sad assay" (*Am.* 63). Petrarch's "candida cerva" eludes him (*Rime* 190), but Spenser's deer is "goodly wonne." After this capture, we may assume that the "sweet warriour" of *Am.* 57 will now give him the "peace" he wants but that Petrarch, like Wyatt after him, cannot find (*Rime* 134). Sounding through the echoes of Petrarch, especially in *Am.* 63 and 67, then, is a certain boastfulness; Petrarch may be among Spenser's poetic progenitors, but the later poet is the more successful lover. Yet despite this possibly playful intertextuality, there remain limitations on the relevance of Petrarch to *Am.* 67. Not only is the hunter a failure, he has every reason to be. As the commentaries of, for example, Gesualdo and Vellutello make clear, the white hind is not merely reluctant but chaste, liberated from enamoured lovers by God and the laws of marriage.[1] The two hinds may be similar in goodness, but the huntsmen differ in their situations.

On several occasions Tasso's "Questa fera gentil" has been cited as Spenser's source.[2] Such a debt would not be surprising, for like the birds in the Bower of Bliss, although presumably with less purely lascivious intentions, the lover in *Amoretti* seems to know Tasso well. There are certainly some parallels between the two poems. Tasso's kindly/noble beast has recently fled among the thorns, brush, and rocks of steep and uncertain paths. But now, its will changed, it wanders modestly and descends to a softer and lower path and, abandoning hardness, makes itself glad and graceful. Henceforth it will smile, says Tasso, and its eyes will shine on its lover. If the lover is so happy now, how will it be when love kisses him with burning pity? Some phrasing anticipates Spenser: *fera gentil* and "gentle deare," *fuggia* and "fly," and *onesta posa* and "mylder looke," if indeed the new mildness in *Am.* 67 is the deer's and not the lover's.[3] Above all, *cangiato voler* is not unlike the "owne goodwill" and "owne will beguyld" of Spenser's hind. Again, however, there are significant differences between Spenser and this "source." Tasso congratualates another man on the animal's change of heart; Spenser speaks in the first person. Tasso has no dogs, no brook, no shade, no binding, and his creature descends whereas Spenser's "returnd the selfe-same way." Most important, there is no indication that the lucky recipient of the beast's favors had despaired or even rested before the animal's desertion of the high thorny path.[4]

Behind Petrarch and Tasso themselves, of course, there is an immense body of literature comparing a relationship to that of hunter and hunted.[5] No one, I imagine, has seen it all, but Renaissance readers would remember the most famous deer. One appears in Horace's lovely reassurance to Chloë, a poem on occasion cited as a source for *Am.* 78 but with a fawn more closely resembling the beguiled and trembling hind of *Am.* 67 observed at a somewhat earlier stage in the process of persuasion. "You avoid me," the lover tells the girl, "like a fawn seeking its timid mother on the pathless mountains, not without vain fear of the breezes and forest; if the coming spring rustles the light leaves or the green lizards disturb the bramble, the fawn trembles in heart and limb. Yet I do not chase you in order to mangle you like a fierce tiger or Gaetulian lion. Cease then at last to follow your mother, now that you are ready (*tempestiva*) for a man."[6] Several words would have struck Spenser's ear: the fawn is filled with *metus* that her pursuer finds *vana*, just what Spenser's lover tells his own quarry elsewhere in the sequence, and because of this fearfulness, like Spenser's deer, it trembles (*tremit*); furthermore, the maturing fawn is *tempestiva*, anticipating one of Spenser's favorite words: timely (and perhaps recalling to him the whole complex of *tempus, tempestas, temperantia* and "goodly temperature" so basic to Book II of *The Faerie Queene*).

Buried in Horace's seductive mildness, however, and in Tasso's man to man congratulation as well, is an unspoken implication. Horace says he has no desire to mangle the fawn, but just what *does* one normally do with a captured deer if one does not want to provide it with a diamond collar? The hunting imagery hints at an almost inevitable anxiety about captivity and dismemberment; deer are not wrong to tremble, even if, like Amoret after her rescue from Busyrane, they later discover that they are, if no longer intact, then not so severely hurt that their wound will not close (*FQ* III.12.38). In other words, the ancient metaphor touches on one of *Amoretti*'s major themes, a feminine fear of imprisonment and wounding that must be put by when it is timely to do so. Indeed, the hunt in *Am.* 67 may itself be "timely," because the capture, death, or even sighting of a deer has often meant a new beginning, a necessary or desirable change in relationships. Such references to deer at moments of transition can be unhappy. When Vergil compares Dido to a pierced hind wandering in anguish through the city (*Aeneid* IV

66–73), he indicates something about the cost of refounding a
dysnasty. For Aeneas, and in this tragic division he differs from
many other heroes, the striken deer and the Italic shores are altogether different quarries. The doe herself finds just what many
hunted animals fear—death—and in Italy the hero will again
have trouble with deer when the killing of a pet fawn starts a war
between the natives and the Trojans, a savagery once more associating empire with blood and sorrow.[8]

Many deer legends, it has been pointed out, have a deep and
archaic connection with the foundation of cities, churches, em-
pires, and dynasties, although the deer seldom suffer as much as
Dido or Silvia's fawn.[9] Stories of Caesar's long-lived and col-
lared deer, the cruciferous deer of saints like Eustace, the deer-
chase leading to sovereignty in Celtic legend, the deer associated
with the beginnings of cities, even the deer who guide Charlemagne or Roland to places of crossing or safety—all tie the establishment or attaining of something new (religious or political) to
a creature whose pursuit nonetheless normally involves pain and
exhaustion. Within the endearing sweetness of *Am.* 67's pastoral
repose, in other words, hide disturbing recognitions of potential
violence and the at least symbolic death involved in any transition from an old to a new life. Acteon, after all, learned from his
own transformation what hounds do to deer, although in at least
one esoteric reading of the story his distribution into a multipli-
city of canine stomachs may be seen as the bliss of mystical disso-
lution into the divine.[10] When Scudamor leads Amoret out of the
Temple of Cupid in *FQ* IV.10.55, her hand trembles in his like a
"warie Hynd" gone to soil (*i.e.* hiding from the dogs in shallow
water; the lover himself is the deer seeking soil in *FQ* III. 12. 44,
1590, but he does not tremble). Scudamor's behavior as a lover
and husband is not beyond reproach, and Amoret may have
more to worry about than the beloved in *Am.* 67, but even the
latter still shivers some at the prospect of what comes next. At
least she is in her weary hunter's charge, not torn by his irrational
dogs, an important consideration for any female meditating
surrender. So too, in a possibly relevant poem by the Petrarchist
sonneteer Sàsso, Acteon offers to submit to Diana, preferring to
die directly at the hands of the goddess.[11].

By the time Spenser wrote *Am.* 67, then, there was not only a
vast herd of classical and medieval deer for a later poet to chase

FIGURE 1. The loving hind of Proverbs 5.19, from the title-page of Thomas Churchyard's *Discourse* (1578). Courtesy of The Henry E. Huntington Library and Art Gallery. San Marino, California.

FIGURE 2. From Valerianus' *Hieroglyphica* (Lyons, 1615). The thirsty deer of Psalm 42 finds God in the water's reflection. Note the double implication: first, that like a good Christian the deer sees Christ in the living waters of Scripture and, second, that the scriptural deer reveals his allegorical significance to us (even as he "reads" or contemplates) through the artist's indication of his two-fold nature. As in patristic commentary and after, the deer *sees* Christ or *is* Christ or both. Courtesy of The Newberry Library, Chicago.

FIGURE 3. David recites Psalm 42 as a deer enacts its part in the opening simile. From Geoffrey Whitney's *Choice of Emblemes* (1586). By permission the Houghton Library, Harvard University.

but considerable ambivalence available as well, ironies and energies generated by the situation of hunter and hunted, man and beast, love as pursuit and love as captivity or destruction. These complexities, furthermore, work as well in religious poetry as in amatory. So, needless to say, Renaissance poetry is also crowded with deer, sometimes indicating the poet and sometimes the object of his desire. Puns on serf/cerf encouraged such poetry in France, and puns on deer/dear or hart/heart proliferated so in England that sometimes it is difficult to know if the author intends his metaphor as anatomical imagery, hunting allegory, or both. Thus Thomas Lodge cries out, "Triumphant eies, why beare you Armes, / Against a hart that thinks no harmes. / A hart alreadie quite appalde, / A hart that yeelds, and is enthrald."[12] If a hunting poem of sorts, there is a certain kinship with *Am*. 67, although yielding deer are not impossible to find elsewhere. Tasso's "fera gentil" condescends to love and one medieval hunting poem ends by begging the deer to grow tame. Closer to home, George Gascoigne, a self-confessed failure at shooting all sorts of game from legal studies to courtly place, manages to hit a doe standing quietly in front of him, an allegorical doe sent by Jehova for his moral and satirical instruction.[13]

Among these hundreds of hunting poems there may be several in which the hunter chases the deer with dogs, gives up, sits down by water to rest, and then finds the deer comes to him to be bound. It would be rash to think that no one during all the centuries from Horace's *tempestiva* trembling fawn to the pleading poetical stag in Gascoigne's *Noble arte of venerie* (1575; sigs. I4$^v$–5) thought of such a variation on the more usual images of escaped deer and captured deer. So far, however, I have found only one poem besides Spenser's that contains all these elements. There are major differences: this poem is explicitly religious, eleven stanzas long, and not so much the story of successful capture as the anticipation of one now that the hunter is initiated into evangelical wisdom. Nevertheless, the lyric is remarkably relevant to Spenser in a number of important ways. Either Spenser knew this lyric, which is intriguing, or two Renaissance poets independently arrived at a similar conceit with similar religious implications embedded in a similar series of poems with seasonal and liturgical significance—and that is intriguing too.

The poem is the sixth lyric in the *Chansons spirituelles* (1547) of Marguerite de Navarre. Although it is long and available in a good modern edition, I give it here for the convenience of Spenserians:

1. Un jeune Veneur demandoit
A une femme heureuse etsage,
Si la chasse qu'il prétendoit
Pourroit trouver, n'en quel Bocage;
Et qu'il avoit bien bon courage
De gaigner ceste venaison
Par douleur, mérite et Raison.
Elle luy a dit: Monseigneur,
De la prendre il est bien saison:
Mais vous estes mauvais chasseur.

2. Elle ne se prend par courir,
Ne pas vouloir d'homme du monde,
Ne pour tourment, ne pour mourir,
Et si ne fault point que l'on fonde
Son salut, fors qu'au Créateur:
Vertu peu vault s'il n'y abonde
Par son Esprit, force et valeur.
Las, vous en seriez possesseur
Si de David aviez la fonde:
Mais vous estes mauvais chasseur.

3. Ce que cherchez est dens le bois,
Où ne va personne infidèle:
C'est l'aspre buysson de la Croix,
Qui est chose au meschant cruelle.
Les bons Veneurs la treuvent belle,
Son tourment leur est vray plaisir;
Or si vous aviez le désir
D'oublier tout pour cest honneur,
Autre bien ne voudriez choisir:
Mais vous estes mauvais chasseur.

4. Lors quand le Veneur l'entendit,
Il mua toute contenance,
Et comme courroucé luy dit:

Vous parlez par grand ignorance;
Il fault que je destourne et lance
Le cerf, et que je coure après;
Et vous me dites par exprès
Qu'il ne s'acquiert par mon labeur.
—Seigneur, le cerf et de vous près,
Mais vous estes mauvais chasseur.

5. S'il vous plaisoit seoir et poser
Dessus le bort d'une fontaine,
Et corps et esprit reposer,
Puisant de l'eau très-vive et saine,
Certes sans y prendre autre peine,
Le cerf viendroit à vous tout droit;
Et pour l'arrester, ne faudroit
Que le retz de vostre humble coeur
Où par Charité se prendroit;
Mais vous estes mauvais chasseur.

6. —Or, ma Dame, je ne croy pas
Que l'on acquière ou bien ou gloire
Sans travailler ne faire un pas,
Seulement par aymer et croire.
De l'eau vive ne veux point boire;
Pour travailler, le vin vault mieux.
La Dame a dit: de Terre et Cieux
Serez Seigneur et possesseur,
Si la Foy vous ouvre les yeux:
Mais vous estes mauvais chasseur.

7. Le cerf est sy humain et doux,
Que si vostre cocur voulez tendre,
Par amour il viendra à vous;
En vous prenant, se lairra prendre:
Et alors vous pourra apprendre
De manger sa chair et son sang
A ceste curée par reng;
Pour estre remplis de douceur
Vous désirs courront à ce blanc;
Mais vous estes mauvais chasseur.

8. En ceste délicate chair
La vostre sera transmuée;
O bien heureux qui peult toucher
A ceste grand teste muée,
A la chair courue et huée,
Mise à mort, rostie pour nous,
Sur la croix pendue à trois cloux!
Hélas, elle est vostre, ô pecheur,
Si vous croyez ces saintz propous:
Mais vous estes mauvais chasseur.


9. Le Veneur entendit la game,
Et descouvrit la Poësie,
Et soudain luy a dit: Ma Dame,
J'abandonne ma fantaisie;
De la Foy mon âme est saisie,
Qui trompe et cor me fait casser,
Colliers, couples et laisses laisser;
Croyant la voix de mon Sauveur,
Autre cerf je ne veux chasser
Pour n'estre plus mauvais chasseur.


10. Empereurs, Roys, Princes, Seigneurs,
A vous ma parole j'adresse;
Vous tous Piqueurs, Chasseurs, Veneurs,
Renoncez travail et destresse,
Dont en lieu de plaisir, tristesse
Vous rapportez le plus souvent.
Las, vostre plaisir n'est que vent;
Laissez comme moy ce malheur:
Autre je suis qu'auparavant
Pour n'estre plus mauvais chasseur.


11. Venez, Veneurs, venez, venez
A la salutaire curée;
A laisser le monde apprenez,
Qui est de si courte durée;
Car charité immesurée

De son Tout vous fait le présent,
Par lequel Rien est fait plaisant,
Remply de divine liqueur:
De moy, je m'y rens à present
Pour n'estre plus mauvais chasseur.[14]

Spenser might have noted several matters here, not least the
shift from a positive to a negative wording in the refrain, the
same device used in his *Epithalamion.* But would he have looked
at so obscure a collection? It would not be surprising. Marguerite
was an important and famous woman, sister of François I, author of the popular *Heptaméron* (which Gabriel Harvey read),
patron of Marot and Rabelais, celebrated by Du Bellay and
Ronsard, and grandmother of the recently triumphant Henri
IV—the Sir Burbon of *FQ* V.xi–xii. Marguerite had encouraged
the belief, not wholly unfounded, that she, the king's mistress
Mme. d'Estampes, and the Cardinal Du Bellay (cousin and em-
ployer of Joachim) formed an English party at the French court,
and her evangelical tendencies, although stopping short of
Protestantism, were so close to what the Sorbonne considered
Lutheranism that one of her early works was briefly banned. The
work in question, the *Miroir de l'âme pécheresse*, was translated
in 1544 by Gloriana herself when she was merely the Lady E-
lizabeth and published several times thereafter.[15] George
Puttenham says of her, "Queenes also have bene knowen
studious, and to write large volumes, as Lady Margaret of
Fraunce, Queene of Navarre, in our time.[16]

The *Chansons* as a whole had much to intrigue a poet like
Spenser. There are thirty-three poems, a good Christological
number, yet some of these pious verses wittily rework popular
lyrics. Chanson 6, for example, parodies an ingeniously obscene
song about a bad hunter who does not know how to chase the
"conin" in a pretty lady's personal forest, hit it right in its moist
middle, and "bien brasser la venoison".[17] Marguerite's Erasmian
piety was intense, but she was no prude. Nor was she reluctant
to describe her longing for God in the sensual terms made available to her (as to Spenser) in the Song of Songs. May God take
her as his wife, she prays; Christ is her "vray amant," and while
she passes the weary hours waiting for her bridegroom she begs
him, "Baisez moy, acolez moy, / Mon Tout en tous." Once

joined to him, she will "se perd et pasme / En son Tout joy-
eusement."[18] The pain of languishing anticipation is less cleverly
worked into the collection's structure than into Spenser's however, and whereas Spenser ends his sequence with anacreontics
about little Cupid, Marguerite ends hers with a noël (it is interesting that each series of poems concludes with images of infancy, the new life). The chief threat during this separation is
not, as in Spenser, venomous tongues, but what Marguerite calls
"cuyder," a belief in one's own virtue, merit, and self-
sufficiency, a false goodness who appears like a hypocrite with
"dévot maintien" and speech of silk, a danger and even an image
found elsewhere in Spenser, of course. "Cuyder" seeks to persuade us that good works can earn us the Bridegroom's embrace;
but to believe this is to join Orgueil's chain of prisoners and to
forget the true "repos"—one of Marguerite's favorite words—
for which the soul aches.[19]

Marguerite's vocabulary is fairly narrow, her symbolic language resonant but repetitive, her allusions chiefly scriptural and
liturgical. If he read the sequence, however, Spenser would have
found pleasant metrical variety and some clever conceits. Certain metaphors parallel his own, such as the siege imagery of
chanson 22 (cf. Am.14), and he might have been especially taken
by chanson 30, which compares the speaker to a thirsty deer, a
ship straining towards harbor, and a captive seeking freedom, all
images found in the Roman liturgy for Good Friday or Easter
Saturday and all relevant to *Amoretti*, particularly as the deer
and ship appear just as the sequence is approaching Easter. Three
poems leap to the eye of any reader of Spenser, not only because
of their similarity to certain Amoretti but because taken together
they acquire a liturgical significance that parallels that of *Am.* 67,
68, and, possibly, 69 and 70.

The first is chanson 6, the deer hunt. The next, chanson 7, is a
ninety-four line Easter poem. Like *Am.* 68 it refers to Christ's
harrowing of Hell and his conquest of death and sin, and it too
ends with an impassioned hope for lover's union: "Je seray
vostre Espoux, vous tous un, mon Espouse: / Venez au vray
repos où sera endormie / Entre mes bras toujours mon Espouse
et amye." The lover who speaks is a pelican, the bird long associated with redemption and cleansing. According to the printer
William Ponsonby, Spenser wrote a now lost poem called "The
dying Pellican," a topic appropriate to the Easter season.[20] Is it

mere coincidence that two poets who described a resting hunter whose deer returns willingly also wrote of dying pelicans? The third, chanson 8, celebrates the new season: "Voicy nouvelle joye," for the dry tree flowers and the soul "devient amoureux."

If Spenser did know this series of poems that moves, like *Am.* 67–70, from a deer's surrender, to Easter victory, to dawn, spring, and love, he must have recognized in it not just a sequence of attractive conceits but a web of scriptural and liturgical allusions, among which the obliging deer is only the most striking. Marguerite's references are fairly obvious because of her explicitly religious matter, but Spenser's sonnets, too, even when primarily secular, have muted biblical echoes particularly audible to readers who take into account recently discovered connections between the sonnet sequence and the church calendar.[21] About *Am.* 68, of course, there can be no doubt. Like Marguerite's pelican poem, it is a brief anthology of scriptural quotations suited to the Easter season. The Harrowing of Hell is never mentioned in the Bible and alluded to only in texts requiring exegetical nudging (*e.g.* Ps. 107: "He broght them out of darknes, and out of the shadowe of death, and brake their bands a sunder"), but many other phrases can be traced to scripture or to its Genevan editors.[22] "Most glorious Lord of lyfe" is from Acts 3.15 ("and killed the Lord of life"), which Spenser had used earlier in *FQ* II. 7. 62, and 3.13 (God "hathe glorified his Sonne") or John 13.31–32. Leading Captivity captive is from Ephes. 4.8 and hence also from Ps. 68, which Paul is quoting. It has not been remarked, I think, that the Geneva gloss on this verse inspired Spenser's second line, "Did'st make thy triumph over death and sin": Christ went "to *triumph* over Satan, *death* and *sinne*, and led them as prisoners and sclaves" (my emphasis). Just before this passage Paul exhorts us to support each other with love, although the end of Spenser's poem also recalls John 13.34–35, 15.12, Ephes. 5.2, and 1 John 4.19. The washing in blood is from Rev. 1.5 and "all lyke deare didst buy," says the Variorum, from the Bishops' Bible: "For ye are dearely bought" (1 Corinth. 6.20). Two psalms with Easter significance also contribute. Ps. 47.5 says "God is gone up with triumph," words the Geneva editors apply to the Resurrection and that may have suggested Spenser's "This joyous day, deare Lord, with joy begin" if he was thinking of the verse as used in the Sarum rite for Ascension Day: *Ascendit deus in jubiliatione*, or in the Edward VI prayerbook: "God is gone up with a mery noyse." Ps. 16, which also refers to "joye," offers the Messianic assurance that "thou wilt not leave my soule in the grave: nether wilt thou suffer thine holie one to se corruption." The next verse, 11, says that with God "are pleasures for evermore," and Spenser's eye may have been caught by the marginal comment: "Where God favoreth, there is perfite felicitie." Verse ("for evermore"), gloss ("felicitie") and context (Easter), I think, lie behind *Am*. 68's "may live for ever in felicity."

The Word quoted with such density of allusion in Spenser's Easter sonnet does not, I think, fall quite silent at the end of the sequence bounded by Ash Wednesday (*Am*. 22) and Easter (*Am*. 68). If Spenser is still remembering his Easter texts in *Am*. 69, furthermore, this reminiscence would help resolve a critical puzzle. The sonnet's vocabulary is close to that which Spenser first used in *The Ruines of Rome*; "anticke," "Trophees," "eternity," "immortall moniment," "posterity," and "spoile" in close proximity, although used by a few Renaissance poets about women (and in Shakespeare's verse about a young man), form a cluster Spenser knew best as ambivalent evocations of Roman or sometimes British glory.[23] There may be ambivalence here, too. Has not the lover, so recently humble and gentle, relapsed into pushiness?[24] Is this the "cuyder" Marguerite feared? And has he not noticed that the lady freely gave herself to him, beguiled by her *own* will and not won, so far as we can see, by labor and toil?

There is no reason Spenser need be consistent, one might reply, for the pleasure of a sonnet sequence is its ingathering of multiple moods and perspectives. The contradiction between the lady's submission and the lover's boastfulness, however, may point to a religious complexity analogous to the psychosexual one. Marguerite's deer poem states explicitly what Spenser's implies: grace and love are unearned (Christ buys us, we cannot buy him), which is why to speak of the successful lover in *Am*. 67 as having become "worthy" is a little off the mark.[25] Yet even if, according to Protestants, we can do no acceptable works without prior faith, God can still congratulate the one to whom he has presumably given that faith, saying "It is wel done good servant and faithful" (Matt. 25.21).

Spenser's two versions of his beloved's capture are not much more contradictory than Christian feeling and experience, whatever the fierce clarities of reformed theology. The lover's juxtaposition of gratitude and pride is, in fact, similar to that in some of the scriptural passages to which Spenser and Marguerite allude in their Easter poems—Ps. 47, Ps. 68, Ephes. 4.8—and in some other related texts. As Marguerite's Pelican puts it, man may be nothing, but when he realizes this then Christ can "En moy le réunis, l'embrasse et l'incorpore" and hence make him partaker in victory. Thus the verses that celebrate Christ's triumph pass that triumph on to us. Ephes. 4.8 says that when God "ascended upon hie" and "led captivitie captive" he "gave giftes unto men." The margin explains that Christ gave his "victorie" over death and sin "as a most precious gifte to his Church." So, too, in 1 Corinth. 15.57, Paul cries, "But thankes be unto God which hathe given us victorie through our Lord Jesus Christ." The top of the page says boldly, "Our victorie." Even Spenser's "happy purchase of my glorious spoile" recalls the "deare didst buy" of *Am.* 68 and perhaps Acts 20.28, in which God has "purchased" the Church. That "purchase" is now ours: in Ephes. 1.14 God has "purchassed" our "inheritance"—"unto the praise of his glorie." So in some sense the lover's claim that this is *his* conquest is not wholly wrong, even if in his pleasure he forgets to mention that his victory is also a gift.

Do these religious echoes reverberate as far as *Am.* 70? Perhaps so. Marguerite's happy chanson 8 welcomes Spring: "voicy le jour" when "L'hyver plein de froid et de pleurs / Est passé" and the new year flowers; the nightingale sings; and the faithful soul, who had trembled hidden in the Law, now sees clearly and falls in love, freed from damnation and drunk with joy at its election; the deadly cross is now a comfort and the soul need no longer lurk at home, for what was dry is now "florissant." Spenser's sonnet, too, celebrates Spring and flowers; the speaker urges the lady to leave her "winters bowre" and since she is "not well awake," he is also asking her to greet new light. For both poets, then, images of sacrifice yield to those of triumph and passionate love and then to new day, new season, flowers, "nouvelle joye" / "joyous time," and love that had been fearful (if not in *Am.* 70 then in earlier sonnets) and will now "les gens hanter" or join Love's "lovely crew." Marguerite has clear scriptural references: to passages like Gal. 3.23 describing the old law as a prison, to speaking in the light (Luke 12.3) or walking in the light (Rev. 21.24, 22.5), and to the Song of Songs ("For beholde, winter is

past: the raine is changed, and is gone away. The flowers appeare
in the earth: the time of the singing of birdes is come," 2.11–12;
the margin reminds us that this means "sinne and error is driven
backe by the comming of Christ which is here described by the
spring time, when all things florish"). Both poems also recall Ps.
104.30: "if thou send forthe thy spirit, thei are created, and thou
renuest the face of the earth," or several passages in Isaiah fore-
telling the day when "the budde of the Lord" (either the Church
or Christ, say the Geneva editors) will be "beautiful and glorious, and the frute of the earth shalbe excellent and pleasant"
(4.2), when Israel "shal florish and growe" (27.6), and when "the
desert and the wildernes shal rejoyce: and the waste grounde shal
be glad and florish as the rose" (35.1; the headnote calls this "the
great joye of them that beleve in Christ" and the "frutes that
followe thereof"; see also Ezek. 17.24).

Read in isolation, *Am.* 69–70 would probably not elicit such
memories, and each sonnet has a secular lineage of its own. Yet
following so hard upon an Easter poem, they may vibrate
sympathetically, so to speak, with what has gone before, even if
they are less insistently scriptural than Marguerite's mélange of
Ps. 104, the Song of Songs, and Isaiah. Like the central temple
scene in *Epithalamion*, *Am.* 68's energies radiate outwards,
alerting us to the analogies and relationships between human and
divine love expressed more metaphorically on either side of the
explicit statement. The Resurrection rends the veil of fable, and
the fictive imagery—deer and moniment/spring—are illuminated by that more direct light.

If this is so, then the thirsty hind of Spenser and the dog-torn
hart of Marguerite should also have biblical relatives, and so they
do. It has been suggested that Spenser's closest scriptural reference is Ps. 42.1, "As the hart braieth for the rivers of water, so
panteth my soule after thee, ô God."[26] I agree that this deer is
important to *Am.* 67, but there is more to be said about it and
about related scriptural *cervidae*. Indeed, certain other texts to
which Marguerite alludes in her deer poem seem relevant here
too, even though they mention no animals. Spenser has no wise
lady (a "Personnification de la Sagesse" as in Prov. 14 and Eccle-
siasticus 14–15, says Marguerite's modern editor), but the juxtaposition of defeated searcher and approaching quarry is not unlike Acts 17.27: we "grope" after God, "though douteles he be
not farre from everie one of us." The brook recalls several

springs such as that of Prov. 5.18 or "the fountaine of living waters" in Jer. 2.13, which the margin calls God's word and contrasts to mere human "invencions, and vaine confidence" (Marguerite's "cuyder").

Several critics have found the deer in *Am.* 67 Christlike, and Marguerite's poem is further indication that they are right—and also support for a reading of the poem that stresses the utterly free nature of the lady's surrender, not the merit, improvement, or psychological development of the lover/speaker.[27] Biblical deer, to be sure, have shifty and multiple identities. Harts in one translation are hinds in another, and it can sometimes be difficult to divide the deer from the goats. Nevertheless, it seems safe to say that incorporated into the deer of *Am.* 67 are the most famous Old Testament harts and hinds, all thought by one or another authority to represent Christ, the Christian, or the Church, and by some to signify more than one of these. Together they form a small family of symbolic creatures who on occasion are pressed *en masse* (and out of context) into exegetical passages of considerable metaphoric intensity. That is to say, the sighting of one deer in a single biblical verse often summons up remembrance of its cousins in other texts. Some of them I have already mentioned: the light-footed deer (hinds in Geneva, harts in Augustine) in Ps. 18 and Ps. 104 and the thirsting deer of Ps. 42. Others who invite study inhabit Proverbs, the Song of Songs, and (more doubtfully) Ps. 22.

Wherever they live, deer have certain well-established habits that explain their usefulness to exegesis, art, and poetry. Even in the Reformation, when biblical commentary had for some time been sobering up after what now seemed its allegorical excesses and was turning more and more to history and philology, the behavior of deer remained well understood.[28] Deer, as almost any reader of classical science, the church fathers, and bestiaries knew well, are thirsty by nature. Their thirst increases after contact with their mortal enemies, serpents, whom they force from their holes with saliva or warm breath and then snuffle up in their nostrils and swallow (either from hatred or as rejuvenating medicine) or trample under foot. Snake-killing can be dangerous and thirsty work; so, filled with venom, deer race to a spring or brook whose waters will refresh and renew them. Deer move quickly, leaping on the hills and rocky places. Although timid, they may be lured by music. Extremely long-lived, they know that to eat dittany will make an arrow fall out. They cross a wide river by swimming in single file, each deer's head resting on the rump of the preceding one; when the leader is exhausted he retires to the rear of the line and the next one takes over. It was not Christian theologians who discovered that deer do these things, but they took advantage of the allegorical possibilities afforded by this particularly compelling chapter in the Book of Nature, and even some Reformation commentary perpetuated the old readings. Luther, for example, agreed that the beloved in the Song of Songs is like a deer because the Word of God leaps from city to city.[29]

Spenser would have come across this deer lore in any number of places, from Pliny to Valerianus, from Hugh of St. Victor to Conrad Gesner. For practical information on how to catch deer, one might consult Gascoigne's *Noble art of venerie*, which also suggests uses for left-over bits of animal; dried deer pizzle, for instance, when powdered and mixed with plantin water, is good for a bloody flux.[30] Furthermore, *The noble art* tells the proper time to hunt each sort of deer; as a hind, the lady of *Am.* 67 is indeed in season, at least if she is "fatte or in good plight." Harts are in season from Midsummer to Holy Cross (Sept.14), and hinds at all other times if they appear healthy (sig. P7ᵛ).

Of all biblical deer the one with the most obvious relevance to Spenser is that in Prov. 5.18–19, although I have not seen the text cited in discussions of the poem: "Let thy fountaine be blessed, and rejoyce with the wife of thy youth. Let her be as the loving hinde and pleasant roe: let her breasts satisfie thee at all times, and delite in her love continually."[31] The Geneva editors say merely that this shows that "God blesseth mariage and curseth whordome," but the loving hind has a richer heritage than this moralizing suggests, for the "cervus amicitiae" of patristic commentary (the creature is a hind in the Vulgate, a hart in Augustine and other fathers) was above all a symbol of Christ or of Christian love and celestial contemplation. God tells us to carry each other's burdens (Gal. 6.2), says Augustine, and deer do just this when crossing a river, so perhaps Solomon was thinking of their habits when he wrote Prov. 5.19 (*PL* 40.80–81). Ambrose calls the deer our lover, Christ (*PL* 14.849–850). The fountain, says Origen, is knowledge and the *cervus*/wife is good doctrine, for the deer signifies contemplation and a love of God that makes us not his servants but his friends. Yet, he says elsewhere, the "cervus amicitiae" is also he who destroyed the serpent who seduced Eve, Christ (*PG* 17.74, 13.171–77). Procopius calls the *cervus*/wife Wisdom, the ancient Word (*PG* 87¹.1266). After such symbolic wealth, it is disappointing to read in works like Thomas Wilcox's *A short yet sound commentarie; on the proverbes of Salomon* (1589) that "these allegories, or metaphores" mean only that we should be loving to wives. Harts, he adds, are known for fondness towards their mates (Wilcox maneuvers the text to stress masculine sentiment, not the wife/hind's own friendliness). The older reading was by no means forgotten, though, and Valerianus cites Eucherius on the hart of friendship as Christ, master of all love and charity.[32]

Still relevant to *Am.* 67 despite their gender are the loving roes and harts of the Song of Songs, symbols of the Bridegroom (*e.g.* 2.9: "My welbeloved is like a roe, or a yong heart"). To marry a deer, as Marguerite's hunter will also do (after he has finished eating it), is to participate in the divine marriage that sanctifies human unions. Needless to say, this hart received much attention in the commentaries. Particularly interesting, because of its implications for *Amoretti*'s sonnets of waiting and separation, is the Geneva gloss to the last verse: "flee away, and be like unto the roe, or to the yong heart upon the mountaines of spices." The editors say the Church asks of Christ that if he leaves he will still be ready "to help them in their troubles."[33] The great answer to this prayer, of course, is Pentecost.

More of a puzzle, but clearly figuring in Marguerite's poem and, I think, in Spenser's, is Ps. 22, the psalm Christ quoted from the cross and which was assumed (with a little help from mistranslation) to foretell the crucifixion. It is said by David speaking for Christ, for as the Geneva headnote puts it, he was "past all hope" but now "recovereth him self from the bottomles pit of tentations and groweth in hope," just as Christ "shulde marvelously, and strangely be dejected and abased, before his Father shulde raise and exalte him againe." David says, "dogges have compassed me" and laments that the wicked have pierced his hands and feet; the note adds, "this was accomplished in Christ."[34] The psalm, assigned in the Sarum Missal for Palm Sunday and in the Edward VI prayerbook for Good Friday, is certainly about a victim, but is it also about a deer? Little cervidological commentary mentions Ps. 22, but St. Jerome says clearly (*PL* 26.931) that this animal is the hart, slayer of serpents, destroyer of poison, and that "nullum alium nisi Christum intelligimus." Richard Sampson's *In priores quinquaginta Psalmos* (1539) says the same, adding that the dogs are bad clergymen. (As a one time close associate of Wolsey, Sampson probably knew what he was talking about, although his own shifts and turns during those difficult years show that he himself was more of a dog than a friendly deer.)

Sampson is led to identify the victim as a deer because he takes the title of the psalm as referring to a "hind of the morning." Some preferred "De susceptione matutina," and Geneva likes "To him that excelleth," although the margin adds, "Or, the hinde of the morning." (Jerome says "Pro cervo matutino," as does Bede; *PL* 26.931, 93.590.) Calvin is unhappy with the title and calls it "darksome"; some have rejected any reference to a literal hind, he says, and because "Chrystes Dignitye could not be avaunced royally inough, onlesse by an allegoricall sense, they transposed the name of hynde unto a sacryfise" (*Commentaries*, trans. A. Golding, 1571). The hind of the morning must be the name of the tune, he says, and twentieth-century scholars are inclined to agree. The fact remains that Spenser knew of an Eastertide psalm thought to concern the hunted Christ and often calling itself a poem about a hind. And, as Bishop Sampson says, "Non absurde, cervo seu cervae, comparatur Christus," for as deer snuffle up serpents and kill them, so likewise Christ killed the serpent when he harrowed Hell and liberated our race "ab illis carceribus," and all this by his own will (sigs. T2$^v$–T7).

Commentators on deer, however, more often cite Ps. 42 and the thirsty hart. True, this creature, too, is probably a hind. Henry Ainsworth argues the point cogently in his *Annotations* (1617, 2nd. ed.) and gives his own less than elegant translation: "As the hind, desirously-brayeth for the streams of waters: so my soule desirously-brayeth unto thee ô God." Hinds, he adds, are more passionate than harts. Earlier translators like Robert Crowley (1549) and Matthew Parker (1567) also knew the animal's likely gender, so Spenser may well have imagined a panting hind. In any case, this deer too was associated with Christ, although it more often represented apostles, saints, the faithful, and penitents.[35] To some commentators the deer is both ourselves and Christ, for Christ as man speaks and acts for us and as his followers we can become him. Like most early exegetes I have read, Augustine is content to equate the deer with the faithful and especially with penitents who have killed the serpents of vice and now run to the waters of baptism and the fountains of life. Let us love each other like deer, he urges, who bear one another's burdens (*PL* 36.464–467). John Chrysostom, whose writing may have influenced *The Faerie Queene*, goes further.[36] In an impassioned meditation of the sort that earned him his name, Chrysostom reverts over and over to this verse. The implied serpents are vices and we too should eat the "intelligible serpent" so as to acquire a holy thirst. After all, we are contracted to God, promising to cherish him more than others and to burn with love. So when in the forum you see silver or golden clothes or other wealth, say to yourself, "Just a little while ago I sang, 'As the hart thirsts . . .'"(*PG* 55.155ff). In other words, the verse is a mnemonic to recall a contract, an engagement; as in the Song of Songs and Prov. 5.19 the deer is our partner in a love affair.

In his own fashion Luther continues this metaphoric pattern. Like Augustine and Jerome, he finds an etymological and mysterious connection between Ps. 42 and the Passion, for the title refers to the "sons of Korah" and, since "Korah" can be read as "baldhead" it anticipates Christ's execution on Calvary, cognate with Latin *calvus*. The whole psalm, he says, is a "sigh of human nature seeking to enter the church of God," but so long as we are outside the Church we cannot speak the word: "Therefore this psalm is ascribed to Christ speaking for mankind," and refers to the exodus from Egypt to the Jordan, from Synagogue to Church, from sin to grace.[37] Calvin's reading leaves behind the ancient fascination with deer symbolism, but he too emphasizes David's longing for the temple. The argument has an odd relevance to *Am.* 67, for Calvin insists that this pastoral scene actually means we should hasten to church, where, indeed, Spenser's lover and lady are soon to be found, certainly in the next sonnet with its liturgical rhythms and eventually in the center of *Epithalamion*. *Am.* 67 is refreshingly rural in imagery, but its implications are not. The point, says Calvin, is to remind us that we are not to live in spiritual isolation, ignoring ceremonies and the congregation: "For he biddeth us not clymb streight up into heaven, but favouring our weaknes, he commeth down neerer untoo us" (*Commentaries*, on what is here verse 2). To Calvin, the deer is David, not the savior himself, but this argument, too,

moves the discouraged human lover towards union with a beloved who comes voluntarily and whose love is not private and
separate but sociable, joining the soul, in the words of *Am*. 70, to
Love's "lovely crew."[38]

One commentary on the psalmist's panting hart seems particularly germane to Spenser: Victorinus Strigelius's often delightful *A proceeding in the harmonie of King Davids harpe*, which
appeared in sections from 1582 to 1598 in the translation of R.
Robinson. The discussion of Ps. 42 (1593) paraphrases the opening verse in words that strikingly anticipate Spenser's own: "*As*
the Hart in *chase* fleeth, and in *long pursute* made *wearie*, doth
most greedily covet and *thirst* after the lively running springs,"
so I thirst not for puddles but for "springs of livelie Water" (my
italics). Standing water is mere philosophical consolation, the
arguments of necessity and virtue; flowing water is curative
evangelical comfort. This consolation is the forgiveness of sin
through Christ, for "The acknowledgement of Gods presence in
calamaties, and the hope of the very last deliveraunce and of
eternall salvation, doo call back languishing soules, as it were
from the jawes of hel, and effectually heale the woundes of the
hart." Sometimes, he adds in commenting on the next verse, we
suppose ourselves abandoned, but God "Sheweth us a gentle and
joyful countenance" through his doctrines and ceremonies, and
"by his Embassadors speaketh familiarly with us, calling and in-
viting us unto everlasting salvation." Let us wait for him.


Strigelius gives his remarks a significant direction, from thirst
for salvation and comfort, to deliverance from Hell, to the anxiety of desertion relieved by the loving "embassy" of messengers.
In other words, he applies the opening verses of Ps. 42 not only
to the Passion but to Pentecost; and rightly so, for the psalm had
long been sung on both Easter Saturday and Whitsun eve, and
was so sung in England until Cranmer's reformation of the
prayer-book confined its special use to the burial service. For the
rest of this essay I will argue, although with some hesitation, that
Spenser, too, relates his deer, and indeed this cluster of sonnets,
to the liturgy, if for the most part less overtly than Marguerite
had done when she created her own filiations between her
chansons and the Roman rite.

This suggestion is not wholly new, but a link between *Am*. 67

and the church calender has been only tentatively proposed and no one, so far as I know, has claimed a liturgical connection for *Am.* 69 or 70. Furthermore, Spenser's calendrical implications and hints have perhaps been investigated too exclusively in terms of the Elizabethan Book of Common Prayer. Spenser must have known the prayer book more or less by heart. Yet even though it seems clear that *Amoretti* is associated somehow with the liturgy, the scriptural allusions that it shares with the Anglican prayerbook are fewer than one might expect. So it is not unreasonable to look as well at the Sarum Missal (readily available to Spenser) and to the first prayerbook of Edward VI. Spenser was no Catholic, and doubtless he agreed with his church's views on ceremonies and on the elements of rigidity, excess, and superstition in the older rite. Yet to a poet, to anyone sensitive to the resonance and energy released by texts structured into a soaring pattern of mutual references and buttressed with reiteration and typological gravity, Sarum's liturgical architecture might seem a good place to visit, even to a Protestant preferring to live in reformed simplicity.[39]

Certain sonnets in the sequence seem at least faintly to recall Sarum. *Am.* 61, correlated by some with Palm Sunday, celebrates the beloved as angel, saint, light, and flowers. As William Johnson says, after making what to my ear are some rather strained comparisons with the prayerbook's readings for that day, Palm Sunday was also called "Flowering Sunday."[40] Whatever actual church practice, the prayerbook has shed the old floral rites, but Spenser's "bud of joy" and "blossome of the morne" recall Sarum's blessing of the flowers and branches, when we are asked to remember the olive leaves of Noah's dove that first announced a world recovered and a journey over (this is suitable, for the forty-day rain and the ship's safe passage fit Sarum's Lenten/Paschal number symbolism and its interrelated recollections of journeys, wanderings, and escapes; not surprisingly, Spenser's own ship reaches safety and "eternall blisse" two sonnets later). Like the Book of Common Prayer's epistle (Isaiah 7) and Gospel (Luke 1) for Lady Day, *Am.* 62 welcomes new life and new light, but the connections are tenuous. Sarum's fragments from Isaiah 45.8 offer a little more: "aperiatur terra et germinet salvatorem."

As these examples make all too obvious, however, attempts at such linkages oversimplify the liturgical context. The Sarum

Missal, and even the Book of Common Prayer, is so rich in *intra*textuality that at the end of each day in the church calendar the reverberating complex of scriptural references merely rotates forward a notch in its emphasis. Anticipation and reiteration are central to the liturgy and to Spenser's sonnets as well. For this reason alone the hunt for direct correspondences may be hopeless. The storm-tossed ship of *Am.* 63 is found in Sarum's Maundy Thursday blessing of the oil as well as in Palm Sunday's celebration. The shiny lady of *Am.* 66 responds to the Passion Sunday prayer, "Emitte lucem tuam" almost two weeks late, and on that same Sunday the dogs of Ps. 22 are already out, if briefly, looking for an animal like the deer of *Am.* 67. This is not to say that certain sonnets have no liturgical referents, only that the connections are more likely to be between two seasons or movements than between one sonnet and one day. From *Am.* 22 and Ash Wednesday, Spenser's sonnets and the prayerbook move through longing and hope, to a series of celebrations involving the beloved's amazing grace and gift of self, a victory, vernal renewal and concord, to a period of waiting. Yet these partial circles, these arcs of the fuller annual rotation which the prayerbook describes and to which *Amoretti* refers, are so complicated by little epicycles of imagery (light, binding, flowers, water, and the like), regressions and foreshadowings, that while the larger similarities are easy to see, plausible specifics are hard to find, as much because of an excess of echoes as because of any dearth.

Sometimes the ground seems a little firmer, to be sure. Spenser's Lenten poem, *Am.* 22, recalls both the Book of Common Prayer and the older rite, as is fitting in a sonnet that naughtily mentions relics, an image, and saint worship. Like Sarum, the Book of Common Prayer's appointed readings have a less idolatrous version of Spenser's sacrificed heart and burnt offering (from Ps. 51), priests around an altar (from Joel 2.17), and averted wrath, although the hope to "apease her ire" may be closer to the Sarum prayers' stress on propitiation and the assuaging of "iracundae tuae." Only in Sarum, however, is there a worshipper "qui meditabitur . . . die ac nocte" (from Ps. 1), whose thoughts attend "day and night" like those of Spenser's lover.[41]

The liturgical connections tighten up somewhat for *Am.* 67, too, although ambiguities remain. William Johnson, who has thought hard about *Amoretti* and the prayer book, says that "There are no parallels between any of the propers for the day and what is contained in the poem. The closest scriptural reference appears in the familiar 'Sicut cervus,'" but he adds that the sonnet "by a remarkable incorporation of liturgics . . . represents the penitents who, during Lent, prepared themselves for acceptance into the body of the Church and who, on Easter eve, were finally baptised." He cites Augustine on the early church custom according to which the catechumens went to the font singing Ps. 42.[42] This is helpful indeed (even when one remembers that a deer *hunt* goes better with Palm Sunday or Good Friday), but Easter eve's use of Ps. 42 was less remote from Spenser's day than Johnson suggests, for, as I have mentioned, the psalm figures prominently in the Sarum Missal for that day and for Pentecost eve. Nor, I think, is it quite right to say, "As the Church accepts the readied Christians, so at this point the lady also quietly and tenderly accepts the now-prepared lover." The panting deer in the liturgy is the accepted one, not the one who accepts, and, as I have said, in much still current deer symbolism the serpent-killing font-seeking hart of Ps. 42 is also Christ, sacrificed for us this season by his own will. The deer can be the accepted penitent or the yielding savior thirsty from slaying vices, or both, but I do not see how it can also be the welcoming Church under these liturgical and metaphorphic circumstances. And Spenser here imagines, as does Marguerite in her own Easter season deer poem, grace and victory coming to us *despite* our lack of deserving, our unpreparedness. For that reason, too, I doubt the lover is the catechumen thirsting for the font. He is just sitting there, tired from fruitless labor.

Spenser might have known one other ancient reason for associating Ps. 42 with Easter eve: according to the Catholic count, this is Ps. 41.[43] The number is wonderfully appropriate because as this ceremony is taking place the forty day fast of Lent is ending, and the prayers and readings also recollect Noah's forty days of rain and the Israelites' forty years in the wilderness; hence the Good Friday prayer that God "famem depellat . . . peregrinantibus reditum, infirmantibus sanitatem, navigantibus portum salutis indulgeat." And Spenser, the forty-year-old lover who has been living under a fantasized planet with (he says in *Am.* 60) a forty-year orbit, is through with his waiting as well, at least for a time, and he too can move on to Easter and the promised land.

The Easter poem, as I have shown, crowds in even more biblical fragments than have been hitherto identified. The relation of *Am.* 68 to the liturgy is, however, more complex than it first appears. The sonnet's rhythms have been rightly compared to those of the Anglican collects, but the "on this day" formula is in fact very rare in the Elizabethan prayerbook, although found in the collect for Whitsun.[44] In this regard, Sarum's chief Easter prayer, ancestor of the Book of Common Prayer's Easter collect, is much closer to the syntactic pattern and content of *Am.* 68, as though Spenser had its shape and rhythm in the back of his mind: "Deus qui hodierna die per unigenitum tuum aeternitatis nobis aditum devicta morte reserasti: vota nostra quae praeveniendo aspiras, etiam adjuvando prosequere." Several prayers later we hear, "Concede nobis famulis tuis ut in resurrectionis eius gaudiis semper vivamus." Combining and condensing these two Easter prayers in effect gives us a structure and even a thought quite like Spenser's: "Lord who on this day didst open for us the gate of eternity, having conquered death (an English equivalent to the Latin ablative absolute), . . . grant that we (concede nobis) may live forever in the felicity of his Resurrection." No prayer I can find in the Book of Common Prayer is as close to Spenser as this, further evidence that whatever his theology he remained moved by the patterns and language of an older time.

Thus *Am.* 68's movement, much of its sentiment, and some of its wording recall the liturgy, especially Sarum. Curiously, however, not one of its scriptural phrases is from readings set for Easter Day in the Book of Common Prayer, although Ps. 16.10–11, which may have generated "live forever in felicity," is appointed for Easter in the first Edward VI prayerbook (words from the same psalm, "Caro mea requiescet in spe," end the Good Friday service in Sarum, an image of mortality resting in hope that adds reasonance to *Epithalamion*'s "So let us rest, sweet love, in hope of this"). The biblical phrases Spenser incorporates certainly refer to Easter, but *liturgically* these are texts associated with the weeks that follow the Resurrection and culminate in Ascension Day. Act 3.15 in all three prayerbooks is set for some time during the week after Easter; 1 Corin. 15.55 with God's (and our) victory is likewise post Easter. Most significantly, Ps. 68 ("captivitie captive") is appointed for Ascension; both Sarum and the first Edward VI prayerbook give

Ps. 47 (God's joyful arising) and the central Ephes. 4.8 to Ascension. What is going on? Is Spenser directing our attention forward, anticipating the great feast day that completes Christ's earthly life? *Am.* 68 is obviously about the Resurrection, but like Marguerite's pelican poem, which in some ways it resembles in content and direction, it foreshadows through allusion the next great feastday in the calendar, day of victory and triumph.

In this regard, furthermore, Spenser's sequence of sonnets follows the movement of the church calendar, for in its secular fashion *Am.* 69 expresses this victorious mood. The vocabulary is drawn largely from Du Bellay and Desportes, but also relevant is Ps. 21, set for Ascension Day in the Book of Common Prayer: "Thou hast given him his hearts desire, and hast not denied him the request of his lippes. . . . His glorie is great in thy salvation: dignitie and honour hast thou layed upon him." (To be sure, Ps. 47, appointed in Sarum and Edward VI, also says that "the shields of the worlde belong to God," a warning not to let victory lead to pride.) And the echoes of the church calendar may linger a while longer, since after the triumph of *Am.* 69 come the flowers and light of *Am.* 70, just as in the church year the next major feast is Whitsun, the day of hope and revival that through the coming of the Holy Spirit confirms and in some sense concludes the earthly events surrounding the redemption. Again, Spenser would have found a precedent in Marguerite's verse; as I have said, the stanzas with which she follows her Easter (and Ascension) poem have recollections of Isaiah, the Song of Songs, and other texts that welcome fertility, joy, and fellowship. The readings in the Protestant prayerbooks have less on renewal and fertility than Sarum, which appoints Isaiah 4 ("the frute of the earth shalbe excellent and pleasant" and the chosen shall "spring up like a bud"), but all three prayerbooks require Ps. 104: "thou renewest the face of the earth." Sarum's processional, a version of "Salva festa dies" echoed several times by Marguerite, exults in flowers, sun, clear sky, spring growth, and painted fields; compare Spenser's Spring, in whose coat "are displayed / All sorts of flowers the which on earth do spring / In goodly colours gloriously arrayd" with Sarum's "vernales . . . opes":"Mollia purpureum pingunt violaria campum prata virent herbis et micat herba comis."[45]

Like the season that finds chief expression in Ascension Day and Whitsun, then, *Am.* 69 and 70 recollect, recapitulate, and

complete the triumphs and renewals of Easter, but like the earlier
sonnets that prepare for Christ's "lesson" of love through erotic
imagery, they disguise these aftershocks of the Resurrection in
metaphor and internalize them in the lover's amatory experience. To point this out is not to suggest modifications of the
symetrical pattern most readers now find in the Amoretti or to
claim that these two sonnets take place on Ascension and
Whitsun the way *Am.* 22, for instance, "happens" on Ash
Wednesday; the two sonnets that follow *Am.* 67 and 68 do,
however, enjoy both seasonal *and liturgical* relevance to their
position in a sequence that makes clear if infrequent reference to
the Christian year.

   There is, moreover, one additional and important piece of evidence that ties *Amorettti* to the liturgy in a general way. So far as
I am aware, no one has pointed out that the number of sonnets in
Spenser's sequence is exactly the same as the number of Sundays
and holy days for which communion collects and readings were
assigned in the reformed prayerbook.[46] The Sundays and holy
days from Advent through Trinity do not correlate by number
with sonnets in Spenser's sequence for at least one obvious reason: some of the forty-seven sonnets from *Am.* 22 to *Am.* 68
must also "count" as ordinary days to give us the central Lenten
pattern. Nor does the sequence's implied narrative, such as it is,
correspond with the church calendar, for the courtship takes
more than one year and ends in a June wedding, although not in
the sequence itself. The period of waiting at the end is not wholly
unlike the end of the church calendar, however, and Spenser refers
to the cold and dark; even his references to slander, common enough
in love poetry, have a parallel in the readings for All Saints. Calen-
dars as gifts to ladies, furthermore, were not unprecedented. Du
Bellay's *Olive* has a Nativity poem near its start and a Good
Friday poem near the end, associating the lady not only with
Christ but specifically with his life in the liturgy.[47] And in 1593
Giles Fletcher had published fifty-two sonnets to "Licia" that
parallel the fifty-two "week"; the sequence contains what one
could call three hundred and sixty-six "days" (1592 was a leap
year and one sonnet has some extra lines to make the numbers
work) together with a pattern of images that suggest increasingly warm and then once more cold weather and thus express not
only the lover's frustration but the lady's solar radiance.[48] Perhaps it amused Spenser to do something similar for Elizabeth

Boyle, although his own poetry has more religious and psychological significance than Fletcher's and more calendrical
specificity than Du Bellay's. He had already made a calendar of
months and was about to give her a calendar of a secular year in
the long lines of *Epithalamion*. Why not press into her lily hands
some happy leaves that form yet one more imitation of the yearly
circle, a sort of engagement ring?

The prayerbook's eighty-nine sets of prayers and readings,
however, take account of fifty-three Sundays, as is required by
that minority of years with an extra Lord's Day. In most years,
of course, there are fifty-two Sundays and thirty-six special
communion days to remember, making eighty-eight; some of
these will coincide, like Epiphany in 1594 and its first Sunday, or
Lady Day and the Monday of Holy Week that year. Fifty-two
Sundays would also be insufficient because Easter's mobility
creates, so to speak, slightly different narratives during its nine-
teen-year cycle, if not in terms of plot then in terms of pacing.
1593/4 has a fairly early Easter, for example, so it skimps on
Sundays after Epiphany and adds one at the end of Trinity to
make fifty-two. Furthermore, the prayerbook's opening list of
lessons for morning and evening prayer services comprises fifty-
five possible Sundays and thirty-three holy days (Ash Wednesday and Holy Week's Monday and Tuesday are omitted) to give
us, again, eighty-eight. The Elizabethan prayerbook, in other
words, contains an opening list of eighty-eight days with lessons
for Matins and Evensong and a long collection of eighty-nine
days with assigned communion readings and collects. Neither
sequence, especially the first, is entirely "real"; for in order to
provide for the calender's annually varying stretches and shrink-
ages, each has too many Sundays for most years (including the
liturgical year 1593/4). Of these two sets of readings, however,
the communion collects and propers form the more important
collection, not only because of the sacrament but also because
they bulk so large in the Prayerbook, taking up more than half of
its pages.

The wavering between eighty-eight and eighty-nine communion services (eighty-nine for possible use, eighty-eight for
actual if sometimes coinciding use in an average year) offers one
additional explanation for Spenser's repetition of *Am.* 35 as *Am.*
83. The repetition, whatever its other purposes or its role in
other numerical structures, converts a total whose number is as-

sociated with a "real" liturgical year (1593/4) of fifty-two
Sundays and sometimes coinciding holy days into one like that
of the usually impossible but necessary calendar of days as given
in the prayerbook. *Am.* 83 thus calls attention to the prayerbook's calendrical ambiguity, for both sequences appear at least
to hover between two numbers, two totals, and if *Am.* 83 is not
in fact quite the same poem as *Am.* 35 because a new context
creates a new text, the same might be said of communion readings omitted during the Epiphany season and used at the end of
the church year. *Am.* 83 thus signals the issue of number and
order; specifically, and in conjunction with Spenser's explicit
references to Ash Wednesday and Easter, it recalls through such
signaling that there are eighty-eight actual communion services
for Sundays and holy days that year (because in one sense there
are only eighty-eight *Amoretti*) and simultaneously reminds us of
the disparity between this pattern and one accomodated to the
exigencies of mortal time (because there are also, after all,
eighty-nine printed sonnets, just as there are eighty-nine sets of
readings in the prayerbook). But what is Spenser's point? Together with any other functions it may have, the repetition
parallels a liturgical wavering between numerical totals that is
necessitated in part by a solar cycle containing one too many
days for a stable number of Sundays from year to year and in part
by Easter's link to a lunar cycle whose mutability is the human
race's own ancient fault—the fault being, of course, the reason
we have Easter. The reappearance of *Am.* 35, in at least this
regard, is not unlike Spenser's numerical manipulations in
*Epithalamion*: it reenacts the imperfections in our fallen world of
time, imperfections for which sexual love and generation offer
some healing consolation and from which divine love redeems
us. [49]

Spenser's *Amoretti* are witty and urbane, often bantering,
playful, and affectionate, never solemn minded. Yet there is no
reason to deny Spenser religious depth and sexual insight as well
as sophisticated charm, and recent critics are surely right to grant
him all these. If I am correct in some of what I have written here,
Spenser composed a sequence that at least on occasion alludes not
only to the reformed prayerbook with its eighty-nine communion days but to the typologically richer Sarum Missal as well.

These scriptural and liturgical allusions, overt in *Am*. 22 and hinted at elsewhere, intensify around *Am*. 68, whose explicitly religious exhortation is flanked by more veiled associations of sexual love with the acts and love of Christ. The deer in whose surrender some readers have recognized Christ's submission to death comes to *Amoretti* from the older liturgy, as well as from classical and Renaissance poetry, either as the animal given to dogs in Ps. 22, recited on Palm Sunday or later on Good Friday in memory of Jesus' returning to Jerusalem to be killed, or as the thirsty hart of Ps. 42, recited on Easter eve to symbolise a burning wish for regeneration—or as both, because the panting hart had long been taken for the savior as well as the saved and equated with other deer who, thanks to their allegorical situation in scripture or their well known behavior in the wild, were also called Christ. Interestingly, some of these deer had recently become better known as females, but nearly all, whatever their gender, served as symbols of a love at once spiritual and erotic and one, in Prov. 5.19, is recommended by Solomon himself as a wife.

Finally, Spenser was not alone in writing of a deer who comes when not chased, and he may well have seen Marguerite de Navarre's similar pattern of paradoxical hunting, Easter victory, invitation to love or marriage, and post-paschal celebration of spring and conviviality. Perhaps Spenser "borrowed" from Marguerite, as mathematical probability and the Pelican speaker would invite one to believe, but to call this "intertextuality" would claim too much. Marguerite was still famous, but her verses were not well enough known to allow the dynamic relationship Spenser could establish with Petrarch, say, or with the Bible and the liturgy. Yet Marguerite's chansons make it even easier to hear the religious overtones of *Am*. 67–70 and to consider Spenser's unusual treatment of the old belief, so often forgotten in all Christian centuries, including our own, but never quite dead, that sexual love can participate in and body forth divine love, that the love that moves the sun and the other stars can move us into each other's arms.

But why a captured deer and not some other pre-Easter symbol? To provide a pastoral moment, maybe, or to show up Petrarch, Tasso, and others. To sound again the theme, apparently of great emotional significance to Spenser, of binding and loosing, of constraint that is liberating because freely choosen.[50]

Also, I think, to make a deeper acknowledgement than some
readings of *Amoretti* allow: the understanding that human sexual love is like divine love also in its experience of pain and loss.
Spenser's sonnet nowhere mentions the dismemberment
Marguerite's deer must experience but the implications may be
there, and feminine anxieties (whether widespread in real life is
probably beside the point) about what follows even loving capture certainly receive ample and sympathetic exploration elsewhere in his poetry. By accepting the risk of suffering, either as
physical intrusion and later parturition or, also scary, as the pen-
etration of an emotional and psychological perimeter, and by
taking on the inevitable and natural sense of some loss, the half-
trembling deer assures for herself and for others—her lover, her
family—a future triumph over doubt, bondage, and fear. It is
hard to imagine what deeper or wiser compliment a poet could
give a young woman.


*Barnard College*


APPENDIX


*Amoretti*


### LXVII

Lyke as a huntsman, after weary chace,
Seeing the game from him escapt away,
Sits downe to rest him in some shady place,
With panting hounds beguiled of their pray:
So, after long pursuit and vaine assay,
When I all weary had the chace forsooke,
The gentle deare returnd the selfe-same way,
Thinking to quench her thirst at the next brooke.
There she, beholding me with mylder looke,
Sought not to fly, but fearlesse still did bide:
Till I in hand her yet halfe trembling tooke,
And with her owne goodwill hir fyrmely tyde.
Strange thing, me seemd, to see a beast so wyld,
So goodly wonne, with her owne will beguyld.

## LXVIII

Most glorious Lord of lyfe, that on this day
Didst make thy triumph over death and sin,
And having harrowd hell, didst bring away
Captivity thence captive, us to win:
This joyous day, deare Lord, with joy begin,
And grant that we, for whom thou diddest dye,
Being with thy deare blood clene washt from sin,
May live for ever in felicity:
And that thy love we weighing worthily,
May likewise love thee for the same againe;
And for thy sake, that all lyke deare didst buy,
With love may one another entertayne.
So let us love, deare love, lyke as we ought:
Love is the lesson which the Lord us taught.

## LXIX

The famous warriors of the anticke world
Used trophees to erect in stately wize,
In which they would the records have enrold
Of theyr great deeds and valarous emprize.
What trophee then shall I most fit devize,
In which I may record the memory
Of my loves conquest, peerelesse beauties prise,
Adorn'd with honour, love, and chastity?
Even this verse, vowd to eternity,
Shall be thereof immortall moniment,
And tell her prayse to all posterity,
That may admire such worlds rare wonderment;
The happy purchase of my glorious spoile,
Gotten at last with labour and long toyle.

## LXX

Fresh Spring, the herald of loves mighty king,
In whose cote-armour richly are displayd
All sorts of flowers the which on earth do spring,
In goodly colours gloriously arrayd,
Goe to my love, where she is carelesse layd,
Yet in her winters bowre, not well awake;
Tell her the joyous time wil not be staid,
Unlesse she doe him by the forelock take:
Bid her therefore her selfe soone ready make,

To wayt on Love amongst his lovely crew,
Where every one that misseth then her make
Shall be by him amearst with penance dew.
Make hast therefore, sweet love, whilest it is prime;
For none can call againe the passed time.

## Marguerite de Navarre

### Chanson 7

Sur l'arbre de la Croix, d'une voix cíere et belle,
J'ay bien ouy chanter une chanson nouvelle.
L'oyseau qui la chantoit esmouvoit le courage
De tout vray Pèlerin, disant en doux langage:
5  Je suis le Pélican qui santé donne et vie
Pour faire vivre ceux que sauver j'ay envie.
La Mort qui eux et moy pensoit ses subjets rendre,
J'ay prise et mise à mort, me laissant d'elle prendre:
Mais estant en ses laz, n'a pas esté sy forte
10  Que n'en soye eschappé en rendant la Mort morte.
Par quoy sur mes enfans n'ha plus nulle puissance,
Qui par mort de vie ont parfaite jouyssance.
Où est ton aiguillon, ô Mort tant redoutée?
Ta puissance par moy de ta force est ostée.
15  Je suis la Vérité et la Vie et la Voye,
Mort n'a plus de povoir en quelque part que soye:
Les pécheurs seulement la trouveront cruelle,
Mais les miens l'aymeront, et la trouveront belle.
Par moy l'horrible Mort est belle devenue,
20  Et les portes d'Enfer n'ont contre moy tenue;
Car au mylieu d'Enfer me trouve le Fidèle,
Qui suys son Paradis et sa joye éternelle.
Mes enfans sont en moy sy très-unys par grâce,
Qu'Enfer, Péché, ny Mort, n'ha plus en eux de place.
25  Adam plein de péchés j'ay mis en croix austère,
Je l'ay crucifié en jouant son mystère;
J'ay prins ce vieil Adam et sa concupiscence,
Lequel j'ay mis à rien par Foy et congnoissance;
J'ay gousté le morceau de Mort en patience:
30  Nul ne le goustera qui ayt en moy fiance.
J'ay entré en Enfer, sentant ses douleurs fortes:
Pour en tirer les miens j'en ay rompu les portes;
Nully ne demourra plus en ces trois limites

Si bien se fie en moy, recevant mes mérites:
35 Mais s'il se veult fier en son labeur et peine,
Estimant mon tourment et ma passion vaine,
Il congnoistra qu'Enfer, Mort et Péché, et Vice
Vaincre ne pourra pas par sa propre justice:
De péchés se verra chargé à sy grand somme
40 Qu'à la fin pourra voir ce que peult sans moy l'Homme.
Mais l'Homme au cœur contrit, petit, humble et infime,
Qui ne sent rien de soy, et nul bien n'en estime,
Qui tout en ma bonté se confie et s'arreste,
A luy tousjours ma main de secourir est preste;
45 Je le mets en Enfer, lui monstrant son ordure,
Et qu'il a mérité par Péché mort très dure;
Je le metz tout à rien, luy monstrant que son Estre
Et sa Vie je suis, son seigneur et son maistre.
Mais quand le Très-petit du tout Rien se confesse,
50 Je le retire à moy, luy monstrant ma promesse:
De ma chair, de mon sang, luy fais présent encore,
En moy le réunis, l'embrasse et l'incorpore:
Luy transformé en moy hors son péché immunde,
Rien que grâce ne voit, qui en son lieu abonde.
55 En moy il voit la Mort sy très-bien acoustrée
Qu'il la désire voir comme de Vie entrée,
Par moy de son Enfer voit les portes brisées,
Là congnoit Paradis et les joyes prisées;
Povreté, faim et soif, travail, peine et tristesse,
60 Trouve, vivant en moy, tout repos et liesse.
Or venez donc, Pécheurs, escouter ma doctrine:
Apprenez ma chanson pleine de discipline.
Je suis monté en hault afin que chascun m'oye,
Et qu'escoutant mon chant soyez remplis de joye.
65 Par Charité j'ay soif du salut de toute âme,
Pour la faire brusler de l'amoureuse flamme.
Las, donnez moy de l'eau de vraye amour à boire
Au vaisseau de voz cœurs par fermement me croire.
De n'avoir fait nul bien, ne craignez ce langage,
70 Car tout est consommé; j'ay gaigné l'héritage;
J'ay accomply la Loy, j'ay gaigné la partie:
Tout est pour vous, Pécheurs, pour lesquelz Eli crie;
A vous tous ignorans pardonner vostre offence;
75 J'ay pour vous délaissé ma vie à mort amère,
Et en très-grand douleur ma très aymée Mère,
Pour vous monstrer que chair, tant soit elle estimée.
Puys j'ay recommandé entre les mains du Père
80 Mon esprit, pour monstrer qu'en luy fault qu'on espère.

Or ay-je le salut de chacun fait sy ample,
Et pour y parvenir me suis mis pour exemple.
Venez, venez, trestous chargez outre mesure
De labeurs et travaux; voyez ma peine dure,
85 Voyez ma croix, mes clous, mes douleurs non petites,
Mon cœur d'amour ouvert et trestous mes mérites.
Tous ces biens sont à vous; par grâce je les donne
A qui par ferme Foy tout à moy s'abandonne.
Venez, embrassez moy, mon troupeau, mon Eglise,
90 Mes Esluz humbles et doux, desquelz fais à ma guise,
Car vous, uniz en moy, estes la mesme chouse;
Je seray vostre Espoux, vous tous un, mon Espouse:
Venez au vray repos où sera endormie
Entre mes bras toujours mon Espouse et amye.

*Chanson 8*

Voicy nouvelle joye.
La nuict pleine d'obseurité
Est passée; et voicy le jour
Auquel marchons en seureté,
5 Chassans toute peur par amour,
Sans que nul se desvoye:
Voicy nouvelle joye.

L'hyver plein de froid et de pleurs
Est passé, tremblant et glacé;
10 L'esté plein de verdure et fleurs
Nous vient plus beau que l'an passé;
Or chacun le voye:
Voicy nouvelle joye.

L'arbre sec et fâcheux à voir,
15 Raboteux et dur à toucher,
Que nul ne dèsiroit avoir,
Maintenant povons le toucher:
Il fleurit et verdoye;
Voicy nouvelle joye.

20 Le rossignol qui s'est fâché
Pour la rigueur de l'hyver froid,
Maintenant il n'est plus caché,
Mais sur la branche se tient droit;
Il gergonne et verboye:
25 Voicy nouvelle joye.

Le Fidèle dedens la Loy
Tout caché, tremblant et peureux,
Par la lumière de la Foy
Voit cler, et devient amoureux
30 De Dieu, qui le convoye:
Voicy nouvelle joye.

Il se congnoit tout délivré
De péché et damnation;
Il se sent de joye enyvré
35 Par la divine Election
Qui tout bien luy ottroye:
Voicy nouvelle joye.

L'arbre de Croix, de peine et mort,
Que tant avoit eu en horreur,
40 Maintenant c'est le réconfort
Où il a attaché son cœur
Afin qu'il ne desvoye:
Voicy nouvelle joye.

Luy qui craingnoit les gens hanter
45 Et cachoit par crainte sa voix,
Maintenant ne fait que chanter
Dessus l'espine de la Croix;
Il fault que l'on le croye:
Voicy nouvelle joye.

50 Il est dehors d'yver et nuict,
Il n'est plus sec, mais florissant;
Mort et Péché plus ne luy nuist;
Il est content dans le Puissant,
Vérité, Vie, et Voye:
55 Voicy nouvelle joye.

## NOTES

1. Petrarch, ed. Alessandro Vellutello (Venice, 1568), sig. P7, and G. A. Gesualdo (Venice, 1581), sig. Dd2, which has more deer lore. On the significance of this commentary to Wyatt and the problematic relationship between "Una candida cerva" and "Who so list to hunt," see Alastair Fowler, *Conceitful Thought* (Edinburgh: Edinburgh University Press, 1975), pp. 2–6. See also Jon A. Quitslund, "Spenser's *Amoretti* VIII and Platonic Commentaries on Petrarch," *Journal of the Warburg and Courtauld Institutes*, 36 (1973), 256–276.

2. Torquato Tasso, *Opere*, ed. Bruno Maier (Milan: Rizzoli Editore, 1963),

I, 453. On *Amoretti*'s sources, see the Variorum edition of Spenser's *Works*, ed. Edwin Greenlaw *et al.*, VIII, *The Minor Poems*, Part II, ed. C. G. Osgood and H. G. Lotspeich (Baltimore, Md.: Johns Hopkins University Press, 1947); Janet C. Scott, "Sources of Spenser's *Amoretti*," *Modern Language Review*, 22 (1927), 189–195; Veselin Kostić, *Spenser's Sources in Italian Poetry: A Study in Comparative Literature*, Filološki Fakultet Beogradskog Univerziteta Monografije: XXX (Belgrade: Novi, 1969), especially pp. 54–56. R. W. Dasenbrock, "The Petrarchan Context of Spenser's *Amoretti*," *PMLA*, 100 (1985), 38–50, says Tasso "describes the capture" of the deer, but the poem makes no explicit reference to capture, only to descent and new friendliness.

3. Edwin Casady, "The Neo-Platonic Ladder in Spenser's *Amoretti*," *Philological Quarterly*, 20 (1941), 284–295, insists that the "mylder looke" is the lover's, which makes sense too. Each syntactic possibility supports an equally plausible understanding of what is going on: the lover is less aggressive and the deer more willing. Perhaps the ambiguity is intentional.

4. The wild animal is now tame, and this in some circumstances could imply loss of sexual integrity. Furthermore, a mountain-going animal on the high trails has specific biblical parallels. Thorny paths on rocky hills are fit for deer and for the "hinds feet" God gives David. See Ps. 18 and 104 and Habbukuk 3.19: "he wil make my fete like hindes fete, and he wil make me to walke upon mine hie places" (Geneva translation). To many authorities the high-stepping hinds meant, as Augustine said in his commentaries on the psalms, that God perfected his love so he might rise above the dark and thorny snares of the world (*Patrologia Latina* 36.152). Peter Lombard, and he was not alone, compares such deer to Christ: like them, Christ steps atop the thorns and entanglements *(foveas)* of sin. See Jean Bayet, "Le symbolisme du cerf et du centaure," *Revue archéologique*, 44 (1954), 21–68, a mine of information about deer in patristic tradition. Whatever Tasso's intended implications, it was possible for Spenser to see a noble animal's abandonment of the thorny hills as a descent in more ways than one.

5. On deer and hunting poems, see especially D. C. Allen, *Image and Meaning* (Baltimore, Md.: Johns Hopkins University Press, 1968), pp. 165–186; M. J. B. Allen, "The Chase: the Development of a Renaissance Theme," *Comparative Literature*, 20 (1968), 301–312; Claus Uhlig, "'The Sobbing Deer,'" *Renaissance Drama*, n.s. 3 (1970), 79–109; Marcelle Thiébaux, *The Stag of Love: The Chase in Medieval Literature* (Ithaca, N.Y.: Cornell University Press, 1974). Less central but useful are Edward S. Le Comte, "Marvell's 'The Nymph Complaining . . . ,'" *Modern Philology*, 50 (1952), 97–101; Nicholas Guild, "Marvell's 'The Nymph Complaining . . . ,'" *Modern Language Quarterly*, 29 (1968), 385–394; Earl Miner, *The Metaphysical Mode from Donne to Cowley* (Princeton, N. J.: Princeton University Press, 1969), pp. 258–266 (on p. 259 Miner says, "no where that I know of in seventeenth-century writing will one find Christ represented by a female type"; I am not sure what "type" means here, but I have found earlier female *deer* representing Christ).

6. *Odes* III.23

7. Thiébaux's opening chapter is particularly helpful on deer and transition. One might add that legends of ghostly riders condemned to perpetual hunt

demonstrate a negative version of this topos; neither capturing the deer nor seeing it escape, the hunter is caught in an infernal and compulsive repetition.

8. Guild and Miner mention the dead deers' implications for empire and change.

9. See Thiébaux; Michael Bath, "The Legend of Caesar's Deer," *Medievalia et Humanistica*, n.s. 9 (1979), 53–66; and Rachel Bromwich, "Celtic Dynastic Themes and the Breton Lays," *Etudes celtiques*, 9 (1961), 439–474.

10. Giordano Bruno's theory, outlined by C. C. Gannon, "Lyly's *Endimion*: From Myth to Allegory," *English Literary Renaissance*, 6 (1976), 220–243.

11. Lars-Håken Svensson discusses Acteon in Renaissance poetry in *Silent Art: Rhetorical and Thematic Patterns in Samuel Daniel's "Delia,"* Lund Studies in English, 57 (Lund: CWK Gleerup, 1980). Like Scudamor, Sir Arthur Gorges is a deer: "Yow are the brooke, and I the Deare Imboste [*i.e.* foaming at the mouth with exhaustion]," in *Poems*, ed. Helen E. Sandison (Oxford, 1953), p. 66.

12. *The Phoenix Nest* (1593), ed. Hyder E. Rollins (Cambridge, Mass.: Harvard University Press, 1931), p. 67. For wordplay in *Amoretti* see William C. Johnson, "Spenser and the Fine Craft of Punning," *Neuphilologische Mitteilungen*, 77 (1976), 376–386.

13. Thiébaux, p. 230; "Gascoignes Woodmanship," in *Works*, ed. J. W. Cunliffe, 2 vols. (Cambridge: Cambridge University Press, 1907), I, 348–352. Gascoigne is also the probable author of *The noble art of venerie* (1575), once assigned to George Turberville.

14. *Chansons spirituelles*, ed. Georges Dottin (Geneva: Droz, 1971), pp. 17–20; the *Chansons* were first published in 1547 as a subsection of the punningly titled *Marguerites de la Marguerite des princesses*. Dottin's notes identify many of Marguerite's biblical and liturgical references.

A young hunter asked a happy and wise woman if the chase he was looking for could be found in that forest, and he said he had plenty of heart to win this venison by grief [or, we might say, by taking pains], merit and reason. She said to him, "My lord, it is indeed the season to take it, but you are a bad hunter."

"It is not to be taken by the chase [by "coursing"], nor by the will of a worldly man, nor through its pain nor through its dying; and so one must base salvation only on the Creator: virtue is worth little if there is no power or strength abounding in the spirit. Alas, you would possess this if you had David's sling—but you are a bad hunter."

"What you seek is in the woods, where no faithless person goes: this is the bitter wood [literally, "bush"] of the Cross, cruel to the wicked. Good hunters find it lovely, and its pains are their pleasure. Now if you wished to forget everything for this honor you would not want to choose any other good—but you are a bad hunter."

When the hunter heard her he screwed up his face as if angry and said, "You speak with great ignorance: I must turn and rouse the deer [make it dash from its hiding place so the dogs will run after it] and must chase it; yet you expressly tell me it cannot be caught by my effort." "My lord, the deer is close to you—but you are a bad hunter.

"If you would please to sit and place yourself on the edge of a spring, and rest your body and spirit, drinking the health-giving and living waters, indeed without your taking other pains the deer would come straight to you, and to take it would require only the net of your humble heart, in which it is caught by Love—but you are a bad hunter."

"My lady, I do not believe one wins either goods or glory or gets anywhere without work or with only loving and believing. I don't want to drink the living waters—for working, wine is better." The lady said, "you will be lord and owner of Earth and Heaven if Faith opens your eyes—but you are a bad hunter."

"The deer is so human/humane and gentle that if you wish to tender your heart [a possible pun: in French one can "tendre" a rope or snare] it will come to you through love. In taking you it will let itself be taken; and then it will be able to teach you to eat its flesh and blood by rank at this curry [i.e. at the ceremony in which the entrails of the deer are given to the dogs on the deerskin; in the allegory we are the dogs]. To be filled with sweetness your wishes will aim at this goal—but you are a bad hunter."

"Into this delicate flesh your own will be transformed: Oh happy he who can handle this great unhorned head, this sought-after and harried flesh, done to death, roasted for us, hung on the cross by three nails! Alas, it is yours, oh sinner, if you believe the holy words—but you are a bad hunter."

The hunter understood the scale [the musical notes] and discovered the idea [the "posie"] and suddenly said to her, "My lady, I give up my fantasy; my soul is seized by Faith, which makes me break trumpet and horn, abandon collars [i.e. dog collars, but also the chains and necklaces of rank and chivalric honor], couples [braces or ties connecting a pair of dogs together], and leashes. Believing the voice of my Savior, I will chase no other deer, so as no longer to be a bad hunter.

"Emperors, kings, princes, lords, I address my speech to you all; you whips, huntsmen, masters—renounce the labor and anxiety which instead of pleasure most often bring you sorrow. Alas, your pleasure is but wind; leave off, like me, this wretchedness. I am not now what I was, so that I might be no longer a bad hunter.

"Come hunters—come, come [a play on "venir" and "venerie"] to the holy deer-feast; learn to leave this world, which is so ephemeral; for the measureless Charity of his All gives you the gift whereby (your) Nothingness is made pleasing, filled with divine liquor. I now give myself over, so as to be no longer a bad hunter."

15. Harvey mentions the *Heptaméron* on fol. 47 of L. Domenichi's *Facetie*, now in the Folger Library. On Marguerite and England, see my "Pearl of the Valois," in *Silent but for the Word*, ed. Margaret P. Hannay (Kent, Ohio: Kent State University Press, 1985).

16. In *The Arte of English Poesie* (1589), *Elizabethan Critical Essays*, ed. G. Gregory, Smith, 2 vols. (Oxford: Clarendon Press, 1904), II, 23.

17. Dottin gives some of Marguerite's originals; as he says, pp. ix–xvii, there was then a fashion for pious parodies. For another laundered hunting

poem, one which makes Christ the hunter, see John Wedderburn's *Gude and Godlie Balates*, quoted in J. M. Gibbon, *Melody and the Lyric from Chaucer to the Cavaliers* (1930; rpt. New York: Haskell, 1964), p. 38: "With hunt is up, / With hunt is up, / It is now perfect day. / Jesus our King, / Is gone hunting— / Who likes to speed, they may." This is a born-again version of Gray of Reading's popular ballad about a friend of Marguerite: "The hunt is up, the hunt is up, / And it is well nigh day; / And Harry our King is gone hunting, / To bring his deer to bay."

Dottin prints thirty-two poems as Marguerite's grouping of spiritual songs, relegating one on the death of François I to an appendix because of its typographical surroundings. I have looked at the Lyons 1547 edition and despite the bar and "fin" I would still include it; the matter is ambiguous.

18. Marguerite, chansons 3, 24, 17, and 21.

19. *Ibid.*, ch. 16, 23 (a fairly dramatic dialogue with the soul tempted by the diabolical Orgueil and "gens de là bas").

20. Spenser, VIII, 33. Marot wrote a less erotic and more anti-Jewish Easter pelican poem, Ballade XIII (1532). On the pelican, see L. Charbonneau-Lassay, *Le bestiaire du Christ* (Paris: Desclée de Brouwer, 1940), pp. 558–568.

21. On Spenser and the calendar (the theory at its most basic is that *Am.* 22 falls on Ash Wednesday, Feb. 13, 1594, and *Am.* 68 on Easter, March 31, the right number of fast days and Sundays later; *Am.* 62 falls, correctly, on the old new year, March 25), see Alexander Dunlop, "The Unity of Spenser's *Amoretti*," in *Silent Poetry*, ed. Alastair Fowler (London: Routledge & Kegan Paul, 1970), pp. 153–169. O. B. Hardison, Jr., "*Amoretti* and the Dolce Stil Novo," *English Literary Renaissance*, 2 (1972), 208–216, wittily calls the resulting pattern a "triptych." More specifically on the liturgy is William C. Johnson, "Spenser's *Amoretti* and the Art of the Liturgy," *Studies in English Literature, 1500–1900*, 14 (1974), 47–61 and his "'Sacred Rites' and Prayer-Book Echoes in Spenser's 'Epithalamion,'" *Renaissance and Reformation*, 12 (1976), 49–54. For some objections, see G. K. Hunter, "Unity and Numbers in Spenser's *Amoretti*," *Yearbook of English Studies*, 5 (1975), 39–45. Carol Kaske's vigorous "Spenser's *Amoretti* and *Epithalamion* of 1595: Structure, Genre, and Numerology," *English Literary Renaissance*, 8 (1978), 271–295, has not dissuaded me from seeing a calendar in *Amoretti*. Her skepticism is sobering, but when she says *Am.* 22 refers to a season and not a day she ignores 1.3 and I am puzzled by the fuss over *Am.* 60's reference to a year spent loving; no law requires the duration of love to correspond to the real or fictional time it took to write the love poems or to that of a calendrical sequence to which the poems might refer. For a calendrical reading that groups Lenten Sundays together, see A. K. Hieatt, "A Numerical Key for Spenser's *Amoretti* and Guyon in the House of Mammon," *Yearbook of English Studies*, 3 (1973), 14–27. James Neil Brown, "Lyke Phoebe; Lunar, Numerical, and Calendrical Patterns in Spenser's *Amoretti*," *Gypsy Scholar*, 1 (1973), 5–15, finds a lunar calendar and references to Elizabeth; the theory is clever but relies too much, I think, on considerations of tone and seems to me overingenious. I will give my own calendrical suggestions later in this essay. Charlotte Thompson's dense and suggestive article, "Love in an Orderly Universe: A Unification of Spenser's *Amoretti*, 'Ancreontics,' and *Epithalamion*," *Viator*, 16 (1985),

277–335, appeared too recently for me to use. Her conclusions complement my own.

22. The Variorum Spenser and Scott mention many but not all of the biblical phrases I cite. I quote the Geneva translation of 1560 (and at Carol Kaske's suggestion I have checked the marginalia against a later revised edition) unless I am citing the biblical passages in an English-language prayerbook.

23. Spenser, however, would also have known Du Bellay's *Olive* 34 (closer to *Am*. 69 than is Desportes's *Cléonice* 11) and Gorges' translation in *Works*, pp. 67–68.

24. Alexander Dunlop, "The Drama of *Amoretti*," *Spenser Studies* I, Patrick Cullen and Thomas P. Roche, Jr., eds. (Pittsburgh, Pa.: University of Pittsburgh Press, 1980), pp. 107–120, sees *Am*. 69 as evidence that the lover's "education is clearly not yet complete."

25. This insistence that the lover earns the lady, *learning* something, is widespread (Spenserians are usually also teachers), even among scholars who recognize that for Protestants there is no justification by works. Thus Don Ricks, "Persona and Process in Spenser's 'Amoretti,'" *Ariel*, 3 (1972), 5–15, says that the lady waits for her suitor "to become worthy" and that he "finally becomes acceptable." Dunlop, "Drama," rightly says *Am*. 67 and 68 show that "True love is . . . ultimately a gift of grace," but in the next sentence he says the "bond of love" depends on "the proven worth of the lover." A. Leigh DeNeef, in a fascinating chapter on *Amoretti* in *Spenser and the Motives of Metaphor* (Durham, N. C.: Duke University Press, 1982), sees that *Am*. 67's deer "reenacts Christ's sacrificial act," but he too finds the lover "reformed," p. 71. Robert S. Miola, in his "Spenser's Anacreontic," *Studies in Philology*, 77 (1980), 50–66, recognizes the poetry's religious significance yet refers to the lover's "well-deserved bliss."

In some sense all this is true, for like Marguerite's hunter, the lover, by giving up his struggle, makes room for the grace that gives him imputed merit. But he is "reformed" and "worthy" only in a negative and possibly unknowing way. Spenser's whole point, it seems to me, is that mercy is above the scept'red sway of education and earning power. For a recent study of Spenser's views on faith and works, see Anthea Hume, *Edmund Spenser: Protestant Poet* (Cambridge: Cambridge University Press, 1984). Arthur F. Marotti, "'Love is not Love,': Elizabethan Sonnet Sequences and the Social Order," *ELH*, 49 (1982), 396–428, says love offered Spenser a realm in which merit, not birth, is rewarded, a provocative argument that also raises this troubling issue.

26. Johnson, "Liturgy," p. 57.

27. On the deer's association's with Christ see DeNeef, p. 67; Robert Kellogg, "Thought's Astonishment and the Dark Conceits of Spenser's *Amoretti*," in *The Prince of Poets: Esssays on Edmund Spenser*, ed. J. R. Elliott (New York: New York University Press, 1968), 139–151 ("the ancient religious and erotic conceit of the beloved as a tame deer" [in fact, such deer are seldom tame]); and especially John D. Bernard's excellent "Spenserian Pastoral and the *Amoretti*," ELH, 47 (1980), 419–432. No one, I think, discusses both the deer's Christlike surrender *and* the scriptural/liturgical deer. Robert G. Benson, "Elizabeth as Beatrice: A Reading of Spenser's 'Amoretti'," *South*

Central Bulletin, 32 (1972), 184–188 discusses the Easter paradox of surrender and triumph, a related topic. Elizabeth Bieman, in "'Sometimes I . . . mask in myrth lyke to a Comedy': Spenser's *Amoretti*," *Spenser Studies* IV, Patrick Cullen and Thomas P. Roche Jr., eds. (New York: AMS Press, 1983), pp. 131–141, mentions Ps. 42 and the habits of deer as snake-eaters. I heartily agree that Spenser is witty and that the deer in *Am*. 67 is "earthly" as well as spiritual (that, after all, is the point of the Incarnation as well as of Spenserian love poetry); that *Am*. 67 has a "Good Friday location in the sequence" (p.139) is less certain if we count by sonnets from Lady Day to Easter (or by Sundays, like A. K. Hieatt).

28. On deer see Thiébaux, Bayet, Charbonneau-Lassay, and Henri-Charles Puech, "Le cerf et le serpent," *Cahiers archéologiques*, 4 (1949), 17–60, which quotes many authorities. For some more eucharistic deer, see Louis Poinssot and Raymond Lantier, "Trois objets chrétiens du Musée de Bardo," *Revue archéologique*, 5th ser. 28 (1928), 66–89. Herbert Kolb, "Der Hirsch, der Schlangen frisst," in *Mediaevalia Litteraria*, a *festschrift* for Helmut de Boor (Munich, 1971), pp. 583–610, shows how the application of allegorized natural history diminished in the late Middle Ages, sometimes further eroded by scientific doubts about deer lore. As Kolb says, however, the symbolic reading of the deer by no means disappeared. I mention here the most famous deer, but there are others in, *e.g.*, Ps. 29, Prov. 6.5, Isaiah 13.14, 35.6, Job 39.4 and Lam. 1.6.

29. Martin Luther, *Works*, ed. Hilton C. Oswald (St. Louis: Concordia Publishing House, 1974), XV, 217–218, commenting on Song 2.9.

30. Sigs. C4ff. Edward Topsell's *History of Four-footed Beasts* (1652), an adaptation of Gesner (1551), cities Pliny saying that "the teeth of a Dragon tyed to the sinews of a Hart in a Roes skin, and wore [sic] about ones neck, maketh a man to be gracious to his Superiors" (p. 92).

31. Breasts may satisfy biblical husbands in Prov. 5. 19 and inspire lovers (see *Am*. 76–77), but they can worry readers. To Peter M. Cummings, in "Spenser's *Amoretti* as an Allegory of Love," *Texas Studies in Literature and Language*, 12 (1970), 163–179, Spenser's delight in them "threatens to warp the poet's view of the lady in favor of fleshly rather than spiritual qualities," and Marotti calls such feelings "an oral longing that has become a predatory greed" (p. 415). Spenser's thoughts may press beyond what he himself quite approves, but passages like Prov. 5.19 would give him some excuse—if any were needed.

32. Valerianus (G. P. V. Bolzani), *Hieroglyphica* VII, 16. I have used the French translation of Jean de Montylard in the Garland series, *The Renaissance and the Gods*, ed. Stephen Orgel. For Eucherius see *PL* 50. 795. Wilcox, *Commentarie*, says "thy youth" can also refer to a young wife.

33. DeNeef, p. 74, compares the separation in *Amoretti* to that in Song. Kaske, pp. 273–280, points out the resemblance to several betrothals in *FQ*, and Dunlop, "Drama," p. 114, associates it with the period after Ascension. I would say after Pentecost, for complaints that one cannot physically see the beloved, the "comfort" (*Am*. 89), are accompanied by awareness of her immage within (*Am*. 88). Carol T. Neely, "The Structure of English Renaissance Sonnet Sequences," *ELH*, 45 (1978), 359–389, discusses inconclusive endings.

Geoffrey Hartman's "'The Nymph Complaining for the Death of Her Fawn': A Brief Allegory," *Essays in Criticism*, 18 (1968), 113–135, connects the hunting theme to the role of the Comforter during Christ's absence: "The end may be near, yet there remains a space of time not redeemed by the divine presence. One can hardly blame the expectant soul for showing impatience" (p. 122).

34. Commentators had long equated the dogs with persecuting Jews, but services ordered by the Elizabethan government in times of trouble sometimes use this psalm with the clear implication that its dogs and lions are foreigners, Turks, and Catholics. William K. Clay prints these services in *Liturgies and Occasional Forms of Prayer set forth in the Reign of Queen Elizabeth* (Cambridge, 1847; Parker Society 27).

35. One reason any given deer could symbolize both parties in a relationship was the tendency of commentators, as I have mentioned, to cite other deer as well and merge their identities. For example, deer huddle together in Origen, *PG* 13. 171–177, Ambrose *PL* 14. 849–854 (who mentions new year games with deer), and Raban Maur, *PL* 111. 204–205.

36. Harold Weatherby, "'Pourd out in Loosnesse,'" *Spenser Studies* III, Patrick Cullen and Thomas P. Roche Jr., eds. (Pittsburgh, Pa.: University of Pittsburgh Press, 1982), argues for Chrysostom's influence on *FQ* I.

37. Luther, X, 194, 197.

38. In this regard, Calvin might applaud William Johnson's observation in "Amor and Spenser's *Amoretti*," *English Studies*, 54 (1973), 217–226 that Spenser's sequence is Christian and not Neoplatonic, although Johnson, I think, Platonizes medieval mysticism too much. I do not mean to deny the pastoral element here, only to add a complexity to those discussed by John Bernard.

39. For the Sarum Missal I have used J. W. Legg's edition (Oxford, 1916, rpr. 1969), based on Medieval MSS, and the less convenient *Missale ad usum. . .Sarum* ed. F. H. Dickinson (Oxford: Clarendon Press, 1861–63), based on later texts. Sarum was not the only use, of course, but it was by far the best known. "Sarum" is Salisbury, whose cathedral was rumored to have a numerological architecture surprisingly relevant to Spenser; see my "Licia's Temple: Giles Fletcher the Elder and Number Symbolism," *Renaissance and Reformation*, 2 (1978), 170–181. For the first prayerbook of Edward VI I have used the Everyman edition (London, 1910) and for the Elizabethan prayerbook Clay and *The Book of Common Prayer*, ed. John E. Booty (Folger Library, University Press of Virginia, Charlottesville, 1976). Harold Weatherby, in a paper read at Kalamazoo in 1984, has suggested a link between Sarum's baptism rite (found in the materials for Easter eve) and *FQ* I.

I agree that *Amoretti* has a liturgical aspect, but like most others I doubt Spenser relates each sonnet to a specific day. A little experiment will show that too often the same sonnet seems to work well with different sets of readings, thus making any one correlation less convincing. By counting backward from Ash Wednesday, Johnson puts *Am.* 1 on Jan 23, citing readings for that day that mention food, eyes, hands, handling, and leaves (see his "'Sacred Rites'"). True enough, although at some expense to context, but suppose *Am.* 1 represented St. Andrew's day, at the start of the liturgical year: *its* readings have eyes, food, leaves, and the laying on of hands, not to mention angels, stars, "might," captivity, and singing to one's beloved. Johnson also says that *Am*. 3 echoes the readings for St. Paul's day, and indeed it does, but if one wanted Spenser to have begun the sequence at Christmas so as to end when both his lover and the faithful are waiting, *Am*. 3 would then seem to recall the St. John's day collect ("Cast thy bright beams of light") and the readings: "God is light," and we grope blinded in darkness; like Spenser, the speaker in Rev. 1 is "ravished," at least in the Geneva translation. Furthermore, Johnson bases some of his argument on psalms he says are set specifically for the Sunday she examines; but in addition to the monthly progress through the psalter, the Elizabethan prayerbook has proper psalms only for Christmas, Easter, Ascension, and Whitsun. The psalms he cites are, however, in the first Edward VI prayerbook as propers for those days. Professor Johnson, who read this article with generosity and attention, told me he is working to resolve some of these difficulties in a book on *Amoretti*.

40. Johnson, "Liturgy," p. 55

41. Ps. 51 in the Elizabethan prayerbook is found in the "Commination against sinners" traditionally used, as the opening words say, on Ash Wednesday. These unusually specific echoes of the Ash Wednesday service are not noted by Dunlop or Johnson, although of course both critics relate the sonnet to the day generally. In the magnificent Sarum Missal published in Paris in 1555 (with, as Harold Weatherby noted in his 1984 Kalamazoo paper, St. George and the dragon on the title-page), there is a woodcut accompanying the Ash Wednesday service showing David, harp laid near by him, kneeling before an altar on which blazes a heart.

42. Johnson, "Liturgy," p. 57.

43. Puech, pp. 39–43, discusses Ps. 42 (*i.e.* Vulgate 41), Easter eve, and number symbolism.

44. The similarity to the collects was first noted by James Noble in 1880; see *Variorum*, VIII, 443. There may be one more possible link between Spenser and the 1555 Sarum. In the Book of Common Prayer, as in preceding uses, the collects and readings for Lady Day (March 25) are placed, like those for other saints' days, after the sequence of readings for Sundays, Christmas, Easter, and so forth. In the 1555 Sarum Missal this is also true, but appearing just before Easter, on Easter eve, there is a mass for Mary. Professor Richard Pfaff tells me that such an anomaly was probably intended to stress the connection between the Annunciation and the Passion, often said in the Middle Ages to have taken place on the same day of the year. The readings are from the Song of Songs on the beloved's beauty and perfumed body, readings not found in other services for the Virgin, passionate though those are in their own manner. Spenser would perhaps have detested the Easter Eve mass for Mary simply as a mass, a papist perversion, but he pays his own lady similar compliments in *Am*. 64. This sonnet corresponds with neither Lady Day nor Easter Eve, but its language seems appropriate to an annual and liturgical season that here, just as in the 1555 Sarum, inspires vocabulary linking human and divine love.

45. *Epithalamion*, too, may echo Sarum as well as the Book of Common Prayer. In Sarum's marriage rite, the priest blesses the bed, a ceremony later played down by the Catholic church, and asks that it be free "ab omnibus fantasmaticis demonum illusionibus." Spenser likewise expels "deluding

dreams" and hobgoblins who "Fray us with things that be not." Here and in st. 23, which like the marriage service in Sarum and the Protestant prayerbook includes prayers for a large posterity and the inheritance of "heavenly taber-nacles" (the prayerbook's "inherit . . . everlasting kingdom") the poignancy lies partly in the husband's assumption of roles traditionally played by others. Just as he needs no Catullus to sing his wedding, he can bless his own bed (the displacement of these prayers to the end of the poem also brings the movement into line with the structure of the classical epithalamion). There is more on the bed-blessing tradition in *The Rathen Manual*, ed. and trans. Duncan MacGregor, Transactions of the Aberdeen Ecclesiological Society (Aberdeen, 1905). Johnson, "'Sacred Rites,'" notes some parallels with the Elizabethan prayerbook but not the "inherit" of st. 23. Hard-core Protestants would not call these associations "sacramental" (p. 53), for Spenser's church did not ac-knowledge marriage as a sacrament, and the prayerbook does not refer to a sign of the cross (p. 52), only to a blessing.

46. By these I mean days in the calendar, both moveable and immoveable, not, *e.g.*, the wedding or burial service. All days had lessons found in the opening almanac plus the collects, epistles, and gospels of the preceding Sun-day, but these are not the special days, Sundays and holy, to which so much of the prayerbook is devoted.

47. V.-L. Saulnier, *Du Bellay* (Paris: Hatier, 1968), p. 63. Du Bellay's scheme involves some symmetry, for each poem is four sonnets from its end of the sequence, but despite a few seasonal references and a total number of sonnets that corresponds roughly to the number of days from Christmas to Good Friday in the years 1549–1550, *L'Olive* has no indication I can find of a particular year; Spenser's calendar is both more complex and more specific than Du Bellay's.

48. Prescott, "Licia." On Spenser's amatory sun symbolism see Richard Neuse, "The Triumph over Hasty Accidents: A note on the Symbolic mode of the 'Epithalamion,'" *Modern Language Review*, 61 (1966), 163–174.

49. I can find no liturgical reason to repeat *Am.* 35 instead of an earlier one. In the church year, of course, no Sunday is repeated, only postponed, not an option available to Spenser (how could we recognize a previously omitted sonnet?). On 83 and 35 see also Dunlop, "Drama," who speculates on Spenser's reasons and summarizes earlier theories of Fowler and Hieatt. On Spenser, numbers, and mutability, see A. Kent Hieatt, *Short Time's Endless Monument: The Symbolism of the Numbers in Edmund Spenser's "Epithala-mion"* (New York: Columbia University Press, 1960).

50. On binding see J. C. Gray, "Bondage and Deliverance in the 'Faerie Queene': Varieties of a Moral Imperative," *Modern Language Review*, 70 (1975), 1–12.

---

I would like to thank A. Kent Hieatt for reminding me of several deer I had forgotten, Edmée de M. Schless for advice on French hunting terminology, Edward W. Tayler for thoughts on the significance of "tempestiva," and my research assistant Anne Himmelfarb for more help with German than I enjoy admitting.

DEBORAH CARTMELL

# "Beside the shore of siluer streaming *Thamesis*": Spenser's *Ruines of Time*

RECENT READINGS of Spenser's *Ruines of Time* have discovered a unity to the poem unnoticed in the first half of this century. In particular, Millar MacLure discusses Spenser's poem in relation to the art of memory, "a process of *imprinting* on the mind virtues, vices, states of being."[1] MacLure argues that the catalogue of "Roman, mediaeval and Renaissance elements not only translates Rome into an archetype but establishes it in memory as a House of Pride."[2] Carl Rasmussen expands on MacLure's interpretation, commenting that the "theme of Verlame's defence—that poetry assures mortals of fame—is from the point of view of traditional morality, abhorent."[3] Rasmussen argues that "poetry is for Verlame the most efficient possible House of Pride."[4] Verlame is closer to Rumour than to Fame, or to the Whore of Babylon than to the Holy Bride of the Apocalypse; and the revelation of her unreliability radically transforms our understanding of the poem.

Verlame rebukes Colin Clout for not remembering the glories of the past, in particular, the dead Sidney: she asks him to memorialize the deceased poet in a poetic house of memory. The 'praise' of the dead to Verlame is analogous to 'raising' an earthly monument, and even more incriminating, to raising the dead

(372–392). She seeks a complicity with the poet, tempting him (or Colin Clout, if they are distinct persons) to sing in a foreign language, that is *her* language of secular praise. It is important to stress that Verlame is the genius of an English city which is Roman—even the Thames is translated into Latin—and the poet finds himself on foreign territory, in a Roman England. In the Geneva Bible, Babylon is glossed as "Rome . . . the sinke of all abomination . . . a kind of hel." More specifically, it is the "Papistrie . . . ful of superstition and contempt for the true god."[5] In the Geneva Bible, Babel and Babylon are interchangeable—and thus, Babylon, Rome, and the Papistry are frequently identified with ostentatious, corrupt edifices, as in John Studley's invective on Roman Catholicism in 1575. Studley introduces his translation of John Bale's *Pageant of Popes* with an assault on Catholicism in general: ". . . most iustley may wee assure men that theyr Babilonicall building must needes come to decaye, being founded on the sande of Tiber banckes, which is dayle washed and eaten away."[6] For a Christian reader, Verlame's lament for her pre-Christian "High towers, faire temples, goodly theaters" etc. (92) inevitably recalls the ironic lament for the fall of Babylon in the Book of Revelation:

> It is fallen, it is fallen, Babylon ye great *citie*, and
> is become the habitation of deuils, and the holde of all
> fowle spirits, and a cage of euerie vncleene & hatefull
> byrde.                                        (Revelation XVIII: 2)

And for a good Elizabethan Protestant, Verlame's account of her once great edifices must be evocative of the Catholic enemy.

In Verlame's section of the poem, the poet (or his persona) remains silent, implying that his is another language. MacLure's and Rasmussen's readings can be extended here to a consideration of the poem as addressing its own originality. It is generally agreed that *The Ruines of Time* is an adaptation of Du Bellay's *Antiquitez* (which Spenser translated and included in the same collection as *The Ruines of Time*); however, Du Bellay's humanist argument for the recovery of ancient texts and the potential of poetry to produce everlasting monuments[7] is certainly not the message of Spenser's poem. In *The Ruines of Time*, the narrator resists Verlame's invitation to join her in the lament for the lost antiquities; that is, he refuses to imitate or translate her song. The refusal to sing implies a Protestant criticism of Verlame's values which, to an Elizabethan, are dangerously close to those of Roman Catholicism. Rather than Du Bellay, I suggest that Spenser's main inspiration comes from the 137th Psalm; and rather than a lament for the fallen Rome, the poem is a celebration of the Elizabethan *break* with Rome. Spenser's poem, in fact, can be interpreted as an allegory of the exodus of the English Protestants during the change-over from Mary to Elizabeth.

At Geneva, the Marian exiles had promoted the singing of the Psalms in English and this custom had become readily accepted in the early reign of Elizabeth. Translating the Psalms into English was a popular meditative practice in the sixteenth and seventeenth centuries; and a favorite Psalm for translation was the 137th, "Super Flumina," the lament of the exiles in Babylon who refuse to sing their song in a foreign land. The Psalm, as translated by the Countess of Pembroke, begins: "Nigh seated where the river flowes / That watreth Babells thanckfull plaine." The Psalm must have reminded Elizabethans of the plight of English Protestants now in exile in a foreign- Catholic-land. It is also reminiscent of the exiles in Geneva and their desire to sing the praises of God in the native tongue of Protestant England. I suggest that Spenser's *Ruines of Time* has as much in common with "Super Flumina" as it has with Du Bellay's *Antiquitez*.

The Psalm begins with the narrator on the banks of a Babylonian river as Spenser's poem begins with the narrator on the side of the "*Thamesis*":

> IT chaunced me on a day beside the shore
> Of Siluer streaming *Thamesis* to bee.

Like the Psalmist, the narrator of Spenser's poem is initially separate or in exile in this strange land. The Psalmist resists the invitation to sing "a Sion lay" to his captors:

> You that of musique make such show,
>   Come sing us now a Sion lay.
> O no, we have nor voice, nor hand
> For such a song, in such a land.
>                         (13–16)

Spenser is also upbraided, as he states in his dedication to the Countess of Pembroke, by "*some friends*" who complain that the poet has neglected his duty of elegizing Sir Philip Sidney; in the same way, Verlame reprimands Colin Clout for not singing the praises of the house of Leicester:

> Ne doth his *Colin*, carelesse *Colin Cloute*,
> Care now his idle bagpipe vp to raise,
> Ne tell his sorrow to the listning rout
> Of shepherd groomes, which wont his songs to praise.
>
> (225–228)

In the first part of *The Ruines of Time*, it is Verlame rather than the poet who speaks. Spenser remains silent, like the Psalmist, he provides a song concerned with a refusal to sing.

The visions concluding the poem provide an alternative to Verlame's lament and the voice is now that of Spenser's own persona. This final section consists of two sets of visions. The first is a series depicting the overthrow of exalted position, stately building, earthly pleasures, bodily strength and works of beauty and magnificence—these pageants can be seen as fulfilling the Psalmist's prophetic vision of the fall of Babylon:

> And Babilon, that did'st us waste,
>    Thy self shalt one daie wasted be:
> And happy he, who what thou hast
>    Unto us done, shall do to thee,
> Like bitterness shall make thee fast,
>    Like wofull objects cause thee see:
> Yea happy who thy little ones
> Shall take and dash against the stones.
>
> (33–40)

The first set of visions concludes with an image of two bears, indicating a movement away from a general meditation on earthly excess towards a personal vision of the house of Leicester (the bears are a part of the Dudley crest). These first visions serve to summarize the futility of Verlame's lament, and an alternative is offered in the second set of visions devoted to Sir Philip Sidney. Verlame's earthly (and, as suggested, Catholic) lament, symbolized by her once great edifices, is replaced by the poet's humble (and Protestant) celebration of the dead Sidney; and, in moving from the earthly to the spiritual kingdom, Spenser's persona overcomes the dilemma of the Psalmist. The poet receives a vision of Sidney unclouded by Verlame's earthly concerns. Unlike the singer of the 137th Psalm, the poet is liberated from foreign captivity (or more specifically, from Verlame's domination) and is able to sing the praises of Sidney in his own voice—in the language of Protestant England.

Spenser's last published poem, the *Prothalamion* can be regarded as a reworking of *The Ruines of Time*. In the later poem, the poet begins, like the narrator of the 137th Psalm, on the river bank, refusing to participate in what has become a strange land:

> When I whom sullein care,
> Through discontent of my long fruitlesse stay
> In Princes Court, and expectation vayne
> Of idle hopes, which still doe fly away,
> Like empty shaddowes, did aflict my brayne,
> Walkt forth to ease my payne
> Along the shoare of siluer streaming *Themmes*.
>
> (5–11)

In the *Prothalamion*, the narrator goes away only to return, seemingly reconciled to a London through his memories of better days under the ideal patronage of Leicester.

When viewed alongside the 137th Psalm, the seemingly amorphous structure of *The Ruines of Time* begins to take shape. The poem re-enacts the movement from Babylon to Sion, or from Marian to Elizabethan England; and the two worlds in the poem are distinguished by the two vioices: the seductive, almost imperceptibly corrupt Verlame, and the divinely inspired narrator of the final visions. *The Ruines of Time* does not imitate Du Bellay's *Antiquitez*; rather, it refuses to imitate it. The poet, inspired by the 137th Psalm, offers his own Protestant original.

*University of Leicester*

NOTES

1. "Spenser and the ruins of time," in *A Theatre for Spenserians*, ed. J. M. Kennedy and James A. Reither (Toronto: University of Toronto Press, 1973), p. 6.

2. Maclure, p. 7.

3. "'How Weak Be the Passions of Woefulness': Spenser's *Ruines of Time*," *Spenser Studies* II, Patrick Cullen and Thomas P. Roche, Jr., eds. (Pittsburgh, Pa.: University of Pittsburgh Press, 1981), p. 170.

4. Rasmussen, p. 171.

5. Gloss to 18:3 and 17:3. *The Bible and Holy Scriptvres* (Geneva, 1560). In "'And nought of *Rome* in *Rome* perceiu'st all': Spenser's *Ruines of Rome*," *Spenser Studies* II, pp. 183–192, Andrew Fichter also suggests that, on close inspection, Spenser's representation of Rome in his translation of the *Antiquitez* is a demonic parody of the kingdom of God.

6. "To the Reader," *A Pageant of Popes* (London, 1575), sig. b ii.

7. See Thomas Greene's analysis of Du Bellay's *Antiquitez* in *Imitation and Discovery in Renaissance Poetry* (New Haven, Conn.: Yale University Press, 1982), particularly p. 222.

8. *The Psalms of Sir Phillp Sidney and the Countess of Pembroke*, ed. J. C. A. Rathmell (New York: New York University Press, 1963). For the popularity of the Psalms, see Rathmell's introduction, pp. xii–xiii.

PAMELA J. BENSON

# Florimell at Sea: The Action of Grace in *Faerie Queene*, Book III

GRACE intervenes often in *The Faerie Queene* to rescue heroes who have reached the limits of their own capacities for virtue. Red Cross knight, in despair in Orgoglio's dungeon, is rescued by Arthur and reunited with Una. Guyon in his faint is succored by an angel as well as by Arthur. Neither hero is out of the woods of his adventures as a result of this intervention, but each man afterwards has the dedication to accomplish his mission. The intervention of grace in both these instances is in keeping with sixteenth-century Protestant doctrine on grace. The heroes desire to be good, but without the gift of grace all external motions to good are of no effect. Only with the gift of grace is the will able to will well.[1] In other words, no virtue can be achieved by man on his own; only with God's grace can one achieve the holiness or temperance he aims at. The frequent interventions of grace to assist Red Cross help to make this clear, and the entrance of Arthur in the eighth canto of all the books except Book Three helps to establish the reliance of the other virtues on grace and not on innate human abilities.

In Book Three the action of grace does not immediately conform to this pattern, and, perhaps as a consequence, its importance has been overlooked. In the eighth canto of this book the agent of grace is not Arthur, but the lecherous Proteus, who rescues Florimell from rape by the old fisherman in whose boat she has sought safety from destruction by the witch's beast who eats ladies' flesh like grass. In this episode grace removes the heroine from immediate physical danger only to place her in danger again, a danger that is more subtle and that threatens spiritual as well as physical damage. In moving Florimell from one danger to the other, grace does not restore to her a supporting character from whom she has been separated, as Red Cross is reunited with Una and Guyon with the Palmer; Florimell is still on her own and at sea, away from any possible help. The situation is further complicated by the fact that Spenser had previously described Florimell's entry into the fisherman's boat as ordained by God, and, therefore, in this sequence of episodes, Spenser seems to be describing God as a sanctioner of rape, or at least, of attempted rape.

Most critics who are interested in the fisherman are not concerned with Protestant aspects of Book Three, and, thus, do not directly consider the problem of grace here.[2] Indeed, Paul Alpers uses this very episode as a cornerstone in his proof that Spenser's assertions of Providential intervention are *not* "literal claims about a world." He reasons that, "if Spenser literally holds Providence responsible for the protection of Florimell, he has a good deal to account for when Proteus puts her in prison."[3] I would like to argue that Spenser is in truth making literal claims about a world—this world. It is a misapprehension to assume that, for a sixteenth-century Protestant, grace necessarily protects one from physical danger. Grace gives the faithful soul the force to withstand the spiritual challenge implicit in the physical attack. In Florimell's responses to the assaults made on her, Spenser reveals the transforming power of grace. A girl so terrified of lust that she runs even from Arthur becomes one who defies Proteus' most seductive strategies with steadfast courage. Because of the action of grace in God's plan, Florimell achieves the virtue of chastity as she could not on her own. Grace turns her from a victim into a heroine.

Although the direct involvement of God and his grace in Florimell's adventure are the two outstanding signals of Spenser's Protestant purpose in this episode, my suggestion really only makes sense if Florimell can be shown to be in need of spiritual grace instead of a mere *deus ex machina* to extract her from a dangerous physical situation. I believe that she can be shown to be in spiritual need. She certainly is physically intact and not lascivious when she reaches the sea shore,[4] but throughout her flight Spenser portrays her as out of control. She gives free rein to her horse and to her will.[5] Her fear has overwhelmed her reason; she is not making a rational defense of her chastity—as she shows when she runs not only from every trembling leaf, but also from Arthur. She is not ready for grace. Thomas Roche sees her wayward palfrey and the fisherman's unsteered boat as symbols that Florimell has subjected herself to the realm of fortune and the vagaries of mutable life.[6] She has abandoned reason and removed herself from human help.

Florimell's arrival at the seashore at this moment continues the theme of the rule of fortune. In Book Three the no man's land of the shore is a place of spiritual danger for many characters.[7] Malbecco's transformation into jealousy takes place on cliffs above the sea. Marinell's retreat to the shore as a haven for his gynophobia and his hoarding there of his treasures retrieved from dead men suggest the sterility of the border between land and sea. Even Britomart seeks out the shore when feeling most low-spirited in her search for Arthegall, and there, in her famous Petrarchan lament, entertains despairing thoughts before directing her discontent outward at Marinell in a most unPetrarchan storm of action. Britomart's action is extremely important here. As Isabell MacCaffrey pointed out, "for Britomart to take the analogy between the tempestuous life and tempestuous sea too seriously would be for her to submit to Fortune rather than co-operate with Providence" which has destined her to marriage and procreation, not an early death.[8] The opposition of unstable Fortune and stable Providence is appropriate to Florimell's state as well as to Britomart's. Although Britomart has the advantage of knowledge of Providence's plan for her, as Florimell does not, and, also, has the added advantage of physical strength, Florimell's helplessness and ignorance are no excuse; indeed, they emphasize her lack of faith. In Book Six Spenser places Serena in a similar situation of danger and utter helplessness, and Serena acts wisely and faithfully: "herself she wholly recommended to God's grace."[9] Florimell in the same situation is passive in the hands of fortune; she does not recommend herself to God's grace. As irrationally driven by her fear as Malbecco will be by his jealousy, she demonstrates a complete lack of faith in the beneficence of Providence and resolves on suicide.

> Not half so fast the wicked Myrrha fled
> From dread of her revenging fathers hond:
> Nor half so fast to save her maidenhed,
> Fled fearefull Daphne on the'Aegaean strond,
> As Florimell fled from that Monster yond,
> To reach the sea, ere she of him were raught:
> For in the sea to drowne her selfe she fond,
> Rather than of the tyrant to be caught.[10]

This stanza portrays Florimell as having reached the limits of human resources. The comparison of her to the Ovidian Myrrha and Daphne suggests that there is no way out of this situation short of a miraculous metamorphosis, and this is, indeed, what occurs. Like the pagan gods who rescued Myrrha and Daphne, the Christian God saves his heroine by transforming her, but with a difference. True Ovidian metamorphosis changes the body into a form that represents the person's spiritual state at the moment of metamorphosis. The myrrh tree weeps and the laurel has tender bark. Spenser's own Malbecco suffers his jealousy eternally. In all these cases the metamorphosis is of the body; the spiritual suffering remains, at least to some extent. Florimell is different. The use of the wicked Myrrha as well as the virtuous Daphne here reinforces all of Spenser's earlier suggestions that Florimell's flight represents the uneasy state of her soul, and thus, a simple, sudden, reductive metamorphosis would leave her frozen in her terror-stricken despair as Malbecco is in his jealousy—it would leave her still on the spiritually sterile seashore. She needs to be transformed spiritually rather than physically. This is what happens in her adventures at sea.

Florimell enters the sea-world by the grace of God: the little boat so attractively pulling at its moorings is there because God did so ordain. She chose Fortune over Providence, but she is being given another chance. This is not the first time that the poet has told us that God is directing the heroine's adventures, and His intervention represents the beginning of the process of spiritual metamorphosis. This change is gradual; the first effective agent of it is the fisherman whose attempt to rape Florimell is the first clear and direct attack on her chastity; up to this point, we have been led to fear for Florimell's chastity by the poet's

accounts of her beauty and vulnerability and by our ability to
read the intentions of the foul forester, but Florimell has been
portrayed as experiencing more general fears for her safety.
When she secretly leaves the old witch's home, she is afraid that
the son or his mother will do her harm; despite the churl's courtship of her, she does not specifically fear deflowering. Her name
suggests fertility, but she as yet seems unawakened to sexuality.
She is committed to the virtue of chastity as a negation of
something she does not know. Her encounter with the fisherman brings her up against the effects of her own sexuality and
fertility, but without damaging her spirit or her body.

The comedy even extends to Florimell herself; her very inno-

This is not the first attempted rape in *The Faerie Queene*; in
Book One, Canto Six, Sansloy attempts to rape Una. In that episode Una's terror and the narrator's pity set the tone for the
scene. The attack is described as an act of war—Sansloy assails
her fort—and imagery from Revelation describes nature's
sympathetic terror. Una's response is immediate: she calls on
Heaven for aid; Heaven's response is equally swift and
completely removes her from the sexual situation. She is rescued
by benevolent satyrs sent by Providence. The sexual attack is finally an allegory of a theological issue and of no real physical
significance.

The Fisher's attempt on Florimell is presented very differently
from Sansloy's on Una. The release of sexual energy that preci-
pitates the attack is one of the main themes of the episode and the
rape attempt is credable as a "real" event, but, paradoxically it
would seem, comedy pervades the description of the event.[11]
The old man's excitement is mocked by such cliched proverbs
as "Hard is to teach an old horse amble true" and broad erotic
puns on his generative organs appear throughout. Of course, in
literature, very old men interested in sex are frequently presented as funny, but usually this is because they are unable to follow
through on their newly aroused desire. The fisherman's proto-
type in the *Orlando furioso*, a hermit who tries to rape Angelica,
cannot get his horse to amble although he tries all night.[12]
Spenser restores the old man's potency, yet maintains a comic
perspective on him. As a result the episode is as bathed in sexuality as Florimell is in fish-scales, but the comic tone reassures the
reader that no substantial harm will be done. She is worried; the
reader is not.

The comedy even extends to Florimell herself; her very innocence is comic. After fleeing lust for so many days, she cannot recognize it face to face in the vulgar leering figure before her. This could be pathetic of course, but Spenser prevents it being so by making what she says comic. As Hamilton has shown and others affirmed, her speech to the fisher, in which she speaks of great waters that "gin apace to swell" and her plea that he guide the "cock-boat well," is full of double entendres.[13] These amuse the reader who feels pleased with his own cleverness in getting the joke and, as they preceed the actual physical rejuvenation of the man's sexual organs, the salacious double entendres cause the reader to anticipate the rejuvenation and to be amused by the description of it in the next stanza in terms that echo Florimell's plea. The reader does not lose sympathy with Florimell, but he, also, does not experience the rape attempt with her. Even her struggle with "hand and foot" is not presented as seriously as Una's simple shrieks. The narrator suggests that at this tense moment Florimell might "reprove her knights of falsehood or of slouth." Reproof is hardly what a woman would have on her mind on this point, the sentiment is too delicate, but the narrator continues for an entire stanza in this gallantly hyperbolic vein.

Previous critics who have analyzed this scene have concentrated on its eroticism and looked for the significance of the scene in its relationship to the portrayal of eroticism elsewhere in Book Three. John Bernard found the source of the comedy to be in Spenser's ability to "distinguish the terrors of Florimell's polymorphous erotic world from the cosmic and comic urge, radiating from her own beauty, that underlies it."[14] In other words, what the fisherman is trying to do to Florimell is terrible, but the force that urges him is universal, natural, and necessary. The comedy enables us to feel the erotic force. This explanation of the comedy ties the episode to Spenser's exploration of eroticism elsewhere in Book Three and accounts for the positive sense of sexuality that comes through despite the violent surface of the narrative, but it does not really explain why this particular adventure of Florimell's is open to comic treatment and it does not account for the significance of the episode in the context of the story of Florimell in particular.

Both the appropriateness of comedy to this episode and its significance in the story of Florimell can be found in God's intervention at the beginning of the adventure. Florimell's flight from the witch's beast is pathetic, not comic; we are made to feel her terror and pity her. The benign comic tone enters only at the moment that Florimell sees the little boat whose presence at the shore God ordained. Una's rape was the work of the devil, an attempt to disrupt God's plan for his truth on earth, and it was treated with appropriate seriousness. Florimell's near rape is thrown in her way by God himself; as a result the outcome of the rape is never in question, and the "cosmic and comic" can show through. Florimell's experience of God's intervention in her affairs is very different from the reader's, however. From her perspective the outcome is in question, of course, and the comedy is not apparent. The experience is as serious for her as it is delightful for the reader; on the verge of suicide, Florimell is offered the opportunity for momentous spiritual renewal and change. Imprisoned on the boat and forced to stop and experience lust's attack directly, Florimell feels angry scorn and fights with vigor though without success; she emerges from her despair, abandons her self-reliance, and calls on Heaven for help as she has never done before in the course of her flight. God responds immediately, as he did to Una. It is here that one might object that God does not intervene so directly in life, that this obviously is not a literal world if maidens in danger of rape are miraculously plucked from danger; but, the truth of miracles aside, Spenser's handling of the second part of Florimell's adventures at sea shows that he is talking of real spiritual changes that can be wrought by grace. He delegates the rescue of Florimell *Proteus* not to a benevolent crowd of satyrs or to a well-meaning knight, but to lascivious Proteus, an Ovidian master of love. Florimell escapes the brute physical assault by the fisherman only to be exposed to tempting erotic pleasures and the physically overwhelming power of a god. This rescue only remains a rescue because of the way Florimell responds to it. No matter what Proteus offers or does, she remains steadfast and calm in her refusal to be moved from her love of Marinell.

Kathleen Williams described Florimell's ability to stand up to Proteus as something new. "In Proteus' cave Florimell, no longer able to take flight, for the first time stands and thinks for herself. . . . She counters each change on Proteus' part with a change of position on her own, but it is purposeful and considered change. She is able to resist, the poet tells us, in her faithful love of Marinell."[15] Although Florimell was prevented from taking flight in the fisherman's boat, this spiritual steadfastness is

different. The god's challenge to her is potentially more morally
damning than the old man's because the fisherman attacked only
her body, but Proteus tries to wrench her from her chastity of
mind, the only chastity over which a woman has any real control
unless she is a Britomart. Florimell's victory over Proteus,
therefore, is a great moral victory.[16]

Although Proteus's attempts to persuade Florimell to his
purposes lead her to a willingness to die, she is in a very different
spiritual state from the one she was in at the sea-shore:

> Eternal thraldom was to her more liefe,
> Than losse of chastitie, or change of love:
> Die had she rather in tormenting griefe,
> Then any should of falsenesse her reprove,
> Or loosenesse, that she lightly did remove.

When Florimell says "die had she rather in tormenting griefe,"
she is expressing the readiness of a martyr for death at another's
hands, not the despair of a person who has given up on outside
help. Florimell's motive in this scene is positive. She desires to be
constant; she thinks of Marinell and refuses to "change" her love.
In her flight toward the seashore, she was headstrong and incon-
stant; she did not think, she only acted out of fear of pain and,
surprisingly, she did not have Marinell in her thoughts. Con-
fronted with Proteus, she is concerned with her reputation and
with the real meaning of chastity, and she does not fear pain; she
is rational and makes a truly virtuous commitment of herself to
another for whose love she is willing to die a martyr's tormented
death.

Spenser's praise of Florimell's steadfast chastity here is bound-
less; he stresses her valorous martyr-like commitment to love by
speaking of her as a saint:

> Most vertuous virgin, glory be thy meed
> And crowne of heavenly praise with Saints above,
> Where most sweet hymnes of this thy famous deed
> Are still amongst them song, . . .

These lines sound as though Florimell has really died because
they speak of her future reception in Heaven as though it has already occurred. They are modelled on an encomium of the hero-

ine Isabella in the *Orlando furioso* who, threatened with rape, managed to get her would-be violator to kill her, thus preserving her chastity and being eulogised by the poet as a saint.

Unlike the Italian heroine, Florimell is not self-reliant; she does not use her wits to defeat her attacker; she holds him off by the strength of her virtue. In the *Orlando*, the episode illustrates active secular human heroism in a moral cause. In his portrayal of Florimell, Spenser completely transforms it into an illustration of heroic passive resistance in a cause that is at once moral and spiritual. Love, not merely a social code of sexual morality, gives Florimell strength.

Spenser's application of the term "saint" to Florimell here is important because it confirms the action of grace and indicates that she is a member of the elect. For the Protestant, sainthood is achieved by the action of grace and not by independent individual merit. The distinction between those who are dead and those who are alive is blurred because the true life, the true "world," about which Spenser is speaking is the life of the spirit. Florimell is now alive spiritually and will be so after her physical death. Her virtuous chastity is a sign of her community with the elect, of her "sainthood." The Protestant heroine, unlike the Catholic one, becomes a saint while still alive by virtue of grace.

Spenser makes us appreciate this spiritual virtue in Florimell by showing us in physical terms how close she comes to losing it. Providence intervenes to rescue her from despair not by removing her from danger but by forcing her to confront it in a terrifying physical form—the fisherman. This confrontation recalls her to her senses, puts an end to her thoughtless self-reliance, and leads her to call for divine assistance. When Proteus appears she does not have faith with her as a companion as does Red Cross Knight when his rescue from Orgoglio by grace restores Una to him; she has grace within her.[17] Hers is a regenerate soul.

This is not to say that the episodes of the fisherman and Proteus are not about sex at all but are merely allegories of the working of grace on any soul. Florimell's experience of sexuality is an essential part of her transformation. Much later, at the end of Book Four when Spenser describes her visit to Marinell, who is languishing for love of Florimell, he describes her effect on Marinell in terms that recall the fisherman's response to her. Marinell is like a

withered weed through cruel winter's tine,
That feeles the warmth of sunny beames reflection
Lifts up his head, that did before decline
And gins to spread his leafe before the faire sunshine.

The language used here is sexually charged; the "withered weed" resembles the fisher's "withered stock" that was refreshed by Florimell's beauty, but here the simile speaks of a spiritual regeneration. The powerful, randomly applied uncivilized sexuality of the fisherman is restrained by love and manners, and this time Florimell recognizes the passion and feels a corresponding warmth. Her spiritual regeneration will make sexual generation possible. Her adventures have brought her to Marinell's bedside, but grace has prepared her for his bed.

*Rhode Island College*

## NOTES

1. I am indebted for this concise statement to Anthea Hume, *Edmund Spenser: Protestant Poet* (Cambridge and London: Cambridge University Press, 1984), p. 68.

2. Most critics read the episode in terms of mythological archetypes or neo-platonic symbolism. Important interpretations are: A. C. Hamilton, who sees Florimell as a Psyche figure representing chastity's cosmic significance in his *The Structure of Allegory in the "Faerie Queene"* (Oxford: Clarendon Press, 1961), p. 147 ff.; Howard W. Bahr, who sees Florimell as representing neo-platonic beauty-in-chastity in his "The Misery of Florimell: The Ladder of Temptation," *The Southern Quarterly*, 4 (1965), pp. 116–122; C. S. Lewis who suggested the episode is an allegory of the descent of the soul into material embodiment in his *Spenser's Images of Life*, ed. Alastair Fowler (Cambridge: Cambridge University Press, 1967), p. 126; Thomas P. Roche, who sees Florimell as the figure of beauty in the alternate myth of the chaste Helen of Troy in his *The Kindly Flame: A Study of The Third and Fourth Books of Spenser's "Faerie Queene"* (Princeton, N. J.: Princeton University Press, 1964), pp. 150–162. Kathleen Williams, *Spenser's World of Glass* (Berkeley and Los Angeles: University of California Press, 1966), includes a brief discussion of the action of Providence, but only sees it as operating in Proteus's cave. An reinterpretation of the exact kind of neo-platonism present is Dwight J. Sims, "The Syncretic Myth of Venus in Spenser's Legend of Chastity," *Studies in Philology*, 71 (1974), 427–450.

3. Paul J. Alpers, *The Poetry of the "Faerie Queene"* (Princeton, N. J.: Princeton University Press, 1967), p. 27.

4. A. C. Hamilton (p. 150) suggests that the loss of her girdle indicates Florimell's loss of chastity, but if her chastity is lost before her struggles to preserve it begin, the rest of the episode hardly makes sense. (Bahr, p. 120, also takes issue with Hamilton on this subject.) At this point it is reasonable to read the girdle as an indicator of Florimell's connection with society and her loss of it as an indication of her separation from all social support. Spenser later tells us that Venus wore it when she was accepting the restraints of society; Florimell's precipitous departure from the court and arrival at the uncivilized sea remove her from society and its ability to protect chastity. When she left the court, alone and in search of Marinell, she gave in to her desire, and now she is absolutely on her own.

5. A. C. Hamilton, ed., *Spenser, "The Faerie Queene"* (London and New York: Longman, 1977), p. 366, note to stanza 2, lines 7–9.

6. Roche, pp. 152–159 *passim*.

7. Daniel M. Murtaugh demonstrates the spiritual dangers of the sea–shore in his "The Garden and the Sea," *ELH*, 40 (1973); he cites the examples of Malbecco, Marinell, and Britomart. He excepts Florimell from the pattern because he does not note a spiritual problem in her.

8. Isabel MacCaffrey, *Spenser's Allegory: The Anatomy of Imagination* (Princeton, N. J.: Princeton University Press, 1976), p. 295.

9. VI. iv. 10. The salvage man whom Serena fears turns out to be no threat; God's grace makes him kind. Serena also gives thanks to God for her deliverance in stanza 15.

10. III. vii. 26. All quotations from *The Faerie Queene* are from the edition edited by A. C. Hamilton cited above.

11. Spenser's comedy has been the subject of much critical endeavor recently. A. C. Hamilton has been especially thorough in his analysis of the verbal humor in this episode both in the notes to his edition and in his article "Our New Poet: Spenser, 'Well of English Undefyld'" in *A Theatre for Spenserians*, ed. Judith M. Kennedy and James A. Reither (Toronto: University of Toronto Press, 1973). John D. Bernard, "Pastoral and Comedy in Book III of *The Faerie Queene*," *Studies in English Literature: 1500–1900*, 23 (1983), 5–20 discusses the narrator's voice and eroticism. Robert O. Evans, "Spenserian Humor," *Neuphilologische Mitteilungen,* 60 (1959), p. 293 notes the distinction between Florimell's point of view and the reader's as comic, but he does not explore its significance, and he, also, mistakenly identifies the aggressor in the boat as Proteus rather than the fisherman.

12. Canto VIII. Ludovico Ariosto, *L'Orlando furioso*, ed. Lanfranco Caretti (Milan and Naples: Ricciardi, 1963).

13. Hamilton, ed., p. 379, note to stanza 24, lines 4 and 7.

14. Bernard, p. 12.

15. Williams, p. 117. See also Roche, p. 159, who argues that Proteus is seeking Florimell's willing consent. His offense is against her love for Marinell. A. Bartlett Giamatti in *Play of Double Senses* (Englewood Cliffs, N. J.: Prentice-Hall, 1975), on the other hand, sees Florimell as still a prisoner of her fear at this point, p. 123. Florimell, in fact, is quite self-possessed with Proteus and confronts his disorderly shape-changing with her steadfastness. To see any

flaw in the stiffness of her "resistance to his wooing" makes it hard to see the value of her chastity.

16. Bahr (p. 122) stresses the difference between Proteus, who represents the subtle and psychological assault on the intellectual and spiritual level, and the fisher, who represents the psychological attack on the physical and human level, but he does not account for Florimell's increased strength; he simply sees the fisher and Proteus as successive challenges.

17. Roche, p. 166, speaks of Britomart's ability to win Satyrane's tournament on the third day as due to her "chastity aided by the grace of God," but he does not analyze the episode in terms of grace.

HAROLD L. WEATHERBY

# *AXIOCHUS* and the Bower of Bliss: Some Fresh Light on Sources and Authorship

*D*ID *Edmund* Spenser translate the 1592 *Axiochus*, which Cuthbert Burbie attributed to "*Edw*. Spenser"?[1] Frederick Padelford, who discovered and published the long-missing book (in 1934), thought so.[2] Subsequent critics—principally Bernard Freyd, Marshall Swan, and Celeste Turner Wright—argued for Anthony Munday's authorship.[3] Half a century after Padelford's discovery the question goes unresolved because neither party to the debate has responded convincingly to the other. Padelford based his opinion on what he heard as echoes in *Axiochus* of Spenserian words and phrases; Rudolf Gottfried, convinced by those parallels, included *Axiochus* in the *Variorum* and there vastly expanded Padelford's list.[4] Neither Padelford nor Gottfried, however, gave much attention to external evidence, most of which supports the case for Munday. Conversely, Munday's champions, while exploiting biographical and historical facts favorable to their position, ignored for the most part the verbal echoes. Reviewing the arguments after twenty years (the last word on the subject was by Professor Wright in 1961)[5] one finds himself a Spenserian or a Mundayite by turns, depending on which body of evidence he considers.

My excuse for breaking a perhaps judicious silence is not expectation of resolving the question but of adding one more echo to Padelford's and Gottfried's list. This echo, however, is a substantial one and more important as evidence of Spenser's authorship than any in the *Variorum*. Most of those are single words or short phrases; somehow both Padelford and Gottfried overlooked an instance of sustained paraphrase—an entire sentence from *Axiochus* carried over into a stanza from *The Faerie Queene*. Here are the passages in question—from *Axiochus*, Socrates' description of the climate in Elysium; from Book Two of *The Faerie Queene*, the weather in Acrasia's bower:

> For the Inhabitants thereof are neither touched
> with force of cold, nor payned with excesse of
> heate, but the moderate Aire breatheth on them
> mildly and calmely, being, lightned with the
> gentle Sunnebeames.[6]

> Thereto the Heauens alwayes Iouiall,
>     Lookt on them louely, still in stedfast state,
>     Ne suffred storme nor frost on them to fall,
>     Their tender buds or leaues to violate,
>     *Nor scorching heat, nor cold intemperate*
>     *T'afflict the creatures, which therein did dwell,*
>     *But the milde aire with season moderate*
>     *Gently attempred, and disposd so well,*
> *That still it breathed forth sweet spirit and holesome smell.*[7]

Resemblance of the italicized portion of Spenser's stanza to the sentence from *Axiochus* is evident at a glance. "Nor scorching heat, nor cold intemperate" parallels, albeit in reverse order, "force of cold, nor...excesse of heate"; "the creatures, which therein did dwell" amplifies "Inhabitants thereof"; "milde aire with season moderate" parallels (again reversing) "moderate Aire...mildly"; and in both passages that air "breathes."

Such resemblances entail two questions: do the parallels constitute proof of influence, and does influence, if demonstrated, prove in turn that Spenser translated *Axiochus*? I shall deal with these in turn.

i

Similarity as such is clearly no proof of influence, for it could be owing to a common *topos* rather than to a common text. *Loci amoeni* are conventionally described in such terms, and the *neither...nor...but* construction to contrast foul weather with fair is very nearly universal. Rather we must discriminate among degrees of resemblance: among several similar passages are two more alike than the rest? is the Spenserian description closer to the Axiochan than to other popular earthly paradises? As a matter of fact, it proves to be. Of the several conventionally cited sources for Spenser's stanza—from Homer, Lucretius, Claudian, Chaucer, and Tasso (suggested by Jortin, Upton, and Warton, and duly noted in the *Variorum*)—none as we shall now see proves to be so convincing a model as the sentence from *Axiochus*. (We should not, of course, forget that the *topos* is indeed widespread and that there may be still some other description hitherto unrecognized and more apt than any of these.)[8]

Jortin's first suggestion—Homer's description of Olympus in Book Six of the *Odyssey*—though resembling Spenser's stanza generally is not in fact very close in detail:

οὔτ' ἀνέμοισι τινάσσεται οὔτε ποτ' ὄμβρῳ
δεύεται οὔτε χιὼν ἐπιπίλναται, ἀλλὰ μάλ' αἴθρη
πέπταται ἀνέφελος, λευκὴ δ' ἐπιδέδρομεν αἴγλη.

Neither is it shaken by winds nor ever wet
with rain nor does snow come near it, but
clear, cloudless air is spread [upon it],
and a shining whiteness hangs over it.[9]

Here is the contrast of harsh weather with pleasant set in the conventional syntax, but Homer does not contrast cold and heat with temperate air as both *The Faerie Queene* and *Axiochus* do; rather he sets wind, rain, and snow in opposition to clear, cloudless air. His precipitation may be a source of Spenser's "storme nor frost," but *Axiochus* affords a much more convincing precedent for "Nor scorching heat, nor cold intemperate." Furthermore Homer's benign air is not only clear rather than moderate; unlike the breathing air of *Axiochus* and *The Faerie Queene*, it does not move: it is simply spread over Olympus.

There is a similar description in Book Four of the *Odyssey*, which commentators (oddly) have failed to note; the prophetic Old Man of the Sea describes the Elysian Field to Menelaus:

οὐ νιφετός, οὔτ᾽ ἄρ᾽ χειμὼν πολύς οὔτε ποτ᾽ ὄμβρος,
ἀλλ᾽ αἰεὶ Ζεφύροιο λιγὺ πνείοντος ἀήτας
Ὠκεανὸς ἀνίησιν ἀναψύχειν ἀνθρώπους.

Neither snow nor much winter nor any rain [is there],
but Ocean forever sends up blasts of shrill-blowing
Zephyr to refresh men.[10]

Here the *neither . . . nor . . . but* syntax serves its customary rhetorical purpose, but again we find nothing so close to Spenser's extremes of climate as those in *Axiochus*. Indeed neither Homeric passage deals with extremes, for neither mentions heat. Therefore the absence of a contrasting reference to temperate or moderate air—the mean between extremes—is scarcely surprising. The logic of the descriptions, however similar their appearances, is in this respect diverse. Indeed "blasts of shrill-blowing Zephyr" sounds anything but temperate.

Jortin's second suggestion is a Lucretian description, which, as he notes, is "an excellent translation" of the Homeric:

                    *sedesque quietae*
*quas neque concutiunt venti nec nubila nimbis*
*aspergunt neque nix acri concreta pruina*
*cana cadens violat semperque innubilus aether*
*integit, et large diffuso lumine ridet.*

The peaceful habitations [of the gods] which
neither winds touch nor clouds wash with rain
nor snow falling white, made hard with bitter
frost, violates; but the air forever cloudless
encompasses them and laughs in light diffused
abroad.[11]

Two elements here, additions to Homer, could be Spenserian sources; Lucretius specifies "frost" (*pruina*)—another possible antecedent for Spenser's "storme nor frost"—and he uses *violat* to describe the frost's action. Spenser's frost also violates. Both moreover describe frost as falling (though in Lucretius it is more precisely snow mixed with frost that falls). In any event *neque nix acri concreta pruina / cana cadens violat* is sufficiently similar to "Ne suffred storme nor frost on them to fall, / Their tender buds or leaues to violate" to qualify convincingly as a source. The resemblance, however, is not so pronounced as that between *Axiochus* and the subsequent lines of Spenser's stanza, for which Lucretius comes no closer than Homer to supplying a convincing precedent. He says nothing of intense heat, intemperate cold, or breathing, temperate air.

Jortin's third suggestion is a *locus amoenus* in Claudian's *Epithalamium of Honorius and Maria*:

> *hunc neque candentes audent vestire pruinae,*
> *hunc venti pulsare timent, hunc laedere nimbi.*
> *luxuriae Venerique vacat. pars acrior anni*
> *exulat; aeterni patet indulgentia veris.*
> *. . .*
>
> *intus rura micant, manibus quae subdita nullis*
> *perpetuum florent, Zephyro contenta colono.*

> Neither the dazzling hoar frosts dare to clothe this place, winds fear to buffet it, clouds to obscure it. It is a place of leisure, for pleasure and for Venus. The harsher part of the year is a stranger; the blessings of eternal spring are everywhere. . . . The fields within glitter; subdued by no [human] hands they flower perpetually, contented with Zephyr as husbandman.[12]

Claudian retains only a vestige of the *neither . . . nor . . . but* syntax; in that respect this passage is less like Spenser's stanza than the others. We do find, however, an emphasis on Venus and pleasure missing from the Homeric and Lucretian descriptions which, if not directly echoed in the stanza with which we are concerned, is certainly appropriate to the Bower of Bliss. Here too, for the first time in the passages we have examined, we find a reference to flora, to which Spenser's "tender buds or leaues" may be indebted. In all other respects, however, Claudian's description seems unSpenserian and clearly no contender with *Axiochus* as a probable source.

A distinct contender, and the most frequent gloss on Spenser's stanza, is Chaucer's *Parlement of Foules*:

> Th'air of that place so attempre was
> That nevere was ther grevaunce of hot ne cold;
> There wex ek every holsom spice and gras.[13]

Besides more vegetation—"spice and gras"—Chaucer supplies, as Homer, Lucretius, and Claudian do not, the juxtaposition of heat and cold as well as Spenser's temperate air—even one of Spenser's adjectives, "attempre." (Chaucer's "holsom" also reappears as Spenser's "holsesome" describing, not grass and spice as in Chaucer, but the sweet smell of the air.) Such similarities are striking, and Spenser almost certainly wrote with Chaucer's lines in mind. On the other hand, there is less rhetorical and syntactical similarity here than in the Greek and Latin passages: the conventional syntax is entirely missing; the reference to temperate air precedes rather than follows the harsh extremes of weather; and Chaucer's air does not "breathe" or indeed move in any fashion. Except the vocabulary—admittedly an important exception—there is nothing of Spenser's in the Chaucerian passage that is not in *Axiochus* and a good deal in *Axiochus* that is not in Chaucer. Surely both contributed to the climate of the Bower, but *Axiochus* seems to have given more.

The latest, chronologically, of the traditional citations is Armida's garden in *Gerusalemme Liberata*:

> Aure fresche mai sempre ed odorate
> vi spiran con tenor stabile e certo,
> né i fiati lor, sì come altrove sole,
> sopisce o desta, ivi girando, il sole;
>
> né, come altrove suol, ghiacci ed ardori
> nubi e sereni a quelle piaggie alterna,
> ma il ciel di candidissimi splendori
> sempre s'ammanta e non s'infiamma o verna,
> e nudre a i prati l'erba, a l'erba i fiori,
> a i fior l'odor, l'ombra a le piante eterna.

> There breezes always fresh and sweet breathe
> with a steady and certain rhythm; neither
> does the sun, circling there, arouse or calm
> their breathings as it does elsewhere; / nor,
> as elsewhere, does it [cause to] alternate in
> those places ice and heat, cloud and clear;
> but the sky mantles itself always with most
> white splendors and is not inflamed or made cold
> by winter; and it nourishes in the meadows grass,
> in the grass the flower, in the flower the scent,
> and it makes eternal the shade of the tree.[14]

Tasso's debt to the tradition is manifest, and like Chaucer he employs the juxtaposition of cold and heat which provides the central logic of the Spenserian and Axiochan passages. In fact the opposition is stated twice—first as "ghiacci ed ardori" ("ice and heat")—and subsequently as verbal action—"s' infiamma o verna" (literally, "inflames itself or winters"). Also like Claudian and Chaucer, Tasso alludes to the effects of a temperate climate on vegetation, and indeed in considerably more detail than either of the earlier poets. Finally we encounter here for the first time in our survey air that "breathes";[15] and this element is also emphasized by duplication—first "spiran" ("breathes") and then "i fiati lor" ("their [the wind's] breathings"). All these characteristics of Spenser's stanza could therefore have come from Tasso, whom we know Spenser knew, rather than from *Axiochus*, which he may or may not have known and translated. One suspects, indeed, that Tasso, like Chaucer, made a contribution to the climate in Acrasia's bower; but like the lines from the *Parlement of Foules*, these stanzas diverge more markedly from Spenser than does the sentence in *Axiochus*. Tasso (unlike Chaucer) employs the traditional syntactical pattern, but that pattern does not stand out in sharp relief as it does in *Axiochus* and *The Fairie Queene*; rather it is overlaid with descriptive and qualifying material which almost obscures it. Moreover, as is the case with Homer's descriptions, the syntax does not set the same terms in opposition; for Spenser and the author of *Axiochus* the *neither* . . . *nor* distinguishes cold and heat, and the *but* applies to the breathing air. For Tasso, *neither* controls the sun's benign influence upon the breezes and *nor* the opposition of ice and heat. Tasso's *but* pertains not to the breezes but to the sky; the breathing breezes introduce the description (as does Chaucer's temperate air). Finally, though we may infer that the climate of Armida's garden is temperate, Tasso does not employ the word or any of its synonyms. On balance, therefore, Tasso looks a less likely primary source than *Axiochus*.

Spenser could have known all of these descriptions and relied upon them. My guess, however, is that his stanza is a composite of *Axiochus*, Lucretius, Chaucer, and Tasso in which *Axiochus* served as the principal constituent—the skeleton which borrowings from those poets fleshed out. (I am dubious about a debt to Claudian or a *direct* debt to Homer, for there is nothing in either which is not to be found in conjunction with more distinctively Spenserian features elsewhere.) Such conclusions are necessarily tentative, the survey of sources being as we have confessed necessarily partial. The *topos* is so common that we can never be certain we have exhausted its representatives; indeed we can be certain we have not. With that reservation, however, we can argue for *Axiochan* influence.

ii

We are brought then to our second question: does influence prove authorship? Not necessarily, for Spenser could have known *Axiochus* without translating it. But we may press the question further: what version of *Axiochus* did Spenser know (or seem to know)? An examination of his phrasing in *The Faerie Queene* suggests that he was drawing from the very same Latin text upon which the translation attributed to him was based. That was, as Padelford showed, the 1568 version by Rayanus Welsdalius.[16]

Here is the sentence in question as Welsdalius rendered it:

*Neque ibi habitantes frigoris vis, nec caloris*
*vehementia infestat, sed moderatus temperatusque*
*funditur aĕr, benignis solaribus illustratus radys.*

Neither force of cold, nor vehemence of heat vex
those dwelling there, but moderate and temperate air

is poured, illuminated with kind sunbeams.[17]

In at least three instances, Spenser seems to echo the Latin phrasing and syntax. The first and most striking of these is the correspondence between "the creatures, which therein did dwell" and Welsdalius's *ibi habitantes.* Spenser's "creatures" admittedly takes a liberty, but there is no way to translate the Latin participle without some such specification—"those dwelling," for instance—and to identify the indefinite dwellers as "creatures" (probably to meet the demands of the meter) in no way alters the sense. The relative clause is probably also owing to the requirements of the line, but that construction is a standard way of rendering Latin participles and usually is more effective English than such a phrase as "creatures dwelling." In fact "creatures, which therein did dwell" is arguably a more accurate rendering of *ibi habitantes* than 1592's "Inhabitants thereof." Spenser (or perhaps we should say, Spenser in his poetic version of the phrase) has retained a verbal construction which, though no longer participial, is by virtue of being verbal closer to the spirit of the Latin than "Inhabitants." Furthermore "therein," as a specification of place, is manifestly a more exact translation of *ibi* than "therefore."

The second noteworthy resemblance is between Spenser's "afflict" and Welsdalius's *infestat.* The Latin is most accurately translated as "vex," "harass," "trouble," or "molest," with which "afflict" is virtually synonymous. Here again *The Faerie Queene* comes closer to the Latin than the 1592 translation, suggesting that the resemblance to Welsdalius is more than mere coincidence. Whoever did the prose version split *infestat* into two verbs, "touched" and "payned" (applying one to cold and one to heat), and substituted the passive for the active voice. In so doing he moved cold and heat from subject to predicate and transformed "Inhabitants" from direct object into the subject. Spenser's version (or his poetic version) while not a literal translation of the Latin is considerably more faithful: heat and cold remain the subjects (though admittedly of an infinitive), and they afflict (actively) inhabitants who keep their place in the predicate.

Finally Spenser seems consciously to have exploited the implications of Welsdalius's *moderatus temperatusque.* The phrase is redundant; why not just one adjective or the other? Evidently

Welsdalius wanted to place heavy emphasis on temperateness, and the 1592 translator probably introduced "mildly and calmely" (adverbs missing in the Latin) to convey that emphasis. *The Faerie Queene* insists even more strongly on the redundant effect of the Latin phrase: "milde," "moderate," "gently attempred," and "disposd so well." All these make the same point—as does, inversely, "cold intemperate" (of which we shall have more to say in another context). One could of course argue that Spenser was influenced in his phrasing not by Welsdalius's Latin but by the theme of Book Two; but that reasoning can cut both ways. He may have been attracted to Welsdalius's version of the sentence in question for that very reason.

The case for Welsdalius as Spenser's source is strengthened by another fact which we have not yet mentioned—that *ibi habitantes . . . infestat* and *moderatus temperatusque* are peculiarities of the 1568 translation. Spenser could not have found these phrases or their equivalents in the Greek original (available in parallel columns in Welsdalius's edition) nor in any of the seven earlier Renaissance versions.[18] For inhabitants and their affliction, for instance, the Greek offers no precedent; it reads simply οὔτε γὰρ χεῖμα σφοδρὸν, οὔτε θάλπος ἐγγίνεται[19] —"neither excessive cold nor fervent heat is there." Since a Latin synonym for ἐγγίνεται is *inest*, to "be in" a place, one can imagine the derivation of *ibi* from the ἐγ- prefix. Of *habitantes* and *infestat*, however, the Greek gives not the slightest hint. Welsdalius probably derived his phrase from the 1544 French translation by Etienne Dolet, which reads, "là on n'est poinct fasché." "Est fasché" is almost synonymous with *infestat*, and *habitantes* could conceivably be extrapolated from "on." Even so Welsdalius must be credited with the imaginative process which produced the Latin phrasing; Spenser reading Dolet's version without previous acquaintance with Welsdalius's would not likely envision "creatures, which therein did dwell" in the indefinite pronoun. *Moderatus temperatusque* is simply unprecedented. The second clause in Greek reads ἀλλ' εὔκρατος ἀὴρ χεῖται, ἁπαλαῖς ἡλίου ἀκτῖσιν ἀνακρινάμενος—"but temperate air is poured, well-mixed with gentle beams of [the] sun." Εὔκρατος means simply "temperate" or (literally) "well-mixed" (there is a pun on εὔκρατος and ἀνακρινάμενος);[20] nothing about the adjective serves as pretext for Welsdalius's emphatic redundancy, nor do the earlier translators (though they render the phrase variously) furnish a precedent.

If, therefore, Spenser's indwelling, afflicted creatures and his heavy stress on temperateness have a source—if they are not (always a possibility) coincidental resemblances—that source is almost certainly Welsdalius. (It is here worth recalling that none of the other *loci amoeni* which we have examined mention inhabitants or the effect of weather upon them; nor, as we have seen, do those descriptions place much emphasis on temperateness.) Hence there is good reason to believe that Spenser knew, and knew rather well, the source of the 1592 translation traditionally ascribed to him. Moreover, the similarities between Welsdalius and *The Faerie Queene* are underscored by one interesting dissimilarity—the proverbial exception that proves the rule. As we have mentioned several times, both in Spenser's stanza and in the 1592 translation the temperate air "breathes": "breathed forth sweet spirit" (Spenser obviously intended a pun) and "breatheth on them mildly and calmely." Welsdalius, instead of "breathed" has "poured" (*funditur*); and in this instance the Latin is faithful to the Greek. *Funditur* is an exact synonym for χεῖται from χέω, "pour."[21] The earlier translations either give us "pour" or construct the sentence so as to omit the verb altogether. Only the two English adaptations substitute "breathe"—an encouragement, certainly, to believe them the work of the same hand.

Belief, however, is unfortunately not proof; Spenser could easily have known and adapted a sentence from Welsdalius's version without being responsible for the translation based on that version. Even the peculiarity of "breathe," given the commonness of the metaphor, is not decisive. Worse still, the discovery of a debt to Welsdalius entails a consideration potentially damaging to a case for Spenser as translator—the possibility of Greek influence. Since Welsdalius's was a two-text edition incorporating the original, whoever was responsible for 1592 had the Greek before him as he worked. One of Padelford's discoveries was that the English relies altogether on the Latin[22]—a fact used to good effect by Munday's proponents, for Spenser presumably knew Greek and Munday only Latin.[23] If therefore we can show that the adaptation in *The Faerie Queene* draws upon the Greek as well as the Latin, we thereby cast doubt on Spenser's authorship of 1592.

Two of his phrases seem, indeed, to indicate recourse to the original—"scorching heat" and "cold intemperate." "Force of cold" and "excesse of heate" in 1592 are literal translations of Welsdalius's *frigoris vis* and *caloris vehementia*, but these phrases take a liberty with χεῖμα σφοδρόν and θάλπος. The former means literally "excessive cold," to which Spenser's "cold intemperate" is a fairly close approximation—considerably closer than Welsdalius or 1592. "Intemperate" for "excessive" could be accounted for as an effort to anticipate the immediately subsequent emphasis on temperate air. Or Spenser may have wished to preserve the Greek word order, and "cold excessive" is not tolerable English. "Scorching heat" for θάλπος requires even less justification; the lexicons suggest "fervent heat" or "summer heat," for which "scorching" is virtually synonymous. "Scorching," moreover, is a favorite Spenserian adjective; Osgood lists twenty-two uses, most of them in *The Faerie Queene*, four of them in Book Two. Welsdalius's phrases convey, of course, the same meanings, but where the Latin varies the original by rendering the Greek adjective as a Latin noun and placing the Greek subject in an oblique case (with 1592 following suit), Spenser appears to have restored the simpler, original construction. Since he follows Welsdalius's Latin in every other respect, these variations could, of course, be his own—for metrical and rhetorical purposes. Given, however, his almost certain knowledge of Greek, that is not likely. We must, therefore, weigh the probability of Greek influence in *The Faerie Queene* against its absence in the 1592 *Axiochus* in drawing any inferences from the evidence before us.

iii

If we return to our two original questions, we may answer the first positively: we have virtually demonstrated influence—and not just Axiochan but specifically Welsdalian influence. Whether that influence constitutes evidence of authorship is, however, less certain. There are, it seems to me, three ways to interpret what we have discovered; and though from here on all is conjecture, we may be able to discriminate among the relative worths of these hypotheses.

It is conceivable that Spenser and the 1592 translator had nothing in common but their source; that so far from being the same person they may have known nothing of one another or of one another's work. Such an explanation would account for the greater accuracy of Latin translation in *The Faerie Queene* and also, of course, for the presence of Greek influence in the poetry; Spenser we can assume was better in both ancient tongues than Munday or whoever the prose translator may have been. No antecedent improbability attaches to such an hypothesis; Padelford demonstrates that *Axiochus* was broadly popular in the late sixteenth century[24]—two unrelated adaptations of a recent translation would not under such circumstances be improbable. Against that explanation stand, however, both the traditional ascription to Spenser (which Padelford was surely correct in regarding as "presumptive evidence in Spenser's favor")[25] and the coincidence (whatever it may be worth) of "breathe."

The latter could be accounted for by a second and more elaborate hypothesis already adumbrated by Professors Swan and Wright: that Munday translated *Axiochus* but modeled his version of the clause in question on Spenser's rendition, whose source he recognized. Munday's proponents have not, of course, discussed this particular passage, but they have suggested that Padelford's and Gottfried's parallels are to be explained by a deliberate intention on Munday's part to imitate Spenser's style and thereby cash in on the poet's popularity after publication of the first installment of *The Faerie Queene*. They even suggest that Burbie's ascription was owing to the same intention and that Munday may have had no scruples about enhancing sales by publishing his work under Spenser's name and in the disguise of Spenser's style.[26] If such fraud were in fact afoot, Munday's discovery of a Spenserian adaptation of a sentence from Welsdalius would have furnished him with just the sort of material he needed for his effort at imitation. The dating, of course, supports such a theory perfectly—Book Two of *The Faerie Queene* appearing in 1590 and *Axiochus* in 1592. The weakness of the hypothesis is not that it does not account plausibly for all the facts but that it is wholly conjectural from beginning to end (and the same objection may be lodged against Swan's and Wright's less explicit development of the same argument). Beyond what we know generally about Munday's and Burbie's questionable literary activities, everything here is supposition.

Less purely conjectural and equally effective in explaining the phenomena is the hypothesis I find most persuasive: that Spenser translated *Axiochus* a very long time before he wrote Book Two of *The Faerie Queene* and either before he learned Greek at all or before he knew it well enough to translate it freely. Everyone who has discussed the question of authorship believes that if *Axiochus* is Spenser's, it is early work. Padelford pointed (though somewhat hesitantly) to the late 1570s on account of what he believed to be the influence of Mornay;[27] but the translation could have been done at any time after the publication of Welsdalius's edition in 1568. Spenser was then still a schoolboy at Merchant Taylors' but sufficiently precocious to publish English versions of French poetry. In the same years in which he translated Marot and du Bellay, may he not have ventured upon Welsdalius as well? Padelford produces evidence that *Axiochus* was used in sixteenth-century England as a school text so it is not impossible that Spenser was assigned translation of the Latin as an exercise.[28] In the perhaps as much as two decades before he wrote the Bower of Bliss, there would have been plenty of time to become "perfect in the Greek tongue";[29] and the maturity which those years would have brought could also account for the greater sensitivity to the subtleties of the Latin which the poetry manifests.

For whatever further light (or shadow) it may throw on the subject, Spenser could have discovered the Greek of the sentence in question—in isolation from the rest of the dialogue and independent of Welsdalius's translation—in the very process of composing Book Two. As long ago as 1957 Harry Berger suggested that the theme of temperance is developed in part through word-play on the Greek κρᾶσις —"mixing" or "tempering." The privative yields ἀκρασία —"bad mixture, ill temperature"—and hence Acrasia, Spenser's personification of intemperance.[30] If Spenser was indulging himself in Greek etymological puns, he almost certainly knew that the antonym of ἀκρασία was εὐκρασία or "temperance," the very virtue of the Book. The adjectival equivalent is εὔκρατος, which in the original *Axiochus* is the adjective describing air—εὔκρατος ἀήρ—the word Welsdalius expands into *moderatus temperatusque* and Spenser into his several synonyms for "temperate." Anyone in the last quarter of the sixteenth century exploring Greek etymologies is likely to have consulted Henri Estienne's *Thesaurus graecae linguae* (Geneva, 1572), the most recent and most authoritative source for such information. (We do not know that Spenser used this thesaurus, but Starnes and Talbert offer good evidence for his knowing other lexicographical productions of the Estienne house.)[31] Estienne's custom is to provide illustrative citations for various usages, and for εὔκρατος he offers the sentence in question from *Axiochus*.[32] If, therefore, as Berger's evidence suggests, Spenser was acquainting himself with various derivatives of κρᾶσις (or perhaps confirming his acquaintance), he could easily have stumbled in Estienne on the very sentence which shapes his stanza. The Greek of that sentence, thus called forcibly to his attention as thematically germane to his poem, would naturally prompt recollection of Welsdalius's Latin and his own youthful translation. A consequence of such a process of association could be precisely what we seem to have in the stanza under consideration—a composite of Welsdalius, of the original ("Nor scorching heat, nor cold intemperate") and of 1592 ("breathed").

There the matter must rest unless (or until) further evidence is forthcoming. We admittedly stop short of a conclusion, and doubt of Spenser's authorship of the English *Axiochus* remains. I think it fair to say, however, that the evidence here educed adds substantially to the argument Padelford advanced fifty years ago.

*Vanderbilt University*

## NOTES

1. Burbie's title-page reads, "Translated out of Greeke by Edw. Spenser." The address "To the Reader" identifies the translator as "that worthy Scholler and Poet, Maister Edward Spenser, whose studies haue & doe carry no mean commendation, because their deserts are of so great esteeme."

2. *The Axiochus of Plato,* translated by Edmund Spenser, ed. Frederick Morgan Padelford (Baltimore, Md.: Johns Hopkins University Press, 1934). Padelford's Introduction contains a full history of the 1592 *Axiochus* from the first known allusion to it, by Thomas Osborne, in 1744. Padelford announced his discovery of the long-missing book in 1932 and spent two years in preparing his edition. The traditional ascription to Spenser has been questioned since the beginning of the nineteenth century; Padelford in his Introduction argued

strongly for Spenser's authorship.

3. The case for Anthony Munday's authorship of the 1592 *Axiochus* was first advanced by Bernard Freyd in 1935 (*PMLA*, 50, 903–908) in response to Frederick M. Padelford's Introduction to his facsimile edition of the recently discovered work (1934). Padelford had argued strongly for Spenser's authorship; Freyd contended that there is no "external authority of any weight" for ascription to Spenser and that "internal evidence of style and content" contradicted Padelford (p. 906). If not Spenser, who? The 1592 title page included an anonymous "sweet speech or Oration, spoken at the Tryumphe at Whitehall . . . by the Page to the . . . Earle of Oxenforde," not in the copy which Padelford edited. This "sweet speech," said Freyd, was almost certainly by Munday, a leading writer of civic pageants and self-characterized as a "servant" to the Earl of Oxford. Munday, who was not "averse to pseudonymity in its boldest form," (p. 906) was in Freyd's judgment the translator of *Axiochus* as well. Only a year later (1936) another copy of *Axiochus* appeared at Sotheby's, this one containing the "sweet speech." William A. Jackson gave a careful description of the book in *The Carl H. Pforzheimer Library, English Literature, 1475–1700* (New York: The Morrill Press, 1940), 3, 995, and proved that the "Speech" could not have been by Spenser. He also showed that another printer, John Charlewood, printed the "Speech." On the basis of that evidence, Marshall W. S. Swan enlarged upon Freyd's argument for Munday's authorship, both of the "Speech" and *Axiochus* in "The *Sweet Speech* and Spenser's (?) *Axiochus*," *ELH*, 11 (1944), 161–181. Charlewood was Munday's printer, and Swan suggested collusion among Munday, Charlewood, and Burbie to cash in on Spenser's popularity. Fifteen years later Munday's biographer, Celeste Turner Wright, in a long article redating Munday's birth ("Young Anthony Mundy Again," *Studies in Philology*, 56 [1959], 150–168), summarized and endorsed Swan's theory of a "literary hoax," which she ascribed primarily to Charlewood. Then two years later in "Anthony Mundy, 'Edward' Spenser, and E. K.," *PMLA*, 76 (1961), 34–39, she supplemented Swan's evidence, demonstrating that Munday could have known Burbie as much as "five years before the *Axiochus* affair." "Mundy, Burby, and their helpers were capable of misusing Spenser's name. In 1592, when the *Faerie Queene* was popular, Mundy may have translated the *Axiochus*, with Spenserian touches, or dug up a youthful version." She found the latter possibility attractive because in 1579 Munday's style "somewhat resembled Spenser's" (p. 35). She also suggested several possible links between Munday and Spenser, the most interesting of which is that they may have had a mutual friend, Edward Knight, who may be none other than "the mysterious editor of Spenser's *Shepheardes Calender*" (p. 34).

4. *Variorum Prose*, pp. 269–277. See Padelford, pp. 26–27.

5. For a convenient summary of the question of authorship, see the entry for "Spenser" in *Evidence for Authorship: Essays on Problems of Attribution*, ed. David V. Erdman and Ephim G. Fogel (Ithaca, N.Y.: Cornell University Press, 1966), pp. 423–427.

6. Padelford, p. 58.

7. *FQ*, II, xii, 51; italics added.

8.  The *locus amoenus* or "pleasant place"—the earthly paradise or golden age—is persistent in Western literature, and so too are studies of the topos. Probably the best account and certainly the most authoritative is Ernst Robert Curtius's in *European Literature and the Latin Middle Ages*, trans., Willard R. Trask (Princeton, N. J.: Princeton University Press, 1953), Chapter 10, "The Ideal Landscape," pp. 183–202. Curtius traces the phrase to Virgil, (*Aeneid*, VI, 638): *Devenere locos laetos et amoena virecta* (p. 192). He examines several classical instances of the topos and its transmission to later literature, in part through rhetorical formulae for landscape description. The best discussion of the motif in the Renaissance is Harry Levin's *The Myth of the Golden Age in the Renaissance* (Bloomington: Indiana University Press, 1969), which includes numerous references to Spenser. A. Bartlett Giamatti's *The Earthly Paradise and the Renaissance Epic* (Princeton, N.J.: Princeton University Press, 1966), Chapter 5 (pp. 232–294) examines Spenser's use of the topos in the Bower of Bliss and the Garden of Adonis. Giamatti is not primarily concerned with sources but makes interesting observations on Spenser's debt to Ariosto and Tasso. Northrop Frye in *Fearful Symmetry: A Study of William Blake* (Princeton, N. J.: Princeton University Press, 1947) throws indirect light on Spenser (a comparison of Blake's Beaulah with the Garden of Adonis), and so too does Stanley Stewart, *The Enclosed Garden: The Tradition and the Image in Seventeenth-Century Poetry* (Madison: University of Wisconsin Press, 1966). Patrick Cullen's "Imitation and Metamorphosis: The Golden-Age Eclogue in Spenser, Milton, and Marvell," *PMLA*, 84 (1969), 1559–1570, though concerned primarily with the *Shepheardes Calender* is suggestive for Spenser's later work as well. Under an index entry for *locus amoenus*, McNeir and Provost list 26 items; for the *loci amoeni* conventionally cited as Spenser's sources for *FQ*, II, xii, 51, see *Variorum*, II, pp. 377–378.

9.  *Odyssey*, VI, 43–45. Greek text is from the Loeb; translation is mine.

10.  *Odyssey*, IV, 566–568. Greek text is from the Loeb; translation is mine.

11.  *De rerum natura*, III, 18–22. Latin text is from the Loeb; translation is mine.

12.  *Epithalamium de nuptiis Honorii Augusti*, ll. 52–55 & 60–61. Latin text is from the Loeb; translation is mine.

13.  ll. 204-206. I quote from F. N. Robinson's edition (Boston, Mass.: Houghton Mifflin, 1957), p. 313. This passage is the only gloss on *FQ*, II, xii, 51, 5–9, in A. C. Hamilton's annotated edition of *The Faerie Queene* (London: Longman's, 1977).

14.  *Gerusalemme Liberata*, XV, stanzas 53–54. Text is that of Tasso's *Opere*, ed. Bruno Maier (Milan: Rizzoli, 1963), III, 515. Translation is mine (with considerable assistance).

15.  One can, of course, translate Homer's πνείοντος as "breathing" instead of "blowing," but the presence of ("shrill") suggests the latter. Both meanings are contained in an undifferentiated form in the Greek.

16.  Padelford examined the Greek original as well as the earlier Renaiss-

ance editions of *Axiochus*. His evidence for 1592's dependence on Welsdalius is conclusive.

17. Welsdalius's text is reproduced by Padelford. For this passage see p. 79; the translation is mine.

18. These are the translations which Padelford lists in his "Introduction," pp. 16–17, and which I have also examined. Actually there were nine translations of *Axiochus*, including Welsdalius, before 1592, but Mornay's (1581), which Padelford thinks Spenser may have known of (p. 14), is abbreviated and does not contain the sentence we are dealing with. The translations in chronological order are: Rudolphus Agricola (Latin), 1477; Marsilio Ficino (Latin), 1497; Bilibaldus Pirckheymer (Latin), 1523; Guillaume Postel (French), 1537–39 (?); Joachimus Perionius (Latin), 1542; Etienne Dolet (French), 1544; Don Giovanni Vincentio Belprato (Italian), 1550; Rayanus Welsdalius (Graeco-Latin), 1568; and Phillippe de Mornay (French), 1581. I am indebted to Robert D. Monroe, formerly Head of the Special Collections Division of the University of Washington Libraries at Seattle, for making photocopies of these translations available to me. Padelford collected them with considerable expense and difficulty in preparing his 1934 edition.

19. Padelford, p. 79.

20. The "well-mixed" air is "well-mixed."

21. Padelford, p. 79.

22. Padelford (p. 17) went so far as to say, "There is not a single phrase or word in which he followed the original at the expense of the Latin." That is slightly stronger language than the evidence allows, for Gottfried found two or three words and phrases which seem owing to the Greek (*Variorum Prose*, pp. 269, 272, and 273). Even so, Padelford is closer to the truth than not; the 1592 *Axiochus* is almost, if not quite, a translation throughout of Welsdalius.

23. Freyd, pp. 906–907. Whether Spenser knew Greek is still debated, but it is difficult to believe that a man of his generation, educated at Merchant Taylors' where Greek was part of the curriculum, holding a Master's degree from Cambridge where Greek was certainly studied, a fellow student both at Merchant Taylors' and at Pembroke, Cambridge, of Lancelot Andrewes, one of the best Greek scholars of the day—that such a man did not know Greek. Nor is there any substantial reason to doubt Lodowick Bryskett's claim that Spenser (at least by 1581) was "perfect in the Greek tongue." (In Bryskett's *A Discourse of Ciuill Life*, 1606 quoted by Alexander C. Judson in *The Life of Edmund Spenser* [Baltimore, Md.: Johns Hopkins University Press, 1945], p. 106.)

24. Padelford, p. 17.

25. See Padelford's rejoinder to Bernard Freyd in *PMLA*, 50 (1935), p. 908.

26. See Swan (1944) and Wright (1959 & 1961).

27. Padelford, pp. 12–14.

28. Padelford, p. 17.

29. Jusdon, p. 106.

30.  Harry Berger, Jr., *The Allegorical Temper* (New Haven, Conn.: Yale University Press, 1957), p. 66. My summary of Berger's thesis, though sufficient for present purposes, scarcely does his discussion justice.

31.  De Witt T. Starnes, "Spenser and the Muses," *University of Texas Studies in English*, 35 (1942), 31–58, and Starnes with Ernest William Talbert, *Classical Myth and Legend in Renaissance Dictionaries* (Chapel Hill: University of North Carolina Press, 1955), pp. 61 ff.

32.  Col. 137.

DAVID O. FRANTZ

# The Union of Florimell and Marinell: The Triumph of Hearing

*F*OR even the most devoted enthusiasts, canto xii of Book IV of *The Faerie Queene* has seemed anti-climactic at best. After the pomp and circumstance of the marriage of the Thames and Medway in canto xi, canto xii appears to be little more than a perfunctory tying up of loose ends, as Florimell is freed from bondage in Proteus's cave and presented to the languishing Marinell. And that meeting itself is understated, a rather disappointing union of lovers who have undergone many trials and tribulations. Marinell is so weak that he can do no more than make "chearefull signes," and Florimell, deeply "in secret hart affected," masks her feeling with modesty, "for feare she should of lightnesse be detected" (IV.xii.35).[1] If the tone is hardly one of full-blown summer celebration, however, it is one of hopeful springtime renewal, and I would argue that Spenser's choice not to compete with the pageantry of canto xi is a wise one, for it serves to give more power to the *way* in which Florimell wins Marinell's love rather than to the celebration of that union, an event which Spenser quite appropriately saves, as many scholars have noted, for the Book of Justice. The *way* in which Florimell wins Marinell, an aspect of the narrative virtually unmentioned in commentary on Books III and IV, is best understood in terms of the neoplatonic debate over which

115

sense is more elevated in apprehending beauty, the sense of hearing or the sense of sight. What Spenser gives us at the end of Book IV is a muted, momentary victory for the sense of hearing. The victory of hearing over seeing in Florimell's case is a fittingly ironic one, since she is one of the females in the poem so persistently pursued and assailed for the physical bearuty that males see. One sight of Florimell sends Arthur and Guyon in hot pursuit, energizes the slothful son of the wicked witch to a lover's service, heats the old fisherman's long dormant blood, and inspires from Proteus a whole pageant of players in his attempts to seduce her. Her love, of course, rests faithfully on Marinell, and she wins his love not when he sees her, but when he hears her complaint in Proteus's cave at the nuptials of Thames and Medway. The coming together of Florimell and Marinell not only provides a fitting conclusion to their relationship, it also provides a fitting conclusion to the Books of Chastity and Friendship as well, for it is one in which we see the "affection vnto kindred" in Cymodoce's gift to her son, "raging fire of loue to woman kind" in Marinell, and "zeale of friends combynd with vertues meet" in Florimell and Marinell. Theirs is the story of Cambell and Triamond writ across a broader canvas.

The particulars of the debate as to which sense enabled the mind to perceive beauty most readily can be traced from Plato and Aristotle through Ficino, Leone Ebreo, Bembo, and a host of other Renaissance philosophers and poets. For purposes of this study, a rehearsal of the debate may be foreshortened by pointing to the issue as it is summarized and made accessible and concrete in Erwin Panofsky's most pertinent study of Titian's paintings of Venus with a musician in his book, *Problems in Titian: Mostly Iconographic.* Panofsky reminds us that the "philosophers were unanimous in claiming that only the senses of sight and hearing but not the senses of taste, smell and touch enable the mind to perceive beauty and thus to gain access to the related worlds of love, cognition and art."[2] Panofsky summarizes the positions of the ancients, with Plato coming down on the primacy of sight and Aristotle on sound, and he directs us to Ficino, who proposed a compromise accepting both senses. Ficino in his commentary on Plato's *Symposium* writes:

> Beauty is, in fact, a certain charm which is found chiefly and predominantly in the harmony of several elements. This charm is threefold: there is a certain charm in the soul,

in the harmony of several virtues; charm is found in material objects, in the harmony of several colors and lines, and
likewise charm in sound is the best harmony of several
tones. There is, therefore, this triple beauty: of the soul, of
the body, and of sound. That of the soul is perceived by the
mind; that of the body, by the eyes; and that of sound, by
the ear alone. Since, therefore, the mind, the sight, and the
hearing are the only means by which we are able to enjoy
beauty, and since Love is the desire for enjoying beauty,
Love is always limited to [the pleasure of] the mind, the
eyes, and the ears.[3]

Panofsky instructs us in how to see this compromise in two
series paintings Titian did of Venus with a musician. In the first
series the musician, an organ player, is disrupted in his playing
by looking at the naked Venus. In the second series of paintings
the organ player has been replaced by a lute player, and he is able
to continue his homage to beauty while she in turn does homage
to music by holding a recorder and keeping a stringed instrument at her side.[4] This compromise, this acceptance of the
power of hearing as sometimes equal to the power of seeing is
also reflected in Book IV of Castiglione's *The Book of the Courtier* and Sidney's *Defense of Poesy* and *Astrophel and Stella*.

In Bembo's discourse on love in Book IV of Castiglione's
*Book of the Courtier*, sight is given primacy in the apprehension
of beauty, but hearing is not neglected and is certainly elevated to
a position close to seeing. Bembo says:

> Therefore let him keep aloof from the blind judgment of
> sense, and with his eyes enjoy the radiance of his Lady, her
> grace, her amorous sparkle, the smiles, the manners and all
> the other pleasant ornaments of her beauty. Likewise with
> his hearing let him enjoy the sweetness of her voice, the
> modulation of her words, the harmony of her music (if his
> lady love be a musician). Thus, he will feed his soul on the
> sweetest food by means of these two senses—which par-
> take little of the corporeal, and are reason's ministers—
> without passing to any unchaste appetite through desire for
> the body.[5]

And later Bembo affirms that both sight and hearing are the
paths by which one gains access to the soul.[6]

Sidney in his *Defense of Poesy* claims that music is "the most divine striker of the senses," and in the Sixth Song of *Astrophel and Stella* he gives us an unresolved debate between the two senses.[7]

When we meet Florimell again near the end of Book IV in *The Faerie Queene*, she has passed through a series of calamitous adventures. Having departed from the court at the news that Marinell has been wounded, she has been pursued and assailed by a host of lustful creatures, finally ending up imprisoned by Proteus. Florimell wins Marinell's love while she is imprisoned in Proteus's cave because he hears her complaint; he is moved; his hardened heart is pierced and softened by her words and tears. In a poem filled with complaints, especially in the middle books, Spenser provides us with a rare instance of a complaint that works, a prayer that is answered. Florimell's complaint has the effect of achieving the ostensible goal of sonneteers and complaint singers, it moves the object of her love. Complaints come in many modes in Books III and IV, from the comic to the pathetic; Venus, Britomart, Arthur, Timias, the Witch's son, the Squire of Dames, Paridell, Scudamore, Poena, the lovers in the Temple of Venus, to name just a few, are heard bemoaning their states. Significantly, Marinell first enters the narrative in Book III on the seashore where Britomart has just completed a complaint filled with Petrarchan imagery of love as a tempest-tossed voyage. She cries:

> Huge sea of sorrow, and tempestuous griefe,
> Wherein my feeble barke is tossed long,
> Far from the hoped hauen of reliefe,
> Why do thy cruell billowes beat so strong,
> And thy moyst mountaines each on others throng,
> Threatning to swallow up my fearefull life?
> O do thy cruell wrath and spightfull wrong
> At length allay, and stint thy stormy strife,
> Which in these troubled bowels raignes, & rageth rife.
>
> For else my feeble vessell crazd, and crackt
> Through thy strong buffets and outrageous blowes,

Cannot endure, but needs it must be wrackt
On the rough rocks, or on the sandy shallowes,
The whiles that loue it steres, and fortune rowes;
Loue my lewd Pilot hath a restlesse mind
And fortune Boteswaine no assuraunce knowes,
But saile withouten starres, gainst tide and wind:
How can they other do, sith both are bold and blind?

(III.iv.8–9)

As with much of the story of Britomart's falling in love, we treat
this with a smile at least. Marinell rides against her at the end of
her complaint, and Britomart defeats him easily. We are then
told Marinell's story, especially how his mother warned him not
to entertain the love of women. His flight from love has led
many ladies to complain "That they for loue of him would
algates dy." We associate Marinell with the sea through his name
of course, but I think Spenser is also careful to associate him with
the complaints of women as well, complaints that often draw
their power from sea imagery.[8]

It might seem odd to argue that Spenser allows hearing equali-
ty with seeing in the winning of love and beauty in a book where
the power of sight is so prominent and powerful a force. At the
center of Book IV, after all, lies the episode where Arthegall sees
Britomart revealed for the first time, and he is transfixed by the
vision (IX.vi.19–22). While it must be admitted that the limitations of seeing are before us too, they are the limitations of the
unvirtuous, who are easily stirred by seeing something as flashy
as the False Florimell, the pursuit of whom culminates in the
wonderfully comic beauty contest at Satyrane's tournament—a
contest where one need only see if Florimell's girdle will stay on
to know whether *Penthouse* will be the next stop. If one looks to
the *Hymnes of Love* and *Beavtie*, those poems which Sean Kane
has said "might almost be called Spenser's Hymns to Amoret
and Florimell," one must admit that Spenser emphasizes what is
seen above all as a positive force.[9] And as if the positive aspects of
the power of seeing are not stressed enough, Spenser makes us
acutely aware that the sense of hearing is one so easily abused in
Book IV: words are especially dangerous; Ate with the
doubleness of tongue, heart, and ears is forever stirring up discord with her malicious tongue; Sclaunder reviles and backbites
Arthur with Amoret and Aemylia; and Arthur himself is so tak-

en by Poena's complaint that he almost gets caught, "halfe rapt" as he is by her lament.[10] Time and again in Book IV we see that once discord is loose and ire given rein, words are seldom sufficient to restore order. "None but a God or godlike man can slake" the sparks ignited by discord, "Such as was *Orpheus*, that when strife was growen / Amongst those famous ympes of Greece, did take / His siluer Harpe in hand, and shortly friends them make" (IV.ii.1).[11] This simile does tell us that music can stint strife, but it takes the efforts of the hero-poet to make it work.

The emphasis on the poet as an extraordinary being should not, however, surprise us, and Spenser follows his example of the successful poet-musician, Orpheus, in canto ii of Book IV with the example of David, the celestial psalmist, who "when the wicked feend his Lord tormented, / With heauenly notes, that did all other pas, / The outrage of his furious fit relented. / Such Musicke is wise words with time concented, / To moderate stiffe minds, disposed to striue" (IV.ii.2). Words are the poet's medium, after all, and if Spenser is going to praise the sense of sight to apprehend beauty and love, he is going to do it through songs of praise, his hymns; if he is going to lament, complain in his sonnets, presumably he hopes they will be efficacious; they will pity win. To read the Marinell-Florimell story as the truimph of hearing over sight may make it the exception in *The Faerie Queen*, but it is a strategically placed and powerful exception, one not inconsistent with Spenser's belief in the power of poetry. Ficino placed poetry above music in those things which we hear because poetry uses words and thus speaks not only to the ear but also directly to the mind.[12] This has relevance for Spenser, I believe.

Canto xii of Book IV begins with an apologia from the poet, "O what an endlesse worke haue I in hand, / To count the seas abundant progeny" (IV.xii.1). The fertility of the sea is captured in the notion "that *Venus* of the fomy sea was bred" (IV.xii.2); this fecudity is what he has conveyed through the pageantry at the wedding of Thames and Medway, a wedding which takes place because Medway has finally relented and listened to the entreaties of Thames. Marinell cannot be present at the wedding celebration itself, since he is half mortal. It is walking about at Proteus's palace that this Adonis-Achilles-Narcissus figure, this "beauteous niggard," owner of prodigious and useless wealth heaped up upon the strand, the male inured by his mother to female beauty, finds that his mortal half is indeed "liuing clay." The association of Marinell with the hardened heart is kept before us in a number of ways throughout this canto, beginning with the statement, given to us before Florimell's complaint itself, that "so feelingly her case she did complaine, / That ruth it moued in the rocky stone, / And made it seeme to feele her grieuous paine, / And oft to grone with billowes beating from the maine" (IV.xii.5). The idea of stone moved, pierced, is repeated within Florimell's complaint proper when she says, "Yet loe the seas I see by often beating, / Doe pearce the rockes, and hardest marble weares; / But his hard rocky heart for no entreating / Will yeeld, but when my piteous plaints he heares, / Is hardned more with my aboundant teares" (IV.xii.7). Florimell believes she is alone, of course. She utters her complaint "hoping griefe may lessen being told" (IV.xii.6). At the midpoint of her complaint, Florimell converts it into a prayer to the "gods of seas" for remedy; we are told that "she wept and wail'd, as if her hart / Would quite haue burst through great abundance of her smart" (IV.xii.11). In this case, however, Marinell has heard all; water spent here is not in vain; Marinell's heart is pierced. We are told:

> His stubborne heart, that neuer felt misfare
> Was toucht with soft remorse and pitty rare;
> That euen for griefe of minde he oft did grone,
> And inly wish, that in his powre it weare
> Her to redresse: but since he meanes found none
> He could no more but her great misery bemone.


> Thus whilst his stony heart with tender ruth
> Was toucht, and mighty courage mollifide,
> Dame *Venus* sonne that tameth stubborne youth
> With iron bit, and maketh him abide,
> Till like a victor on his backe he ride,
> Into his mouth his maystring bridle threw,
> That made him stoupe, till he did him bestride:
> Then gan he make him tread his steps anew,
> And learne to loue, by learning louers paines to rew.
> (IV.xii.12–13)

It is significant that Marinell's heart is pierced not by what he has seen but by what he has heard. He is won not by Florimell's beauty but by her profession of faithful love—the very quality that has kept others who pursued her physical beauty from possessing her.[13] Hearing has allowed Marinell to understand a truth about Florimell that no vision could ever grant him.

However, the triumph of hearing over seeing is only a beginning in bringing about the union of these lovers. While "ruth" has moved both the "rocky stone" of Proteus's cave as well as Marinell's "stony heart," this is not enough; Marinell still must learn "loues paines to rew," and he wastes away for love of Florimell since he can find no way to rescue her. Tryphon, who cured Marinell of the wounds inflicted by Britomart, proves a useless physician in this case, for now Marinell has been wounded by love, not merely proven defenseless against chastity. If that earlier encounter with Britomart means that she has overcome the temptation to withdraw into herself as Roche suggests, it also means something for Marinell. In part, his defeat at the hands of chastity is first step, a sign, I think, that he will be vulnerable to chaste love; Florimell's complaint is testament to precisely that kind of love. Apollo is brought in after Tryphon, and it is he who discovers that love is the cause of Marinell's malady, not destructive love but love "that leads each liuing kind." When Cymodoce learns this and gets from Marinell the name of the object of his affection, she goes to Neptune to "complaine," asking him in one gift to save three lives—her own, her son's, and Florimell's. It has been noted that Spenser's language here is full of legality, but we should also note that in a canto in which supplications are heard, Neptune, in hearing Cymodoce "plaine," finds truth discovered "plaine," and Proteus is compelled to deliver up Florimell, a gift won by a mother for her son.

The happy ending of this story allows the reader some sense of closure at the conclusion of Book IV even though the wedding will not be performed until Florimell is restored to society in the Book of Justice. Florimell and Marinell become exemplars, in a sense, for many of the love relationships that remain unresolved. We have seen Britomart involved with Marinell and Florimell through her battle with Marinell and her complaint that is so like Florimell's. We know through the prophecies that her complaint too will eventually be answered, though she will have to take a more active role in bringing about its happy resolution. Amoret too has her associations with Florimell. It is Amoret, we must remember, who can wear Florimell's girdle. She gets associated in our minds with Florimell not only through this symbol of her chaste love in canto v of Book IV, but in other significant ways as well. As Nohrnberg has pointed out,

> the third book begins with the flight of Florimell, and ends with the deliverance of Amoret seven months after her abduction by Busirane. The fourth book begins with the wanderings of Amoret, and ends with the deliverance of Florimell seven months after her imprisonment by Proteus. The seventh canto of the earlier book shows Florimell escaping from the hyena-monster and falling into the clutches of Proteus; the same canto of the later book shows Amoret excaping from the savage identified as "greedie Lust."[14]

That Spenser has both Amoret and Florimell freed after seven months, the shorter period of human gestation in the Platonic scheme, the period after which Adonis returns to Venus in the zodiacal scheme, the number of mutability and the number of man (ruled by seven planets, living through seven days and seven ages) as Fowler reminds us, is surely significant in this story about renewal and regeneration on the human level.[15]

There are other associations with the Amoret story; we should recall that Spenser moves us back to Florimell's narrative in canto xi of Book IV immediately after giving over canto x to Scudamore's narrative about the winning of Amoret at the Temple of Venus. Scudamore has been urged by Britomart to "take on . . . that paine" of telling; it is a story about the "pound of gall" that redounds to "euery dram of hony." Scudamore's retrospective story is about the beginning of a love relationship, one that has already had its share of impediments, but I would argue that the close association of Amoret with Florimell gives us hope that this relationship too, tempered through pain, will have a happy outcome.

Cymodoce's role in the story epitomizes Agape's love of "kindred sweet." That kind of love lies at the heart of the story that ostensibly characterizes the book, the story of Cambell and Triamond. Cambell is able to triumph in battle through the powers of his magic ring, a gift from his sister Canacee.

Triamond gets his strength from the souls of his brothers, a gift from his mother, Agape. Agape must accept the mortality of her sons; she is able to extend the life of Triamond through the lives of the other two when the "three fatall sisters" hear her entreaty.

Cymodoce, protective mother that she is, must learn to accept her son's mortality and his place in the natuaral process. This she finally does with efficacious results, surpassing the witch's gift of the False Florimell to her son.

Roche, Blissett, Nohrnberg, Hamilton, Kane and others have all helped us see the Marinell-Florimell story as Spenser's reworking of the Prosperina myth, the Venus and Adonis myth, the Achilles-Helen story, the Narcissus story.[16] It is a story about the power of love extending to the sea and the union of land and sea, much interpreted in light of neoplatonic doctrine. The final stanzas of canto xii are indeed cast in terms designed to remind us of natural processes, of rebirth, of the beginnings of Spring: Florimell is brought into the languishing Marinell:

> Who soone as he beheld that angels face,
> Adorn'd with all diuine perfection,
> His cheared heart eftsoones away gan chace
> Sad death, reuiued with her sweet inspection,
> And feeble spirit inly felt refection;
> As withered weed through cruell winters tine,
> That feeles the warmth of sunny beams reflection,
> Lifts vp his head, that did before decline
> And gins to spread his leafe before the faire sunshine.
>
> (IV.xii.34)

I must confess that while this stanza and the one following it provide a most fitting ending for Book IV, they also mark the return of sight as the predominant sense. "Chearefull signes" are all that can be managed at the end, no words, although we should note that Marinell's viewing of Florimell is "inspection": he can see the true Florimell, inside her, because of what he has heard.

Spenser's articulation of the debate about the power of seeing and the power of hearing does not end with canto xii of Book IV. The power of seeing is so pervasive in the poem as to make it inseparable from the essence of the work. But the poet's investigation of the power of hearing, and by extension the power of speaking, becomes increasingly important through the two final public books, being most prominent, of course, in Calidore's pursuit of the Blatant Beast. It is worth noting that Spenser's friend Lodowick Bryskett, in his *Discourse of Ciuill Life*, speaks of hearing and seeing as the primary senses in this life, and he stresses the sense of hearing as being of more help "towards the learning of a ciuill life, as the sentences of wise men passe thereby into our vnderstanding. And whereas the things which we learne by the eyes, are but dumbe words: so do the eares heare the liuely voices, by which we learne good disciplines, & the true manner of well liuing."[17]

It should not surprise us then to find at the heart of the most visionary moment of *The Faerie Queene* an allegory about the power of words. Calidore is drawn to what he sees by what he hears—Colin piping on Mt. Acidale; and he learns about what he has been able to see from what Colin himself *tells* him. The moment itself is auditory as well as visual, for it is that moment when the harmony of the universe is both seen and heard in the dance of the graces to the song of the poet—all testament to the power of love. This is the lesson for which the ending of Book IV prepares us, as we gain access to the worlds of love, cognition, and art.

*The Ohio State University*

## NOTES

1. Edmund Spenser, *The Faerie Queene*, ed. Thomas P. Roche, Jr. (Bungay, Suffolk: Penguin, 1978). All subsequent *Faerie Queene* citations are from this edition.

2. Erwin Panofsky, *Problems in Titian: Mostly Iconographic* (New York: New York University Press, 1969), p. 119.

3. Sears Jayne, trans., *Marsilio Ficino's Commentary on Plato's Symposium*, The University of Missouri Studies, No. 19 (Columbia: University of Missouri, 1944), p. 130.

4. Panofsky, *Problems*, pp. 124–125.

5. Baldesar Castiglione, *The Book of the Courtier,* trans. Charles S. Singleton (Garden City, N.Y.: Doubleday & Company, Inc.: Anchor Books, p. 347.

6. Castiglione, *The Book*, p. 348.

7. Sir Philip Sidney, *The Defense of Poesy* in *Sir Philip Sidney: Selected Prose and Poetry*, ed. Robert Kimbrough (San Francisco, Calif.: Rinehart Press, 1969), p. 134. The Sixth Song from *Astrophel and Stella* follows:

O you that hear this voice,
O you that see this face,
Say whether of the choice
Deserves the former place;
Fear not to judge this bate,
For it is void of hate.

This side doth Beauty take,
For that doth Music speak,
Fit orators to make
The strongest judgments weak;
The bar to plead their right
Is only true Delight.

Thus doth the voice and face,
These gentle lawyers wage,
Like loving brothers' case,
For father's heritage;
That each, while each contends,
Itself to other lends.

For Beauty beautifies
With heavenly hue and grace
The heavenly harmonies,
And in the faultless face
The perfect beauties be
A perfect harmony.

Music more loftly swells
In speeches nobly placed;
Beauty as far excels
In action aptly graced.
A friend each party draws
To countenance his cause.

Love more affected seems
To Beauty's lovely light,
And Wonder more esteems
Of Music's wondrous might:
But both to both so bent,
As both in both are spent.

Music doth witness call
The Ear his truth to try,
Beauty brings to the hall
The judgment of the Eye;
Both in their objects such
As no exceptions touch.

The Common Sense which might

Be arbiter of this,
To be forsooth upright,
To both sides partial is;
He lays on this chief praise,
Chief praise on that he lays.

Then Reason, princess high,
Whose throne is in the mind,
Which Music can in sky
And hidden beauties find,
Say, whether thou wilt crown
With limitless renown.

8. James Nohrnberg, drawing on an unpublished essay by Stephen Barney, suggests that we should see in Marinell's name "'unwillingness to marry.'" *The Analogy of "The Faerie Queene"* (Princeton, N. J.: Princeton University Press, 1976), pp. 572–573.

9. Sean Kane, "Spenserian Ecology," *ELH*, 50 (1983), 463.

10. See *The Faerie Queene*, IV.ix.6.

11. We are also reminded, however, of *Amoretti* 44 where the poet's song is not able to stint the strife as Orpheus's is.

12. See Paul Oskar Kristeller, *The Philosophy of Marsilio Ficino*, trans., Virginia Conant (New York: Columbia University Press, 1943), p. 308:

Ficino treats of poetry in close connection with music, since poetry also appeals to the ear and, in addition to using words, often incorporates melody and always has rhythm. But poetry is superior to music, since through the words it speaks not only to the ear but also directly to the mind. Therefore its origin is not in the harmony of the spheres, but rather in the music of the divine mind itself, and through its effect it can lead the listener directly to God Himself.

13. See Thomas P. Roche, Jr., *The Kindly Flame: A Study of the Third and Fourth Books of Spenser's "Faerie Queene."* (Princeton, N. J. : Princeton University Press, 1964), pp. 152–162.

14. Nohrnberg, *The Analogy*, p. 599.

15. Alastair Fowler, *Spenser and The Numbers of Time* (London: Routledge & Kegan Paul, 1964), pp. 37, 46–47, 139.

16. In addition to the works already cited see A. C. Hamilton, *The Structure of Allegory in "The Faerie Queene"* (Oxford: Clarendon Press, 1961), pp. 138–169 and William Blissett, "Florimell and Marinell," *Studies in English Literature, 1500–1900*, 5 (1965), 87–104.

17. Lodowick Bryskett, *A Discovrse of Civill Life* (London, 1606; rpt. Amsterdam: Theatrum Orbis Terrarum Ltd., 1971), p. 55.

LOUISE SCHLEINER

# Spenser and Sidney on the *Vaticinium*

*E* ARLY in the *Apology for Poetry*, Sidney declares that we can recognize poetry as a praiseworthy art by the poet's names among the
ancients. The Romans used the term *vates*, one inspired by the
*vaticinium* or divine source of inspiration, that is, a "diviner, fore-
seer, or prophet," whose "high-flying liberty of conceit...did
seem to have some divine force in it."[1] And the Greeks had the
word "maker," from the verb *poiein*, to make—a producer of
artifacts in words. That these two versions of the creative process
are incompatible does not for the moment concern Sidney, nor
does he yet limit their applicability. He needs these two high names
of honor to pin on the poor defamed art of poetry. But later he will
distinguish between them as referring, respectively, to ancient divine poetry and to most other, "right" poetry, then will qualify this
distinction, reconciling the two concepts of poetic creation in an
Icarus metaphor of power and rational control in poetic flight
(*Apology*, p. 72). In a work of Spenser's about the nature of poetry
we find another way of reconciling these two concepts of the poet,
and it can be instructively compared with Sidney's.

*Vates* and "maker" do reflect incompatible models for the creative process. Is the poet given words by some 'voice,' some unac-
countable source of inspiration, flowing into the creative mind
from a region beyond conscious access or control—as the oracular
priestesses were said to pour forth Apollo's words, which they

129

themselves later marvelled at? Or is the poet a rational artisan, who forms a controlled plan of a work, exercising conscious choice, then executes the plan by known constructive principles—as a cabinet-maker produces an original piece? When people try to explain the creative process, they usually encounter some such dichotomy of inspiration vs. artisanship. Plato, having said in the *Ion* that poets have their beautiful words not of themselves but from the gods,[2] exiles them from his Republic for too elegantly recounting false and harmful stories of the gods. At the threshhold of Romantic theorizing, Schiller classifies poets as either naive or sentimental—the poet of un-self-conscious, inspired genius vs. the painstaking poet of self-critical craftsmanship.[3] The dichotomy remains with us in many forms, including that of right brain and left brain functioning.[4]

The Renaissance had its own versions of how the powers of mind and spirit interact in poetic creation. Most Renaissance thinkers were, like Sidney, devoted admirers of analytical reason, even when they wrote about poetics, and liked to ascribe to it the greater share of credit.[5] But they were aware of the dichotomy—or perhaps we could say bifurcation—of creativity, and the *vaticinium* was their most frequent way of crediting the inspiration side, even though it was problematic because based, in Sidney's phrase, in "a full wrong divinity" (pp. 18–19). *The Shepheardes Calendar's* and Sidney's versions of poetic inspiration make an especially instructive contrast because Spenser and Sidney were both fervent Protestants of the Leicester circle and both drew upon the same sources and traditions in poetics—Plato, Cicero, Horace, Minturno, Scaliger and other neo-Platonists[6]—and yet their works express rather different conclusions.

Spenser's "booke called the English Poete," promised in *The Shepheardes Calendar*, never appeared. But we have a report of its stance on inspiration in the "October" eclogue, as it is mediated by the *Calendar's* "E. K." apparatus.[7] The commentator "E. K." was purportedly a friend of Spenser, a scholarly, usually knowledgeable but sometimes obfuscating, sometimes comically pedantic voice, giving prefatory matter and notes after each eclogue.[8] Certainly we cannot always regard what "E. K." says as Spenser's own straightforward view. But "October" is not one of the places where we find "E. K." being archly secretive, or obtusely pedantic in a manner perhaps being satirized (or deserving satire): on the contrary, his gloss there presents a concept of inspiration deriving from Julius Caesar Scaliger that, as we shall see, mediates subtly between Piers's and Cuddie's conflicting claims. Since there is no satiric or reductive way to read it and since it is consistent with the debate conclusion of "October," we may take it as a seriously intended view on inspiration. Piers credits poets like Cuddie with the power to inspire youth to virtue and to "pricke them forth with pleasaunce of thy vaine" (ll. 21–23), the powers, he says, of Orpheus. "E. K." glosses this passage as follows:

> Plato, . . . in his first booke de Legibus sayth, that the first inuention of Poetry was of very vertuous intent. For at what time an infinite number of youth vsually came to theyr great solemn feastes called Panegyrica, which they vsed euery fiue yeere to hold, some learned man being more hable then the rest, for speciall gyftes of wytte and Musicke, would take vpon him to sing fine verses to the people, in prayse eyther of vertue or of victory or of immortality or such like. At whose wonderful gyft al men being astonied and as it were rauished, with delight, thinking (as it was indeed) that he was inspired from aboue, called him vatem: which kinde of men afterwarde framing their verses to lighter musick (as of musick be many kinds, some sadder, some lighter, some martiall, some heroical: and so diuersely eke affect the mynds of men) found out lighter matter of Poesie also, some playing with loue, some scorning at mens fashions, some powred out in pleasures, and so were called Poetes or makers.
>
> (*Shepheardes Calendar*, p. 458)

If Spenser did not himself write at least some of the "E. K." gloss and at times purposely incorporate amusing inconsistency into it, then we have here a notable reversal of opinion on "E. K."'s part (from the "Prefatory Epistle" of the whole *Calendar* to the "October" gloss), just on this issue of the *vaticinium*. "E. K."'s epistle (to Harvey) had praised Chaucer's "wonderful skill in making" and ridiculed modern poets' overuse of easy, thoughtless devices such as alliteration (never mind that plenty of alliteration will occur in the eclogues to come). "E. K." speaks scornfully of such "rhymers," who he says "rage and fome, as if some instinct of Poeticall spirite had newly rauished them aboue the meanenesse of commen capacity . . . as that same Pythia [*i.e.* the Sybyll], when the traunce came vpon her: *os rabidum fera corda domans etc.*" ["overpowering her raving mouth and wild heart"—Virgil, *Aeneid,* 6:80]. He goes on to say that Colin Clout is nothing like these supposedly 'inspired' poets: he does not know the Muses at all and writes only "to paint out [his] vnrest." Thus "E. K." at this introductory point speaks in the strictest rationalist strain of humanism; he has taken a dim view of poetry's claim to prophetic inspiration, if he has not outright rejected it. (Harvey characteristically sounds like this, as when he writes to Spenser ridiculing "Cogging deceitfull . . . Sooth-sayers" who claim "so familiar acquaintance with God" as to "reveal his mysteries" and "purposes."[9])

But what line does "E. K." later take, in the note already quoted and in his "Argument" to the "October" Eclogue?

> Poetry . . . [is] indede so worthy and commendable an arte: or rather no arte, but a diuine gift and heauenly instinct not to bee gotten by laboure and learning, but adorned with both: and poured into the witte by a certaine ENTHOUSIASMUS and celestiall inspiration, as the author hereof elsewhere at large discourseth, in his booke called the English Poete. . . .

"E. K." has changed his tune about the *vaticinium,* perhaps having been converted by reading the said treatise, and also by his own 'enthusiasm' for Cuddie's poetry here. In his Glosse note quoted above, "E. K." tells how he now accounts for poetic inspiration. Referring to an alleged passage from Plato's *Laws* about the origin of lyric poetry at religious festivals,[10] he explains that a poet singing "in prayse eyther of vertue, or of victory or of immortality or such like" has been "inspired from above" and thus is rightly called *vates*; but when poets treat "lighter matter . . . some playing with loue, some scorning at mens fashions, some powred out in pleasures," then they are called "Poetes or makers." "E. K." believes, however, that inspiration is present even in "Makers": he glosses as follows "October's" concluding passage, where the longed for poetry does not fit his category of the directly vaticinal but only of the

"poetic." Cuddie waxes eloquent about his hopes to write tragedy under the inspiration of "Bacchus's fruit," and "E. K." comments:

> He seemeth here to be rauished with a Poetical furie. For (if
> one rightly mark) the numbers rise so ful, and the verse
> groweth so big, that it seemeth he hath forgot the
> meanenesse of shepheards state and stile.

Cuddie has just replied to Piers's praise of Love as an inspiration to poetry by claiming that Love, so far from inspiring high
poetry, outright prevents it because the "crabbed care" that Love
causes drives out the Muses. Cuddie (whom "E. K." has linked
with Colin Clout by suggesting that he may be another persona
for the author) continues as follows, and this is the passage "E.
K." finds inspired:

> Who euer casts to compasse weightye prise,
> And thinks to throwe out thondring words of threate:
> Let Powre in lauish cups and thriftie bitts of meate,
> For *Bacchus* fruite is frend to *Phoebus* wise.
> And when with Wine the braine begins to sweate,
> The nombers flowe as fast as spring doth ryse.
>
> Thou kenst not *Percie* howe the ryme should rage.
> O, if my temples were distaind with wine,
> And girt in girlonds of wild Yuie twine,
> How I could reare the Muse on stately stage,
> And teach her tread aloft in bus-kin fine,
> With queint *Bellona* in her equipage.
>
> But ah, my corage cooles ere it be warme . . . (etc.)
>
> (*Shepheardes Calendar*, "October," ll. 103-115)

"E. K." says this part swells with a divine breath, though its inspiration is vinous, not vaticinal (*i.e.*, the inspiring god is
Bacchus, not Apollo). And as for Cuddie's concluding Embleme
from Ovid's *Fasti*, "*Agitante calescimus illo etc.*" ["We grow
warm while that [god] agitates"], "E. K." interprets it as
follows: "Hereby is meant . . . that Poetry is a diuine instinct and
vnnatural rage passing the reache of comen reason."

Cuddie's tone of aspiration even after his earlier bitter complaints shows that he is not being satirized as a mere wino or 'pot poet.'[11] Rather, in a neo–Platonic vein deriving from Scaliger, Cuddie the poet is shown seeking a level of inspiration suitable for his next efforts. For "E. K." the previously skeptical commentator has followed Scaliger in reconciling *vates* and "maker" by dividing up the turf of poetry between them, considering both to be inspired but in a 'higher' and a 'lower' way. If we should skip "E. K."'s officiously pleased, learned, and hand-rubbing commentary, we miss part of the *Calendar*'s dynamics, for through contrasting voices, it shows an aspiring poet, as yet unrecognized, but energized by the discovery of his emerging power, looking forward to further uses of it, and able to excite and convert even a sometimes pedantic soul like "E. K." (be he real or fictional).

Scaliger's *Poetices libri septem* (1561) had described poetic inspiration as a case of being "seized on by the divine madness" and said that poets "invoke the Muses, that the divine madness may imbue them to do their work."[12] They are, then, "divinely possessed," but there are two different kinds of this possession: the divine power may come directly "from above," as with Hesiod and Homer, or it may come indirectly, through "the fumes of un-mixed wine, which draws out the instruments of the mind, the spirits themselves, from the material parts of the body," as with such poets as Ennius, Horace, Aristophanes, and Aeschylus. One might suppose this to mean that the inspiration in the second case, though powerful, is not really divine but rather a matter of naturally heightened consciousness and expressive potency: the spirits or *spiritus*, in Renaissance physiology, were supposed heated vapors of the blood, thought to supply a person's power of thought, and these could be "drawn out" into the brain and concentrated by alcohol or some other agent, creating a state of sharpened wit and creativity. But Scaliger has taken pains to insist that both kinds of poet are "divinely possessed"—the second then through the agency of "wine" rather than through direct indwelling of a higher divinity, "from above." While Scaliger does not list all the genres specific to either class, his chosen examples indicate that hymns, cosmological poems, panegyrics, and epics are of direct divine inspiration, while satires, epigrams, lyrics, comedies, and even tragedies (he cites Aeschylus) are inspired through "wine."

Spenser is following this distinction closely in Cuddie's effusion, quoted above, and throughout "October": the young poet hopes that when "with wine [his] braine begins to sweate" he can write great tragedy, can "rear" the tragic Muse onto the stage with "thondring words." "E. K.," as we have seen, likewise glosses "October" with Scaliger's distinction between lofty divine and lower inspiration; and he adds something to Scaliger's concept: he applies the terms *vates* and maker to the respective levels of inspiration, mentioning heroic and panegyric verse as examples of the vaticinal, lyric, and satiric for the other kind of inspiration. Seen in this light, most of Piers's idealistic declarations to Cuddie are just as valid as Cuddie's rejections of them, but represent a level of inspiration which Cuddie is right not to claim for himself—at least not yet.

Cuddie and "E. K." are in agreement throughout "October," both consistently following Scaliger. Thus Cuddie rejects Piers's claim that Love's power can raise the poet to the greatest heights of inspiration, replying that lofty verse and love verse are "two webbes" that can not be woven simultaneously. Love poetry, he implies, proceeds from a lower kind of inspiration, mediated through a physiological stimulus. Likewise following Scaliger, "E. K." insists nevertheless that *all* poetry is inspired: it is "no arte, but a divine gift and heauenly instinct not to be gotten by laboure and learning, but adorned with both: and powred into the witte by a certaine ENTHOUSIASMUS, and celestial inspiration . . ."—that is, either by enthusiasm kindled by the stimulus of some lower-ranking divine power (as Bacchus or Eros) or that kindled by Apollonian inspiration to a higher theme.

While Cuddie and "E. K." in "October" have both followed Scaliger, the cumulative impression the eclogue gives is one of more positive, energized affirmation of the vatical concept than one gets in reading Scaliger. Taking the eclogue and gloss together, we can see that Spenser has managed to celebrate the *vaticinium* in glowing terms here, as the original well-spring of all poetry and its shining *aegis*, and yet claim only that lofty poetry is of oracular vatical inspiration, the rest being inspired by lower powers.

In this context, "E. K."'s metaphor for the interaction of artisanship with inspiration must be closely inspected; we want shortly to compare it with Sidney's metaphor for the same case. "E. K."'s concept is of a liquid being poured into a container ("a divine gift . . . powred into the witte"), a gift which must be "adorned with . . . laboure and learning." Work and skill shape a beautiful container for the liquid, but the balance, in such an image, seems to be tipped in favor of inspiration, which must fill the poet—he must wait and hope for it. We may be sure that what "E. K." said about the *vaticinium* in "October" was of interest to the *Calendar*'s dedicatee, Sir Philip Sidney, who would soon express a different view.

Sidney, as Spenser did, follows Scaliger in working out a distinction of higher and lower; and like Spenser he applies the terms *vates* and 'maker' to the two levels, though when Sidney introduces the term "vates" as *the* Roman name for poet and explains its meaning of inspired prophet, he allows his readers to suppose it applicable to all poetry (*Apology*, p. 10). That proves to have been a rhetorical strategy for his introduction, later to be qualified. His precise distinctions or "more ordinary opening" of the nature and kinds of poetry begin with Aristotle's definition of it as mimesis or imitation (*Apology*, pp. 18 ff.). The first kind of poets, who "may justly be termed *vates*," are such as "imitate the inconceivable excellencies of God," as did David and other biblical poets, or among the Greeks Orpheus, or "Homer in his Hymns." The second kind 'imitate' or set forth human knowledge in verse—metaphysical or scientific (as Lucretius)—and Sidney concedes these may not be "true poets" because they are bound by their subject matter. The third kind, "indeed right poets" are the "makers," who imitate man and nature "both to delight and teach . . . and to move men to take . . . goodness in hand" (*Apology*, p. 20).

Sidney has here differed from both Scaliger and Spenser's "E. K." in a major point: he has limited the scope of the *vaticinium per se* only to biblical tales or lyrics and other ancient religious lyrics ("Homer in his Hymns"), while Scaliger listed Homer in general—thus also his epics—as among things "inspired from above," and "E. K." likewise counted as vaticinal all "prayse of victory" and "prayse of virtue" (the latter being classed by Sidney as within moral/philosophical poetry—his second "kind"). Post-reformational Protestant suspicion of subversive *Schwärmer* and allegedly inspired enthusiasts of all kinds may be at work in Sidney's formulation here, coupled with his own inclination to trust human reason, the "erected wit," as God's best gift, rather than any extra-rational state of "fury" or inspiration.

Officially, then, Sidney has fenced off for the *vaticinium* a very small plot, where it brings forth only explicitly religious poetry, mostly hymns. All other genres—even the high ones Scaliger and "E. K." call vatical, such as epics, heroic romances, odes and other epideictic poems—all these are within the province of "right poetry," where the "maker" will "range only reined with learned discretion into the divine consideration of what may be and should be" (*Apology*, p. 20). "Only with learned discretion" means that no other force than educated reason will guide the true poet.

However, Sidney has already qualified or extenuated this strict rationalist view of poetry, and will do so more notably before his treatise is over. Following earlier Renaissance theorists in comparing the poet as earthly "maker" with God as divine "Maker," Sidney has said that the poet, made in God's image, himself "makes" a "second nature" in poetry, "when with the force of a divine breath he bringeth things forth far surpassing her [Nature's] doings" (*Apology*, p. 17). As Andrew Weiner and others have noted,[13] Sidney here ascribes to the poet's "erected wit" the power to overcome any corruption of the mind caused by original sin and thus both to know aright and to "figure forth" true goodness. In effect, then, Sidney has all but banished the *vaticinium*, substituting for it a Protestant view that the poet's "erected wit" or reason can perceive and depict a golden world. Yet a veiled tribute to inspiration remains in his formulations. Instead of the *vaticinium* with its associated liquid imagery of bubbling, foaming, and pouring, Sidney hints rather at the dominant biblical imagery for inspiration: that of moving air, wind, or breath. God breathed into Adam, and he became a living soul; the Spirit came upon the disciples in a great wind, and they prophesied; God spoke to Job from the whirlwind; Jesus compared the Spirit to a wind that blows where it will; one could multiply examples. Sidney's ingenious strategy here is never to name the tenor of the biblical metaphor but only to evoke it through its vehicle: he never claims that the Holy Spirit *per se* inspires "right poets," but only that they speak "with the force of a divine breath," they soar in a "high flying liberty of conceit [that] did seem to have some divine force in it," they are not "tied" down but "lifted up with the vigor of [their] own invention." These airy metaphors are sprinkled subtly through the early part of the *Apology*, introducing a concept that gets elaborated near the end of the work, where Sidney finally concedes an essential role to inspiration in all true poetry, though denying it the name of the *vaticinium*.

In a subtle and self-aware analysis, Sidney depicts the two forces of inspiration and skill in poetic creation, in a single metaphor of Icarus and Daedalus. He begins the paragraph in question by saying that he had never planned nor studied to be a poet. How, then, did he come to be one?

> Only, overmastered by some thoughts, I yielded an inky tribute unto them. Marry, they that delight in poesy itself should seek to know what they do, and how they do, and especially look themselves in an unflattering glass of reason, if they be inclinable unto it. For poesy must not be drawn by the ears; it must be gently led, or rather it must lead; which was partly the cause that made the ancient-learned affirm it was a divine gift, and no human skill; sith all other knowledges lie ready for any that hath strength of wit; a poet no industry can make, if his own genius be not carried unto it; and therefore is it an old proverb, *orator fit, poeta nascitur.* [An orator is made, a poet is born.] Yet confess I always that as the fertilest ground must be manured, so must the highest flying wit have a Daedalus to guide him. That Daedalus, they say, both in this and in other, hath three wings to bear itself up into the air of due commendation: that is, Art, Imitation, and Exercise.
>
> (*Apology*, ed. Robinson, p. 72)

The poet, Sidney is saying, begins with a set of "thoughts" which he never sought nor hoped for. They feel like intruders in his mind. They possess and pressure him until he pays them tribute in some written invention answerable to their urging. Such "thoughts" cannot be taken up or learned but are a "divine gift." They come over the poet and lift him into flights of fancy, as the mythical Icarus was carried aloft and flew with ingenious wings that had been given to him. Thus much the role of inspiration. It is a gratuitous gust that lifts the poet into flight; then the Icarus figure or poet must make full use of the navigational and aeronautical (read "rhetorical") skills of his father Daedalus, namely "Art, Imitation, and Exercise"—those practiceable, learnable skills of organization, story-telling, and varied language use. If this "highest flying wit" attempts to carry through his flight without such aid, he will, like Icarus, fail and crash miserably. Conversely, whoever tries to fly without the gift of wings, will never get off the ground. Sidney goes on to observe that English poetry is currently in a bad state because the poets usually either lack inspiration (they try to "draw [poetry] by the ears" when instead "it must lead"), or having that windy *afflatus* of inspiration, lack the "maker's skill, "never marshalling [their works] into an assured rank, that almost the readers cannot tell where to find themselves."

Thus while Spenser's "E. K." imaged the poet as the stationary creator of a vessel to be filled with the golden liquid of inspiration, its shape being at the same time adorned with jewels of learning and rhetoric, Sidney, instead, sees the poet as an Icarus figure, an active, mobile being, who without any volition of his own is blown into flight by the breezy *afflatus* of inspiration, but from there on out depends solely on artificial Daedalus wings of knowledge and rhetorical skill to sustain his flight.

In an earlier passage closely related to this one, Sidney has said:

> the skill of the artificer standeth in that *Idea* or fore-conceit of the work, and not in the work itself. And that the poet hath that *Idea* is manifest by [his] delivering them forth in such excellency as he hath imagined them.
>
> (*Apology*, p. 16)

The seeds of this "fore-conceit" have been given the poet in the set of poetically fertile "thoughts" from which he will evolve it. Sidney then illustrates the point with Xenophon's described ruler Cyrus of the *Cyropaedia*. Cyrus's character as ideal ruler, in its planned concrete embodiment within the action of a specific narrative, was the "fore-conceit" of this particular work by Xenophon. Notice that the "fore-conceit" intended here is not purely a high-level abstraction—say, a list of abstract qualities requisite to an ideal ruler. Xenophon's "fore-conceit" included both that abstraction and the image of its concrete embodiment in a man within a fictive world—a world of colors, deeds, politics, sweat, and blood. All these concrete things are present as images in the "fore-conceit." They must be present there, because Sidney attributes to the "fore-conceit" that same poetic "excellency" that will characterize the completed work.

And what is that "excellency" specific to poetry, differentiating it from philosophy? It is the power to move the reader through concreteness—not just to teach but to delight the reader through the vivid concreteness of the "feigned" images projected by the work. The poet first imagines the "Idea" or "fore-conceit" already imbued with that special "excellency" and delivers it forth with that "excellency." Thus the "fore-conceit" is both abstract and concrete, in Sidney's view. We could call it an ideational construct that includes both abstractions and their planned correlated embodiments at different levels of concreteness, a multilayered, multi-dimensional, moving model of the planned work, in the poet's mind before ever the pen is put to paper.

We must avoid oversimplifying Sidney's subtle analysis. While Forrest Robinson's study and edition of the *Apology* have given us much useful commentary and apposite reference material (such as the excerpts from Thomas Cooper's *Thesaurus* and Phillipe de Mornay's *Trewnesse of the Christian Religion*), and while he is surely right that Sidney was influenced by Ramism and other concepts of visually diagrammatic intellection,[14] I must suggest a different interpretation of the term "fore-conceit" (p. xxii). Robinson says it is the poem's "conceptual structure," a "scaffolding" on which the concrete work can then be "suspended." For example, in writing a hypothetical piece about the legendary Roman Lucretia who committed suicide in order to denounce the man who had raped her, Robinson says the poet would first "organize his ideas about constancy" into a kind of mental "diagram" or "abstract picture" of this "moral abstraction," constancy.[15] Such a diagrammatic abstraction then serves as the poet's "fore-conceit," and the reader will later be able to decode and exactly reproduce it, says Robinson. Sidney would indeed have approved of such a procedure, but the resulting abstraction, in this case 'constancy,' he would see as one element of the fore-conceit, not as the whole fore-conceit. Otherwise he would not have ascribed to *it*—just as he does to the resulting actual poem—that specifically poetic excellency, the power of moving concreteness, the power to fix images in a reader's mind and move the reader to act upon them for virtue. Not Lucretia as a stick figure comprised of all the abstract sub-types of constancy, as in a Ramist word-picture diagram, but a different Lucretia would be needed as "fore-conceit": namely, a red-lipped, pale and frowning Lucretia, with nut-brown hair disarrayed, breathing lightly and oozing constancy from her every pore, that would be the poet's "fore-conceit." He would plan to paint, as Sidney puts it, "in colors fittest for the eye to see . . . the constant though lamenting look of Lucretia when she punished in herself another's fault. Wherein he painteth the outward beauty of such a virtue" (p. 20). Exactly that *outward* beauty, as well as the *inner* or abstract beauty of the concept constancy, must be already present in the artist's "fore-conceit," or he could not paint it. For, as Sidney says, "the skill of the artificer [*i.e.*, the poetic "maker"] standeth in that Idea or fore-conceit of the work," that ability to conceive of it in advance, as it will be in its moving concreteness, a piece of "heart-ravishing knowledge" (p. 10) such as only poetic art can create. The abilities requisite to getting the "fore-conceit" down on paper—skills of narrative organization, rhetorical devices, etc.—those the poet has in common with any other intelligent writer, say the historian or the philosopher.

Let us now review the creative process as Sidney conceived of it. Certain "thoughts" crying out for "inky tribute," thoughts that are a gratuitous gift of inspiration, enter and "overmaster" the poet's consciousness. The element of concrete intellection, the rudimentary fusion of abstract with concrete, is evidently already present in these pestering, activating, initiating "thoughts" of the poet, since exactly that fusion of abstract with concrete is not present in the planning concepts of the historian or the philosopher; each of them, says Sidney, conveys only the concrete, or only the abstract. Under the impetus of these "overmastering thoughts" then, and before anything is written down, the organizational and developmental "skill of the artificer" goes to work on those first "thoughts" to hammer them and build them up into a well-ordered "fore-conceit of the work," including the leading qualities of its planned "excellent" concreteness. The "maker's" work must then continue, as the "Idea" is carried into embodiment on paper by the poet's acquired skills of "Art, Imitation, and Exercise." In sum, inspiration has only the function of blowing Icarus into flight; from there on, Daedalus the ingenious, rational inventor and craftsman takes over.

Some readers may recognize that I am reading Sidney's "*Idea* or fore-conceit of the work" as close in meaning to what certain modern theorists—such as the aesthetician Susanne Langer—have similarly termed the "'idea' in a work of art," or "ma-

trix of the work-to-be," a complex, pre-existing ideational construct, guiding the artist at work, a construct whose embodiment or expression can only be the work itself: no verbal
description could capture it, which is to say, the meaning or
'concept' of the work is not paraphrasable nor even capable of
schematic representation.[16] Sidney would have agreed. No
"wordish description," as he calls it, of an abstract thinker has
the specific "excellency" of poetry, its power of concrete intellection, that "feigning notable images of virtues, vices, or what
else . . . which must be the right describing note to know a poet
by" (p. 21).

Have I made Sidney into a modern theorist? Hardly. His
preponderant Renaissance devotion to the rational, analytic
mind and to ideal virtues is entirely clear. Virtues and vices,
abstractions though they be, are to him as real as stars or stones,
and should be clearly evident in good literature, in full definition. Furthermore, quantitatively speaking, he has assigned to
inspiration a very small part in creativity, even denying it its divine name of *vaticinium* for any but explicitly religious poetry.
He has done so quite consciously: he says he cannot agree with
Plato, who "attributeth unto poesy more than myself do,
namely, to be a very inspiring of a divine force, far above man's
wit" (p. 67). Spenser, by contrast, does go along with Plato
there, though he needs the help of Scaliger's distinction between
higher and lower divinities of inspiration to make palatable the
claim that all poetry is inspired. "E. K.," who started out to the
right even of Sidney on this issue by ridiculing the *vaticinium*
concept in his prefatory epistle, has by "October" been converted to Spenser's ardent, thoughtful neo-Platonic view. But to
Sidney, swayed by the humanist devotion to Reason above all, it
seems that inspiration supplies only the initial "over-mastering
thought," the initial gusty breath of the creative process. All the
rest is rationally directed effort, including the mental task of or-
ganizing and developing the work's at once abstract and concrete
"fore-conceit."

The contrast between the ideas of Sidney and of Spenser/"E.
K." on this matter illustrates a characteristic difference of tem-
perament and thought. Spenser was far more committed to and
more enamored of the *vaticinium* concept than Sidney was, and
he followed Scaliger and other neo-Platonists in trying to ensure
its claim to validity by safely restricting its direct application to

the realm of 'high' genres such as hymn, panegyric, and epic. Sidney kicked it upstairs even further, to make room for his own Protestant rationalist concept of the "erected" (rather than inspired) wit.[17] While he thus banished the *vaticinium per se* to the small and ancient realm of biblical tales and poetry and Homeric lyric, he nevertheless, in the Icarus passage and other 'flight' images, paid an even more notable, because grudging, tribute to inspiration than Spenser did: for when he 'looked into his heart and wrote' about writing, he had to concede that inspiration is the initiating force in the creative process.

*Washington State University*

### NOTES

1. Philip Sidney, *An Apology for Poetry*, ed. Forrest G. Robinson (Indianapolis, Ind.: Bobbs-Merrill, 1970), p.11. All references are to this edition and will be cited in the text.

2. Plato, "Ion," trans. W. R. M. Lamb, Loeb Classical Library, vol. 164, (Cambridge, Mass.: Harvard University Press, 1925; rpt. 1962), pp. 420–425.

3. See Friedrich von Schiller, "Naive und Sentimentalische Dichtung," in *"Sämtliche Werke* (Munich: Winkler, 1968), vol. V.

4. Nietzsche inverts the Renaissance opposition of vaticinal (Apollonian) vs. Bacchanalian inspiration when he contrasts the Dionysian with the Apollonian artist, and in our own century, Croce distinguishes intuitive knowledge from logical knowledge. More recently, certain theorists using medical evidence have said that the left brain lobe controls conscious language use and performs analytical operations of math and logic, the storage, sort, and modeling commands of consciousness. The right brain lobe apparently accesses information in affectively determined patterns and generates integrative insights, intuitions, and perhaps the very urge to artistic creativity—these are, then, the rational/analytic vs. the intuitive/synthetic powers: "making" vs. divining. See Benedetto Croce, *Aesthetic as Science of Expression and General Linguistic*, trans. Douglas Ainslie (London: Farrar, Straus & Giroux, 1909); and Earl Miner, "That Literature Is a Kind of Knowledge," *Critical Inquiry*, 2 (1976), 487–518, especially pp. 502–506.

5. Useful studies of Sidney's poetics in its contemporary contexts include the introduction to Geoffrey Shepherd, ed., *An Apology for Poetry* (London: Oxford University Press, 1965)—challenged by Craig (see below); A. C. Hamilton, *Sir Philip Sidney: A Study of his Life and Works* (Cambridge: Cambridge University Press, 1977); Forrest G. Robinson, *The Shape of Things*

Known: *Sidney's Apology in Its Philosophical Tradition* (Cambridge, Mass.: Harvard University Press, 1972); Dorothy Connell, *Sir Philip Sidney: The Maker's Mind* (Oxford: Clarendon Press, 1977); Andrew D. Weiner, *Sir Philip Sidney and the Poetics of Protestantism: A Study of Contexts* (Minneapolis: University of Minnesota Press, 1978), who disagrees on certain points with Robinson (pp. 43–44); O. B. Hardison, Jr., "The Two Voices of Sidney's *Apology for Poetry*," *English Literary Renaissance*, 2 (1972), 83–99; and D. H. Craig, "A Hybrid Growth: Sidney's Theory of Poetry in *An Apology for Poetry*," *English Literary Renaissance*, 10 (1980), 183–201.

6. On the background of Sidney's poetics see the above works; on Spenser's see especially Robert Ellrodt, *Neoplatonism in the Poetry of Spenser* (Geneva: Libraire E. Droz, 1960) and *The Works of Edmund Spenser: A Variorum Edition*, ed. Edwin Greenlaw, *et al.* (Baltimore, Md.: Johns Hopkins University Press, 1943), VII, pt. 1, 371–374.

7. *Spenser, Poetical Works*, ed. J. C. Smith and E. De Selincourt (London: Oxford University Press, 1912), pp. 417–418 and 456–459. All references are to this edition and cited in the text.

8. In the first of the *Three proper wittie familiar Letters* (London, 1580) of Spenser and Harvey, Spenser described "E. K."'s glosses on his forthcoming "Dreames" as comparable to those in his "Calendar" and further as "some things excellently and many things wittily discoursed of E. K." If this is not a tongue-in-cheek reference to an apparatus he himself partly or wholly composed, it certainly at least indicates authorization of "E. K."'s statements. Thus for my present purpose I regard "E. K."'s commentary as authorized by Spenser, whose close supervision of the whole production of the book has been shown by Ruth S. Luborsky in "The Allusive Presentation of *The Shepheardes Calendar*," *Spenser Studies* I, Patrick Cullen and Thomas P. Roche, Jr., eds. (Pittsburgh, Pa.: University of Pittsburgh Press, 1980), pp. 69–93.

9. Spenser/Harvey letters, Variorum *Works*, IX, 454–458.

10. The is no such passage in Bk. I of the *Laws* as "E. K." claims, but perhaps the reference is to *Politics*, Bk. IV or *Laws*, Bk. XII, as Renwick suggests (ed. cited above).

11. Richard Hardin, "The Resolved Debate of Spenser's 'October,'" *Modern Philology*, 73 (1976), 257–63, thus denigrates Cuddie.

12. Julius Caesar Scaliger, *Poetices libri septem* I, 2 (1561), trans. F. M. Padelford, rpt. in Hazard Adams, ed., *Critical Theory Since Plato*, (New York: Harcourt, 1971), p. 140. The passage is:

Iccirco igitur invocant Poetae Musas, ut furore imbuti peragant quod opus est. Horum autem Θεοπνευστως duo adhuc genera animadverti. Unum, cui caelitus advenit illa divina vis, aut ultro nec opinanti, aut simpliciter invocanti. Quo in numero seipsum ponit Hesiodus: Homerus autum ponitur ab omnibus. Alterum acuit meri exhalatio, educens animae instrumenta, spiritus ipsos a partibus corporis materialibus. Talem ait Ennium Horatius: talem nos Horatium. De Alcaeo atque Aristophane idem memoriae proditum est. Nec Alcman caruit ea calumnia. Sophoclem quoque Aeschylo id obiecisse: Vinum, non ipsum, esse illius authorem Tragoediarum.

On Scaliger's own poems on the same themes see Robert J. Clements, "Literary Theory and Criticism in Scaliger's *Poemata*," *Studies in Philology*, 51 (1954), 560–584.

13. See Weiner, pp. 34–50; Connell, pp. 46–47; and Morriss H. Partee, "Anti-Platonism in Sidney's *Defense*," *English Miscellany*, 22 (1971), 7–29, who says Sidney rejects Plato's concept of the *vaticinium* because it "allows poets a lofty, yet unwarranted relationship with God" (p. 7).

14. See Robinson, especially pp. 99–128.

15. Forrest Robinson, ed., *An Apology for Poetry*, "Introduction," p. xxii.

16. See Susanne K. Langer, *Philosophy in a New Key* (1942; rpt. New York: Mentor, 1948), pp. 188, 199, and 222; and *Feeling and Form* (New York: Scribner's, 1953), pp. 386–389.

17. Milton was evidently influenced by Scaliger, Spenser, and Sidney in his concept of chaste or higher vs. Bacchic inspiration (see his "Elegia Sexta"), but drew the line between higher and lower genres, in this sense, differently from where any of them had drawn it: Sidney allowed only religious poetry to be vatical, while Milton and Spenser included heroic poetry as well (part of Spenser's "praises of victory") among the vatical genres; however, Milton cites Pindar's victory odes as Bacchic, though Spenser's "praises of victory" would include them. Thus Milton drew his line between higher and lower genres lower than Sidney's but higher than Spenser's. On the passages that influenced Milton in Scaliger and Minturno, see John M. Steadman, "Chaste Muse and Casta Juventus': Milton, Minturno, and Scaliger on Inspiration and the Poet's Character," *Italica*, 40 (1963), 28–33.

DAVID J. BAKER

# "Some Quirk, Some Subtle Evasion": Legal Subversion in Spenser's *A View of the Present State of Ireland*

I. "Discourse of the overrunning and wasting of the realm"

On April 14, 1598, the Secretary of the Stationers' Company, upon request of the Warden, entered a manuscript copy of Edmund Spenser's *A View of the Present State of Ireland* into the Stationers' Register on behalf of the bookseller "Mathewe Lownes. . . . Uppon condician that hee get further aucthoritie before yt be prynted."[1] Lownes did not get that authority. Elizabeth's Council did not want the treatise published. Recently, it has been claimed that the *View* was suppressed because it lays bare "the premises upon which sovereign power operates. . . . Genuine power would not admit its savagery, and although the *View* speaks the official language of law and reformation, it does not fail to reveal that decapitation, destruction, and constant surveillance are the facts upon which the language rests."[2] This phrasing, however, implies a distinction between language

147

and facts, the one an ideologically biased idiom which refers
with more or less accuracy to a world standing beyond it, the
other the brute residuum left after language has done its mysti-
fying work, the stuff language cannot shape. I am going to assume that facts—including politically charged facts like decapitation—are defined by and within the language brought to bear,
and political language especially does not recognize facts for
which it cannot account or which it cannot justify. Indeed, this is
its purpose. When, for instance, Spenser relates that

> at the execution of a notable traitor at Limerick called
> Murrogh O'Brien, I saw an old woman which was his fos-
> ter mother took up his head whilst he was quartered and
> sucked up all the blood running there out, saying that the
> earth was not worthy to drink it, and therewith also steeped
> her face and breast, and tore her hair, crying and shrieking
> out most terribly (62)

he is not revealing a brute and brutal fact which exceeds the capacity of official language to redeem it. This horrific spectacle
came to Spenser already constituted by his official language, and
he presents it already interpreted and justified. (Here he has implicitly claimed that the Irish resemble the blood-drinking Gauls
Caeser described and so display their barbarism and suitability
for another Roman conquest.) The only savagery which he
admits is the savagery of the primitive Irish themselves.

The brutishness of the "meere" Irish, the superior civility of
the English, these were facts for Spenser and his official readers.
Their official language rested, like any language, not on irreduc-
ible, nonlinguistic realities—the self-evident horror of a bloody
head and a screaming woman—but on premises, assumptions
with the force of fact which gave shape and significance to such
"realities," but were themselves beyond proof or disproof. In the
1570s, it was the practice of Sir Humphrey Gilbert to order that

> the heads of all those . . . which were killed in the day
> should be cut off from their bodies and brought to the place
> where he encamped at night, and should there be laid on the
> ground by each side of the way leading into his own tent, so
> that none should come into his tent for any cause but
> commonly he must pass through a lane of heads, which he

used *ad terrorem* the dead feeling nothing the more pains thereby. And yet did it bring great terror to the people when they saw the heads of their dead fathers, brothers, children, kinsfolk, and friends lie on the ground before their faces.[3]

Official terrorism like Gilbert's leads more than one historian to conclude that "Elizabethan officers in the closing decades of the century 'believed that in dealing with the native Irish population they were absolved from all normal ethical restraints.'"[4] But Gilbert, and Spenser equally, *were* restrained (and compelled) by norms, the normative premises, that is, undergirding their official language. Within the premises of Irish savagery and the absolute rightness of enforced civilization, servered heads were not incontrovertible evidence of official depravity, but yet another means of articulating the official language of terror. Colonial officials inscribe their language on the Irish; decapitation is one of the ways this is done. Since such practices do not stand beyond the official language but are themselves articulations of that language, it seems improbable that the *View* states for English brutality a case "that cannot be stated."[5] For Spenser it is not a case that needs to be made. Wretchedly cruel as colonial policy seems, to Spenser it was not repugnant, simply because according to the political consensus within which he moved and had his being it was justified, or more precisely, needed no justification at all. As W. B. Yeats remarked, "Spenser had learned to look to the State not only as the rewarder of virtue but as the maker of right and wrong, and had begun to love and hate as it bid him."[6]

Spenser's *View*, then, does not "judge" because Spenser does not have available to him any place outside of his justifying beliefs from which he could judge. Nor does it "expose"[7] a distasteful truth underlying and concealed by an official ideology because that ideology itself shaped what Spenser could see as true of Ireland even as he encountered it. His view never encompassed the brutal realities of English colonization because for him they were neither brutal nor real. "When Spenser wrote of Ireland," Yeats said, "he wrote as an official, and out of thoughts and emotions that had been organized by the State. He was the first of many Englishmen to see nothing but what he was desired to see."[8] Though I would add that there was nothing just there for him to see, at least not from the point of view from which he wrote his *View of the Present State of Ireland*, nor was there any but the official language in which to declare what he saw.

Now, if the *View* was not a critique of the distortions of the official language, why was it suspect? Why, as we are asked, "should the government suppress a work that states its case?"[9] This crucial question asks us, in effect, to account for Spenser's purpose in the *View*, his relation to the authorities for whom he wrote it, the reading to which they subjected it, and their baffling rejection of a text which claimed to articulate their ideology. My essay is an attempt to answer it. I have a speculative argument to put forward. Consider the implications of this suppression. Spenser submitted his text to Elizabeth's Council; presumably, he believed it would be accepted. He intended and expected the *View* to be read as an authoritative statement of royal policy, authoritative because it was framed in the language of the authorities and articulated their version of the truth. But it was not so taken; it was denied publication. The authorities, presumably, did not think it expressed what they believed in a way they approved. They read the *View* as in some way unacceptable. There was, then, a disparity between the *View*'s purpose and its effect. Unless Spenser meant his treatise to go unpublished—and I will assume he did not—the *View* must represent a miscalculation on his part. He misjudged the effect his text would have on its intended readers—and those readers, for their part, misread (or disregarded) his intent.

This is not to say that we ourselves cannot surmise Spenser's purpose. To make sense of the *View* at all we must attribute some intention to it, and I will do so here. Even apart from the text, Spenser's intent can be plausibly inferred: he submitted the *View* for the Council's approval; he rendered sixteen years of loyal service in Ireland to Elizabeth and her colonial administration; he willingly accepted the Queen's rewards of land and position in the colony and was concerned to defend them. Spenser surely meant the *View* as a royalist polemic. He was a royal servant, not just by employment, but as a self-appointed apologist and theorist. His *View* is a work of compelling, even overweening ambition. Though Spenser has fashioned the *View* for the official readers on the Privy Council, almost certainly, the reader he most wants to reach is Elizabeth herself. Spenser means to vindicate Elizabeth's colonial policy—despite her better impulses if need be—to expose, and then negate the contradictions in the royal view of Ireland. In "A Briefe Note of Ireland," another document submitted to the Council, Spenser addresses the Queen directly. Her English subjects in the colony have suffered grievously, he says, and he wants to

> vnfoulde vnto your Maiestie the feeling of theire miserie and to seeke to impresse in your Princlie minde the due sence thereof whereby some meete redresse may be tymelie provided. . . . But our feare is leste your Maiestes wonted mercifull minde should againe be wrought to your wonted milde courses and perswaded [that] by some milde meanes either of pardons or proteccions, this rebelliouse nacion may be againe brought to some good conformacion which we beseech allmightie god to averte and to sett before your gracious eyes the iuste consideracion howe that possiblie may be.[10]

In the *View*, among Spenser's purposes is to aid almighty god in averting a royal blunder, to tutor his Queen, to set before Elizabeth's very eyes the impossibility of mercy, to impress on her princely mind the confused misery which, because of her misplaced benevolence, corrupts her Irish colony. There is no reason to believe Elizabeth ever read the *View*. Quite possibly, Spenser miscalculated there too. But this hubristic, brutally rigorous purpose helps us to account for the relentless verbal excess of his text. In the *View* we see a powerful literary intelligence working within, struggling within, sometimes overwhelming the conventions of official truth which must shape the larger motions of its thought, but which it must sometimes deform to accomplish it purpose: to tell the intolerable truth of Ireland.

Now, I propose that it was this deformation of official conventions for the sake of official truth which elicited a dubious reading. It was what seemed the disquieting ambiguities of the text which elicited the Privy Council's suppression. It was the authorities, not the author, who rendered the *View* suspect. Elizabeth's officers read this text according to their own code and for their own purposes. They brought to their reading an official hermeneutic, a hermeneutic of suspicion. They read to detect ideological deviance and in the confidence that they knew

the officially sanctioned truth. They suspected whatever called
that truth into question by whatever means. Spenser's official
readers thought the *View* objectionable, I think, because their
reading practices prepared them to find failures of orthodoxy
even in texts purporting to declare official truth—and Spenser
offered them a text in which, given a suspicious reading, they
could detect a tacit critique of English legal verities. Given the
prevailing conventions by which official truth was to be
produced and received,[11] the *View* could not look like the univo-
cal, consistent statement of policy that authority demanded. Its
equivocations and excesses overwhelmed whatever purposes the
Council may have had for an official text. As a vehicle for official
truth, it seemed unstable, and, therefore, threatening.

Nowhere would this have been more so than in Spenser's
opening treatment of the law in Ireland. There he does not expose the brutal rigor of English policy; he reveals that policy as
less rigorous than its adherents would want to think. He in-
sinuates the distasteful ambiguities involved in trying to recreate
the verities of English law in an alien land; he argues obliquely
for the incoherence of the law, the chosen instrument of official
policy.

"[I]t is dangerous," says Irenius, Spenser's spokesman,[11] "to
leave the sense of a law unto the reason or will of the judges who
are men and may be miscarried by affections and many others
means, but the laws ought to be like to stony tables, plain, steadfast, and unmoveable"(33). If these lines are ironic—and I do not
think they are intentionally so—it is because the dialogue they
are set within can be read as a circuitous demonstration that law
in Elizabeth's colony cannot be plain, steadfast, and unmoveable, that, for the English, Ireland has become a chaos of
legal ambiguity, subversive equivocation, and pervasive uncertainty. This treatise involves Spenser in a disquieting analysis of
the authority of English law on the margins. And because the
*View* does not declare that authority unequivocally, the *View*
itself comes to be a dangerous text. Far from being like to stony
tables, its meaning plain, its argument steadfast, and its premises
unmoveable, it testifies to the present impossibility of conduct-
ing the Queen's policy in Ireland within a legal discourse of fixed
terms and unquestioned truths. Again and again, the *View*
reveals the uncertainties of English law even as it condemns
them, displaying its susceptibility to manipulation from within

and its inability to warrant its own authority. In prose that does not straight-forwardly articulate legal verities, but twists through manifold arguments, taking into account far more than it should, the *View* both castigates and exemplifies the conflicted, disorienting discourse of English law in Ireland.

Writing from within that discourse, Spenser's relation to the royal authority he tries to serve is difficult and unavoidably critical. He is acutely aware of the ungovernable complexities of making a coherent argument for royal authority when, in Ireland at least, it is precisely the tenability of that authority which is in question. As we will see, Spenser realizes that without a secure "center" of authority, the terms of law are always under pressure. Even within an English court, those terms are subject to various motivated interpretations. Some affirm them; others deny them. Their meanings are negotiated, altered, and disputed. The "reason or will" of men who "may be miscarried by affections or many other means" cannot be excluded, though their contention over the sense of English law leaves it incoherent and uncertain. Consequently, the truths which for Spenser must be established and guaranteed by an authoritative, stable legal discourse are nowhere to be had. In Ireland, servants of the Queen like himself must administer a legal code whose jurisdiction is indefinite and fluctuating in courts where testimony is suspect and judgment unsure. Worst of all, the royal authority on which adjudication must rest is brought into question by its apparent inability to halt the chaotic struggle over the law within the precincts of its own tribunals.

This legal flux horrifies Spenser, and the *View*, I think, should be read as a plea to the government to assert Elizabeth's rightful prerogative and prevent her law from devolving into formlessness. The solution Spenser expects is the immediate and definitive establishment of English law on royal authority. This would require an incontrovertible demonstration from the throne of the absolute centrality of the prince's will and the utter dependence of every legal doctrine on its conformity to that will for its validity. To completely secure itself, regal authority must show that invincible power flows from its inherent prerogative—and this is why Spenser eventually pleads for a full-scale military invasion of Ireland and the eradication of those who deny the Queen's supremacy. Royal truth must not only be the unrivalled truth, it must be capable of ordering the world so that its truth cannot be denied. As Yeats put it, "Like an hysterical patient [Spenser] drew a complicated web of inhuman logic out of the bowels of an insufficient premise—there was no right, no law, but that of Elizabeth, and all that opposed her opposed themselves to God, to civilization, and to all inherited wisdom and courtesy, and should be put to death."[12] The very existence of those who can think otherwise than officials would have them is threatening; the possibility of denial must be eliminated, especially in Ireland, where, on the periphery of the kingdom and far from the locus of authority, royal truth dissipates and unsettling thoughts can be contemplated, even spoken.

The *View*, in sum, is a contradictory invocation of authority; it summons the "presence" of the Queen to invest her system of law with her own inherent sovereignty. But in order to convince Elizabeth of the necessity for her authorizing "presence," Spenser must repeatedly point up the malignant effects of her "absence" from the legal system, while, at the same time, never explicitly acknowledging that her legal authority is lacking at all. We need not doubt that Spenser devoutly believes that royal authority alone is capable of guaranteeing legal certainty and halting the confused play of interested judgments he castigates, but all the evidence of unregulated indeterminacy he brings forward can only go to prove that the royal authority he is invoking has failed to establish even the conditions of its own intelligibility. That actual royal influence extended only so far beyond the Pale, that the Queen's writ ran only here and there, no one could deny. But that even within the domain of the English and for a colonial official like Spenser English law in Ireland had become so concussed with uncertainty that its authority—the Queen's authority—had effectively come into question was not, I suspect, something the royal apologists who sat on Elizabeth's Council could accept. That, I think, is why the government suppressed a work that stated its case.

## II. "Some quirk, some subtle evasion"

What especially bothers Irenius, Spenser's spokesman,[13] is that the Irish can maneuver within the procedural boundaries of the common law and yet escape its jurisdiction. He persistently charges that native custom allows the Irish to escape into an inaccessible domain where common law does not work and treason is devised. Eudoxus, his interlocutor, wants to assume that brehon law "is not now used in Ireland, since the kings of England have had the absolute dominion thereof and established their own laws there." But Irenius assures him that even the natives who "seem to acknowledge subjection, yet the same Brehon law is privily practised amongst themselves . . . they may do what they list, and compound or altogether conceal amongst themselves their own crimes" (5). For official readers, this could have a disturbing implication: the imposition of common law did not insure royal sovereignty, not only because there were "many wide countries in Ireland in which the laws of England were never established" (5), but because even though every mark of adherence to English law might be apparent, the Irish could somehow withdraw into an inner precinct where only their own rules pertained. The disturbing result was that two laws were in effect at once. They were in contradiction (what was legal by brehon law was crime to the English), but the contradiction could not be eliminated because, once allowed into the legal system, the Irish had a vexing way of demanding that its rules be applied to them while covertly following their own. When Eudoxus suggests having English judges handpick Irish jurors "of the soundest disposition," Irenius tells him, "then would the Irish party cry out of partiality, and complain he hath not justice, he is not used as a subject" (23). A barbarian is allowed to name himself a subject, permitted to appropriate a legal language and manipulate it to his own purposes. If this were a simple matter of an alien acting a bad part as something he cannot inherently be, an official reader might be horrified enough. But more, this role-playing could imply that within the system of common law, there were no longer any essentially barbaric or civilized selves. Common law in Ireland had degenerated into legal spectacle. Selves slipped in and out of categories which should fix them, and the declarations of these shifting shelves took on different meanings within the conventions of different legal codes simultaneously.

Consider the legal disarray which attends an Irishman's appeal to native custom in an English court. "For myself have heard," complains Irenius, "when one of that base sort which they call Churls, being challenged and reproved for his false oath, have answered confidently, that his Lord commanded him, and that it was the least thing he could do for his Lord to swear for him"

(24). Whatever this man said, when he said it before a common law bench there were two legal codes constraining and compelling him, each a set of conventions which could be invoked to determine what he should say and how it would be taken. First, the code of common law; it required him to take an oath and attached import to that oath as a guarantor of veracity. Common law prescribed the rules that were to shape his speech and it dictated that what he said and the "truth" should be one. Common law procedure was used to rivet in place a set of rules for making and interpreting statements within the precincts of the court. They were to be what the judges could recognise as true or false.

Then there was the native code of clan obligation and hierarchical responsibility, and it too dictated what the witness was to say: whatever would satisfy his lord's requirements. As he testified, he spoke within both codes at once. He employed the language of English truth and the speech of Irish loyalty. What he said had two simultaneous meanings, each depending on what his listeners were capable of hearing; they heard him make a true (or false) statement, or they heard him demonstrate his loyalty to his lord by pragmatically declaring the "truth" that would serve him best. Only one of these meanings, probably, was accessible to most English. Under the conventions of legal interpretation they themselves had established, such testimony could only be taken as truth or deliberate inversion of truth. But Irenius takes it differently. Though he disapproves, he realizes that the witness' declarations are entirely consistent with his legal obligations under native custom. Even "false" Irish testimony can be more than mere prevarication. Irenius implies that the Irish rebel can, even standing in a common law court where his very speech is governed, call upon quite another legal code within the rules of which his utterances take on meanings completely lost to the English. Officials literally do not know what the Irish mean when they speak. Since they cannot test Irish statements for veracity, they cannot know the truth when they have heard it. As Irenius realizes, this undecidable testimony makes it impossible to conduct a trial. In any working court, some kind of truth (or some consensus on what will count as truth) must be ascertainable if verdicts are not to seem wholly specious. But in Ireland, "were it so that juries could be picked out of . . . choice men" guaranteed to interpret as the English would have them, still "there would nevertheless be . . . bad corruption in the trial,

for the evidence being brought in by the base Irish people will be
. . . deceitful . . . sure their lords may compel them to say anything" (24). When anything might be meant by what is said, the
certainty which should be enabled by fixed rules of interpretation is hopelessly absent. And if, as Eudoxus asks, "the proof of
everything must needs be by testimonies of such persons as the
parties shall produce; which if they shall corrupt, how can there
ever any light of truth appear?" (24). Within the far too accom-
modating bounds of the common law, no certain verdict can be
achieved.

In Ireland, Irenius reveals, the authorities have lost control of
their ideological machinery; they cannot establish and protect
official truth. They confront an interpretive problem: they find it
impossible to stipulate a set of rules for legal interpretation so
rigorously binding that in their courts meaning will always
remain fixed and their consensual truth always inviolate. Their
rules themselves succumb to interpretation; others who stand
outside their rules, who appear to act within them, reconstrue
their precepts to serve their own alien purposes. They can follow
the letter, but mock the spirit. "[N]ow that the Irish have
stepped into the realm of the English" (22), as Irenius says, they
can do their work of subversive re-interpretation from within.
But the English cannot, from the edges of Irish culture, reach
inside to reshape the customs of their adversaries. They possess
their own code, brehon law, and it fashions them, gives them
their purpose, and dictates the meaning of their actions and
words even in an English court. As Irenius forces his readers to
realize, English law does not provide the authorities procedures
with which to govern the reading of testimony and the discern-
ing of truth. Its rules of reading do not stand prior to or independent of their employment. Any reader may seize and redirect
them. As Irenius laments,

> though they will not seem manifestly to do it, yet will some
> one or other subtle-headed fellow amongst them pick some
> quirk, or devise some subtle evasion, whereof the rest will
> lightly take hold, and suffer themselves easily to be led by
> him to that themselves desired; for in the most apparent
> matter that may be, the least question or doubt that can be
> moved will make a stop unto them, and put them quite out
> of the way, besides that of themselves they are for the most

part, so cautelous and wily headed, especially being men of
so small experience and practice in law matters, that you
would wonder whence they borrow such subtleties and sly
shifts (23).

The Irish, Irenius complains, can conduct themselves within the
common law all too well. They manipulate its rules; they take
hold of some point of legal procedure, some quirk which the law
itself authorizes, and force English officials to play by their own
rules for Irish ends. They make legal arguments, but though
their conclusions seem wilful evasions of the patent truth, the
authorities cannot legally deny them. In short, these rebels'
crime is that they abide by the law in order to exploit it, not that
they break it.

Eudoxus offers various remedies for this subversion from
within, but Irenius demonstrates that none will stop Irish dupli-
city. Packing juries will not work; even fixed jurors, Irenius
knows, will be defeated by unfixable testimony. Told that a
quirk of the common law allows receivers of stolen goods to escape punishment, Eudoxus considers that "this . . . might easily
be provided for by some Act of Parliament" (26). He wants to
prevent the rebellious Irish from interpreting the law for themselves by appealing to a body of official interpreters whose
pronouncements will organize the rules for those under them.
He tries to transcend the problem by locating authority above it,
but, as Irenius must tell him, he only displaces the problem up-
ward. What Eudoxus suggests "is almost impossible to be
compassed" because by law "the said parliament must consist of
the peers, gentlemen, freeholders, and burgesses of that realm
itself" (26) and these are just as likely to misconstrue the
common law as any of the Irish. Later, Eudoxus thinks to put his
trust in another body of interpreters, the judges. Even in a
doubtful case, he thinks, "the judge when it cometh before him
to trial, may easily decide this doubt and lay open the intent of
the law by his better discretion" (33). Eudoxus' expectation
would have seemed reasonable, and Irenius' rejection of it
reveals the depth of his distaste, not just for the corruption inflicted on the common law, but for that law itself. Even without
a fully elaborated doctrine of judicial review, it was thought that
a judge should conjecture the purposes Parliament (acting
according to common law) had meant a statute to serve. The ex-

ercise of his "better discretion" was required of him. But Irenius
will not tolerate the vagaries of any interpreter, even an English
judge. The judges "are men"; their reason or will may "be
miscarried"; the "sense of a law"[14] must not be left to their discretion. Since "it was less . . . the content of the law than the
judicial process itself—usage, judgment, and statute—that was
immemorial,"[15] Irenius' renunciation of this ongoing elabora-
tion of common law by its practitioners amounts to a dismissal
of the common law itself. He rejects it precisely because its
practices are ongoing instead of "steadfast . . . and unmoveable," because within it the law is not self-evidently
"plain" in its sense, but must be elaborately interpreted.

Once interpretation starts, he implies, it does not stop. No
matter where placed in the court, behind the bench, before it,
within the jury, every interpreter of the law offers his own self-
interested account of undecidable texts. Some "statutes are so
slackly penned, and [some] . . . so unsensibly contrived, that it
scare carrieth any reason in it, that they are often and very easily
wrested to the fraud of the subject" (32). They can be read to any
purpose. Their slack penning allows an unlicensed play of exegesis in the spaces opened up as they lose shape and definition
under the pressure of rigorous, but ill-motivated readings. No
amount of contrivance, however sensible, could halt the mis-
appropriation of these texts. Irenius is no believer in textual fash-
ioning which constrains the reader to read for an inherent meaning. He sees that, as one official reader put it, "every thinge is as
yt is taken,"[16] and, in Ireland, it is possible to take a text, not just
wrong, but any way you want. Irenius condemns more than the
misreaders themselves; he blames the rules which allow misreading. Eudoxus wants to believe that legal disarray "is no fault
of the Common Law, but of the persons which work this fraud."
But Irenius replies that "the Common Law hath left them this
benefit, whereof they make advantage, and wrest it to their bad
purposes" (p. 28). Ireland is engulfed (perhaps only an official
poet would have thought of it this way) in a crisis of reading.

### III. "Some secret meaning"

Irenius despairs of English mastery because he believes Irish
misreading cannot be governed. But not every administrator assumed this. Later, under James, military conquest would make it

possible to assume that official truth had established itself incontrovertibly. Faced with a trial in which the "proof of everything" seemed unsure, Sir John Davies, James's Attorney General in Ireland, would find himself able to fix the rules by fixing, as it were, the interpreters themselves. Once he "had punished one jury with good round fines and imprisonment for acquitting some prisoners contrary to direct and pregnant evidence" he wrote a correspondent, "another jury being impanneled for the trial of others found two notorious malefactors guilty . . . both which were presently executed."[17] It was to shatter the mirror in which English law saw itself parodied and to pull the Irish out from behind the looking glass that Davies sent the "Law . . . [to] make her progress and Circuit about the Realme, vnder the protection of the sword . . . vntill the people haue perfectly learned the Lesson of Obedience, and the Conquest bee established in the hearts of all men."[18] Davies is sure that common law, properly enforced, can be brought to bear upon inner selves; "hearts" can be fashioned into those of true subjects. His confidence amounts to a certainty that English law will secure the hegemony of English truth; its power will create knowledge by infusing official verities into thought of the Queen's "subjects"—subjected equally in their submission to the crown and their re-definition as selves, as "subjects" who think of themselves only according to categories of official truth informing their every thought. Davies administered a brutal military government, but his conquest was finally epistemic. "[W]hereas the greatest aduantage that the Irish had of vs in all their Rebellions," he wrote,

> was, *Our Ignornace of their Countries, their Persons, and their Actions*: Since the Law and her Ministers haue had a passage among them, all their places of Fastnesse haue been discouered and laide open; all their paces cleard; and notice taken of euery person that is able to do either good or hurt. It is knowne, not only how they liue, and what they doe, but it is forseen what they purpose or intend to do: Insomuch, as *Tirone* hath been heard to complaine, that he hadde so many eyes watching ouer him, as he could not drinke a full Carouse of Sacke, but the State was aduertised thereof, within few houres after.[19]

For Davies, law grants officials irresistible entry into the inner precincts of Irish treachery. Rebellious selves sequestered within a code of alien law can be reached, observed, and above all known. Law passes among them, separating and categorizing, assigning every Irishman a niche within the official scheme. Fixed in place by the cognitive machinery of "the State," every intention is open to surveillance and coercive refashioning.

Irenius has a theory of cultural refashioning too, but while Davies's certainty was borne out by the circumstances he was able to impose, the project which Irenius articulates for Spenser is a desperate denial of the conditions he faced as a colonial officer. Spenser thought, as he had Eudoxus say, that "the original cause of this evil" lay in England's failure to impose on Ireland its "language"—language in a large sense. "[F]or it hath been ever the use of the conqueror to despise the language of the conquered, and to force him by all means to learn his" (67).

As I began this essay by arguing, Spenser did not distrust his ideological language and could not have "spoken" any other, but he could sense, and lead his suspicious readers to sense, that in Ireland another tongue was spoken and another truth given voice. To dismantle this alien language he would silence its speakers, literally taking the words out of their mouths, for "the words are the image of the mind, so as they proceeding from the mind, the mind must needs be effected with the words; so that the speech being Irish, the heart must needs be Irish, for out of the abundance of the heart the tongue speaketh" (68). Irish selves articulate their language and their language in turn articulates them; they fold into one another, mutually constitutive. To alter the one is to alter the other, so the Irish must forget their tongue. Within their language, the unreconstructed Irish achieve a different order of being. Bound up in alien words, they set themselves apart from official truth in a realm which, in its autonomy and corrupt resplendence, may have seemed to resonate with the fascination and repulsion of idolatrous art. It could not be shared; it must not be tolerated. Spenser must eradicate it for the sake of pure truth. "Spenser's art," as Stephen Greenblatt asserts, "does not lead us to perceive ideology critically, but rather affirms the existence and inescapable moral power of ideology as that principle of truth towards which art forever yearns. It is art whose status is questioned in Spenser, not ideology."[20]

In the *View*, Spenser reaches for that principle of truth, dragging his recalcitrant readers after him, investing himself in its verities, and obliterating, when he can, whatever opposes it. But, we infer from his text and conclude from his last days that he failed to achieve the final certainty of sanctioned truth. Ireland up in arms, his plantation burned, Spenser, in London, pleaded with Elizabeth in the "Briefe Note" "to receive the voices of a fewe moste vnhappie Ghostes, of whome is nothinge but the ghost nowe left which lie buried in the bottome of oblivion farr from the light of your gracious sunshine."[21] Rendered insubstantial by the failure of received truth to sustain itself or him, Spenser also presented Elizabeth, the sole unquestioned incarnation of truth left him, a treatise entitled, *A View of the Present State of Ireland*. His dialogue is a resolute declaration of official truth, but in it can be heard the voices of more than a few unhappy ghosts.

*The Johns Hopkins University*

## NOTES

1.   Quoted in the "Bibliographical Note" to Edmund Spenser, *A View of the Present State of Ireland*, ed. W. L. Renwick (Oxford: At the Clarendon Press, 1970). All future references to this text will be given parenthetically.

2.   Jonathan Goldberg, *James I and the Politics of Literature: Jonson, Shakespeare, Donne, and Their Contemporaries* (Baltimore, Md.: The Johns Hopkins University Press, 1983), p. 9.

3.   Quoted in David B. Quinn, *The Elizabethans and the Irish* (Ithaca, N. Y.: Cornell University Press, 1966), pp. 127-128.

4.   Karl S. Bottigheimer, "Kingdom and Colony: Ireland in the Westward Enterprise 1536–1660," in *The Westward Enterprise: English Activities in Ireland, the Atlantic and America 1480–1650*, ed. K. R. Andrews, N. P. Canny, and P. E. H. Hair (Detroit, Mich.: Wayne State University Press, 1979), p. 52. Bottigheimer is quoting Nicholas Canny, "The Ideology of English Colonization: from Ireland to America," *William and Mary Quarterly*, 3rd Series, 30 (1973), 583.

5. Goldberg, p. 9.

6.   "Edmund Spenser," *Essays and Introductions* (New York: Collier Books, 1968), p. 371.

7.   Goldberg, p. 9.

8. Yeats, p. 372.

9. Goldberg, p. 9.

10. *The Works of Edmund Spenser*, ed. Edwin Greenlaw *et al.*, (Baltimore, Md.: The Johns Hopkins University Press), IX, 241–242.

11. From one point of view, the conventions by which an official text like the *View* was read in this period were peculiar to their historical moment and irrecoverable. From another, they are as available to us as the text itself, just as much a "matter" of conjecture and inference, no more present, but no more absent, equally constituted by the interpretation brought to bear. We can read readers as well as texts. My own sense of these conventions derives from texts which I take to have satisfied the requirements of authority at the time: dispatches (read, usually, in part), but especially Sir John Davies's *Discovery of the True Causes Why Ireland was Never Entirely Subdued* (1612; Shannon: Irish University Press, 1969).

12. Yeats, p. 361.

13. In an expanded version of this essay, I argue that Irenius is not Spenser's spokesman in a simple sense, but one voice in a dialectic Spenser constructs between inadmissible scepticism of royal policy and articulations of the official "view," articulations Spenser usually puts in the mouth of Eudoxus.

14. For full quotation, see p. 7.

15. J. G. A. Pocock, "The Ancient Constitution Revisited: a Retrospect from 1985," unpublished ms., p. 25. Within the common law, "immemoriality" was the prime criterion of legal validity.

16. Quoted in Annabel Patterson, *Censorship and Interpretation: The Conditions of Writing and Reading in Early Modern England* (Madison: The University of Wisconsin Press, 1984), p. 44.

17. "A Letter from Sir John Davies, Knight, Attorney General of Ireland to Robert, Earl of Salisbury Touching the State of Monaghan, Femanagh, and Cavan, Wherin is a Discourse Concerning the Corbes and Irenahs of Ireland," *Ireland Under Elizabeth and James I*, ed. Henry Morley (London: George Routledge and Sons, 1890), p. 359.

18. *Discovery*, p. 74.

19. *Discovery*, pp. 270–271.

20. *Renaissance Self-Fashioning from More to Shakespeare* (Chicago, Ill.: The University of Chicago Press, 1980), p. 192.

21. "Briefe Note," p. 236.

MARGARET P. HANNAY

# Unpublished Letters by Mary Sidney, Countess of Pembroke

*F*OUR holograph letters by Mary Sidney, Countess of Pembroke, have recently come to light. Overlooked by Frances Young in her 1912 listing of Mary Sidney's correspondence, the basis for subsequent references to her letters, they have never been published. [1] The first is a letter written to Robert Devereux, Earl of Essex, on behalf of her husband, Earl of Pembroke; it sheds some light on the tortuous relationship between the two great Welsh lords. The other letters, two to Sir Julius Caesar and one to the Earl and Countess of Shrewsbury, concern a "fowl abuce" committed against her by "that bace Mathew." Together, the letters demonstrate that in addition to her achievements as writer, translator, and patron, the Countess was active in politics and administration.

The first of these unpublished letters is unrelated to the others and to any known correspondence of Mary Sidney. In this brief undated letter to Essex she explained that, for want of a secretary, Pembroke asked her to write on his behalf. It is unclear why he did not write himself, but his other correspondence is in a secretarial hand; his reliance on a secretary probably resulted from lack of time rather than illiteracy, as his enemies charged. [2]

165

My Lords ernest desire to vnderstand of your
Lordships safe ariuale at Plimoth, as allso your
happy dispach thence, hath made retorne of this
wise post to feche a better satisfaction, & by
these few, for want of a secretary, to Lett you
know his thankfullnes conceued of your honorable &
so kind passage by him, of which coold he by
fitter means make better testemony, your
Lordship, he saith, shoold therof be as fully
assured as hee wishes his praiers may be effectuall
for your most fortvnate & blessed succes. my selfe
beeing willing to repete the arrant. Lest the
messengers naturall inclynation shoold cawse him
forget it, haueing trobled you thus may well sort
my praiers with the best that ar for you.


                    Your  Lordships  frend that wishes you
                         all honor & safty


                    Pembroke & M. Pembroke[3]

Mary Sidney first signed the letter, in her usual small script,
under the closing. Pembroke then added his signature to the left
of hers in letters twice as large. However, he did not put hatch
marks across the bottom of the page to fill the space as he often
did in other letters to prevent unauthorised additions; "this wise
post" must have been trustworthy, if forgetful. The messenger
was apparently someone sent by Essex to Pembroke, bringing
welcome news. Unfortunately, the Countess did not follow her
usual practice of inscribing her letter with place and date; Essex
would know that already.

It is difficult to know just where this undated letter fits into the
relationship between Pembroke and Essex. The earliest plausible
date would be 1589, when Essex sailed with Drake to support
Don Antonio of Portugal; the obvious *terminus ad quem* is
Pembroke's death on 9 January 1600. The letter could refer to
1591, when Essex was given command of the English forces sent
to assist Henri IV against the French Catholics, a project dear to
the Sidneys, or to 1596, when Essex sailed from England in June

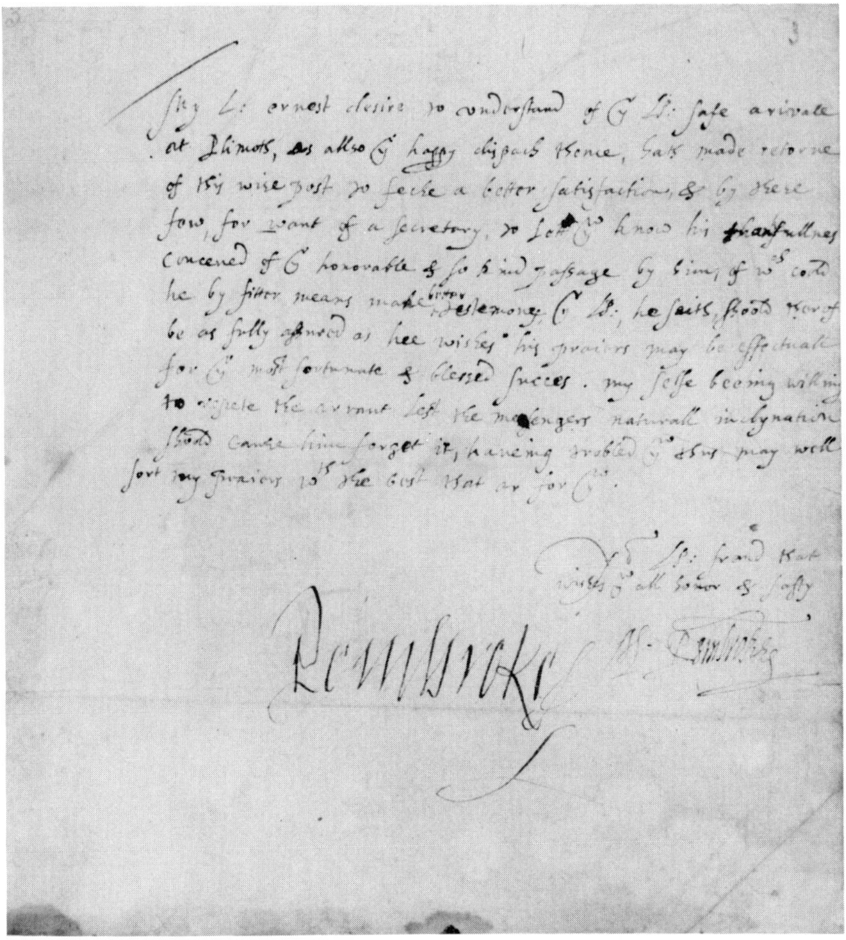

FIGURE 1. Letter from Mary Sidney to the Earl of Essex. Reproduced by permission of Robert H. Taylor and the Princeton University Library.

to reopen campaign against the Spanish, during which he sacked Cadiz; Essex returned to Plymouth in August. Another possibility could be the disastrous sailing in August of 1597, when Essex left from Plymouth to attack the new Spanish armada and capture treasure vessels returning from South America.[4]

The dating is particularly problematic because Essex and Pembroke—despite their close ties by marriage—were constantly vying for power in Wales and quarreled seriously over the ownership of Norwood Park in 1595.[5] Our most vivid contemporary source of information about the quarrel is the extensive correspondence between Robert Sidney, serving as Governor of Flushing, and his agent Rowland Whyte. Whyte was Welsh and apparently came to the Sidneys through his connection with the Earls of Pembroke, so he was particularly careful to report any news about Robert's sister Mary and her husband.[6] Because the Sidney and Herbert families usually acted as a political unit, any quarrel involving Pembroke was of serious professional, as well as personal, concern to Robert. He depended on his sister and her husband to obtain his leave to return home and also hoped that they could secure his permanent release from Flushing—preferably by giving him Pembroke's position in Wales.[7] On the other hand, Robert naturally wished to maintain his friendship with the powerful Essex, then near the apex of his career.[8] The Norwood Park quarrel put Robert in an exceedingly awkward—if not dangerous—position.

In one of his regular reports from court, Whyte wrote that "The vnkindness between 1000 [Essex] and 2000 [Pembroke] continues; but the Queen takes the matter in hand and mightily favouring the Western knight, is angry with 1000 for taking so uiolent a course, and tells 2000 he shall . . . have the thing in question. But away he [Pembroke] is gone, being at his departure graciously used. Here are many storms like to fall vpon him . . . and he has here no friend."[9] Although the queen promised that "he shall haue his money back again," Pembroke was not mollified. He sent a letter "that Arthur Massinger should find means to deliuer it to the Queen . . . which being very well considered upon by Massinger he found it would be his Lordships overthrow to have soe passonat a letter deliuered." Lady Warwick and others of Pembroke's friends also wisely refused to deliver the letter. Pembroke, Whyte concluded, "hath very few frends or none left here hymself so careless of them when he hath them."[10]

Despite this 1595 quarrel, which did far more harm to Pembroke than to Essex, 1596 is the most plausible date for Mary Sidney's letter to Essex. In that summer "Lord Herbert" accompanied Essex to Cadiz, took part in the assault, and was subsequently knighted. "Lord Herbert" was certainly Mary Sidney Herbert's relative and may well have been her sixteen-year-old son William. He first went to court in 1595 but left late in the year and did not return until 1597; in 1596 there is a complete hiatus in his biography. In 1598, before he inherited the title of Pembroke, he was apparently referred to as Sir William Herbert.[11] Another suggestive piece of evidence is that young William was intimate enough with Essex during this period to joke with him; "I am glad you have lost none of your limbs in your late conflict; if you had been maimed, a good tennis player had been spoiled."[12] Significantly, William's uncle Robert Sidney demonstrated particular concern for this 1596 voyage in his letters to Sir Francis Vere and George Gilpin.[13] Although there is no conclusive proof that William Lord Herbert went on the Cadiz voyage, such an explanation certainly fits the tone of this letter from the Earl and Countess. Gratitude for Essex's "so kind passage" and repeated concern for Essex's success, honor, and safety, would be an appropriate expression of parental concern. It is even conceivable that the trustworthy but forgetful post could be young William himself. If Essex did take him on the voyage and include him among those he knighted, he might have been seeking reconciliation after the Norwood Park quarrel. Since the capture of Cadiz made Essex one of the most powerful men in England, it would have been a politic time for Pembroke to make peace with him.

Pembroke, however, was an irascible man not always able to judge his own best interest. By 1598 that earlier quarrel over land deteriorated into well-defined factions in Wales, with Pembroke and Essex vying to place their own servants in power. On 26 June, for example, Pembroke complained to Cecil of the way his letters of patronage were "received with scoffing laughter by my Lord of Essex."[14] Pembroke and Essex remained bitter enemies from this point on, making 1596 the most logical time for the letter.

That the letter is in Mary's hand is particularly appropriate, for the Sidney/Herbert women took no part in the quarrel and con-

tinued to treat Frances Walsingham, Philip's widow and Countess of Essex, as a sister.[15] After Essex was arrested, Whyte's
reports to Sidney still demonstrate an affectionate family concern for Frances: confined in York house, Essex "often walkes
vpon his open leades, and in his garden, with his wiffe; now he,
now she, reading one to the other."[16] On 3 May 1600, when
Essex was in disgrace, in debt, and still in confinement awaiting
trial, Lady Essex came to see Lady Barbara Sidney and her children: "Methought to see her clad as she was, was a pitifull
spectacle," Whyte reported.[17] While Pembroke lay dying, his
enemy Essex was acquitted, released, and then openly rebelled
against the Queen. Although Mary Sidney was at Wilton with
her husband, the Sidney family continued to play an important
role in protecting both Frances Walsingham, Countess of Essex,
and Penelope Devereux, Lady Rich. When Essex's rebellion
failed, he and his supporters "took boat at Queenhithe to Essex
House, and shut themselves in, resolving not to come alive in
their enemies hands." Robert Sidney persuaded them to yield,
offering "two hour's respite for the ladies and gentlewomen [in-
cluding those dear to the Sidneys—Frances and Penelope] to be
removed." Then Robert asked Essex, "And yourself, my Lord?
what mean you to do? for the house is to be blown up with gun
powder vnless you will yield." After some time, Essex "yielded
the house" and was taken off to his eventual execution.[18]

Essex, "the Elizabethan Icarus," was destroyed, but because
relations between Pembroke and Essex had been acrimonious
from 1598 on, the Herberts were not implicated in his fall, as
were so many of their Welsh countrymen. This undated letter
which Mary Sidney wrote on behalf of her husband must have
been composed before that decisive break in 1598—probably in
July 1596, anticipating the triumph at Cadiz.

The other three unpublished letters are written in 1603 and
1604, after the death of Pembroke and of Queen Elizabeth. They
evidence the increasing frustration Mary Sidney felt in her
attempts to obtain justice against her former employee Edmund
Mathew, who had defied her authority in Cardiff, stolen her
jewels, planned the murder of her trusted servant—and yet
succeeded in convincing the new king that she was merely an
hysterical woman slandering Mathew himself. For recourse, she
turned first to Sir Julius Caesar, Knight of His Majesty's
Requests, and then to her son's prospective father-in-law, the

Earl of Shrewsbury.

The unpublished letters to Caesar are included in the collection of holograph letters at the British Library bound as *Caesar Papers: Letters of the Nobility*.[19] Her letters of 4 July 1603 and 8 July 1603 are printed in Young's biography, *Mary Sidney*; the letter of 14 July 1603, although listed in the seventeenth-century index in the front of the *Caesar Papers*, was overlooked by Young; the letter of 6 September, in a secretary hand, has never been noted.[20] "The fowl abuce" of "that bace Mathew" is never spelled out in the letters and can be reconstructed only from the Star Chamber records of a lawsuit she eventually brought against him.

Her first attempt to gain Caesar's help, dated 4 July 1603, is inscribed "To my honorable good friend Sr. Julius Cesar knight. geue these." The letter was endorsed on receipt, "The Countess of Pembroke tuching Mathew."

> Sr. to make good unto his maiestie, the reasons and
> truth, that I haue apprehended and iustilie
> accepted against Mathew. I haue to their great
> charge, as standinge ingadged uppon myne honor,
> unto his highnes, Mathew to bee the uery author, of
> soe foule an indignitie offred. as also to make
> good to the whole worlde, I would not possesse his
> princely eares with any vntruth. I haue I say to
> their great trouble and charge, brought upp those soe
> sufficient, and honest men, and of good reputation
> as will directlie vpon their oathes depose the
> truth. I haue tendred them, to the Lord Wotton.
> whose answere is. the matter is past their hands.
> I will not say a strange answere unto mee. but soe
> farr from my expectation, as the miracle hath
> brought, a strange Intelligence to mee. Soe as
> nowe I ame left onlie vnto you. that you will for
> my sake, and at my earnest request, for a thorowe
> satifaction of his highnes, to take these men
> sworne. and that by your honorable meanes, at
> least it may remayne vpon record. Vntill aptlie
> you may possesse, his maiestie, with the truth.
> soe as the sooner, you shall doe it, the sooner you
> shall make mee infinitelie beholdinge vnto you. as

an argument of the true feeling you hold of myne
honor heerin wherof I ame but to full. and so
restinge

Your euer thankfull and most assuered frend

M. Pembroke[21]

This letter was addressed from "Winsor." According to
Nichols, Mary and her daughter Anne were present at the Feast
of St. George on 2 July 1603, when Prince Henry was invested as
Knight of the Garter along with several other young men, including Mary's son William, the new Earl of Pembroke.[22]
Counting on Lord Wotton's long association with her brother
Philip, the Countess obviously expected him to take her part by
hearing her witnesses in Windsor and then bringing them directly before the King.[23] She believed that his response ("the matter
is past their hands") was merely an excuse to avoid bringing her
case before the king. Irate at Wotton's refusal to listen to the
witnesses she had brought at such expense, she was forced to set-
tle for written testimony instead of the more persuasive oral testimony. She therefore asked Caesar, as Master of Requests, to
conduct a formal examination of her witnesses before they had to
return home. (Under English law, an examiner may be appointed to take down the testimony of witnesses who cannot appear in
court because of distance or ill health; this documented examination can be used as trial evidence.)

Apparently both Wotton and Caesar brushed aside her case as
a troublesome interruption of the festivities. The Windsor letter
is followed four days later by one from the town of Burnam,
which makes it clear that Caesar was not taking her request
seriously. Although he formally examined the witnesses and
sent her a copy of his findings (the "examination" she mentions),
he recommended that she forget the entire matter. More omi-
nously, although she and her witnesses were prevented from
reaching King James, Mathew had told the king that she was
maliciously slandering Mathew's reputation. Like the letter of 4
July, this letter dated 8 July is addressed "To my honorable good
frend Sr. Julius Cesar knight. master of his highnes Requestes
geue these" and is endorsed in another hand, "The Countess of
Pembroke touching Mathew."

Sir. I thank you, for your great paynes and
kindnes, in this troublesome business of myne. the
which I assure you, I will not nor cannott forgett.
and nowe I ame further to pray you. to acquaint
his highnes, that you find, I did nothinge
maliciously against mathew. which I hope is proued
before you. and of the effect of that prooff.
which is against him, I pray you enforme his
majesty or otherwise I shall not be righted.
according to the truth and my expectation. Thus
euer restinge most thankfull unto you, I bidd you
hartelie farewell.

The Windsor and Burnam letters were both neatly written by a
secretary and then signed "M. Pembroke" by the Countess. This
Burnam letter, however, concludes with a postscript in the
Countess's own hand:

My trust is onely in you now lett me craue your
thorow frendly proceeding tuching this fowl abuce
that his Majesty may iustly conceue the
vnworthines of that bace Mathew so as he may not
receue any Grace here, nor hold the place of a
Iustice in the contrey. haueing so aparently
transgresd therein. it is the Sister of Sir
Ph[ilip] Sidney who yow are to right & who will
worthely deserue the same.

Yr affectionat frend

M. Pembroke[24]

Significantly, the Countess based her request on her relationship
to Philip rather than her position as Dowager Countess or
mother to the young lord who had been just honored at the Feast
of St. George; aside from personal considerations, a reminder
that she was a Sidney would ally her both with her brother the
Protestant martyr and with her father, Sir Henry Sidney, a more
popular governor in Wales than his successor, Pembroke. Even

that ploy did not work, so a week later she wrote to Caesar again. Inscribed "To my honourable frend Sr. Julious Ceasor Knight . . . of his majesties requests" it is endorsed in another hand "14 July 1603. The Countess of Pembrok—argument [against] Mathew." Caesar still had not presented the record of his examination to King James. This letter, in her own hand, has no opening salutation and appears to be written in haste and under considerable stress:

> This day had that most iniurious bace comepanion
> preuailed had not strangers to me preuented my
> dishonor therein. My hope, nay my confidence was
> that you woold haue fownd time with his majesty
> to haue putt this matter owt of further question by
> fully enforming him of the truth of my cawse & this
> phelows aproouen viloney towards me But I
> perceuve though you ar willing you can gett no
> oportunety which is no small cross vnto me. Well
> then must I worke otherwise what I may & to that
> end do post away this berear praying you to deliuer
> him the origenall examanation which is vnder your
> hand & which is still in your owne hands you haueing
> sent me onely the coppy that I may gett it
> presented to his majesty thereby to give his
> hyghnes ocation to call you vnto it. Not dowting
> then of your frendly proceeding according to your
> promis & my beleef in you which now is come to the
> tuch: faile me not I beceech you it consernes me
> neerely to vrge thus to be righted by you: it is
> needless to tell you againe & againe I shalbe
> more then thankfull. In hast I rest

> Your frend

> M. Pembroke[25]

Two more letters in this volume of Caesar's correspondence, filed out of order and separated from their inscriptions, further explain her frustration. The case had not come to the king's

attention because on 21 June 1603, Edmund Mathew himself had
written to Caesar:

Right worshipful: it pleased the kings Majestie to referr a matter
depending in question, Betweene the right Honorable the
Countese of Pembrooke, and my selfe to the hereing of the Lord
Wooten and Mr. Vicechamberline whoe hauing harde the matter
at large, haue made the reporte and diliued in unto you to be
prefered to the Kings highnes, which report as I ame enformed,
dothe not so well satisfie her Ladyship as she expected, In regard
whereof my desierye, for that I woold be lothe to agrevate her
Ladyship further disfauor. and wold guie her all the satisfaccon
which Lyith in my powr, that if her Ladyship willbe so pleased
to haue the matter reexamined, by whome it shall please her
Ladyship to appointe, I shalbe exceedingly contented, or if it
wold please her Ladyship to accept me into her presenc and to
undertake the hearing thereof her selfe, you being present, whoe
I knowe can better iudge thereof then anie other, and then if she
in her Ladyships wisdoome shall see cause for me to endure her
displeasure, and to haue this imputation remaine upon me, I shall
submit my self to endure yt or what els she in her discresion shall
seme expendient; And if I maie be so bould to entreate your fauor
so farr at your leasure as to signifie this much vnto hir, and in the
meane time to make stey of the report to the kinges highnes, you
shall tye a poore gend in all hee maie euer to be readie to doe you
service. And so rest

Your assured at comaundement


Edmund Mathew[26]

from my lodgeing at Courte
the 21th of June 1603

His letter, a masterful display of aggrieved innocence,
achieved its objective, for the case did not come to trial that year.
On 6 September 1603 the Countess wrote to Caesar from Green-
wich. This letter, in a secretary hand with a holograph signature,
begins with another administrative problem:
    Sir, I ame, to praye your aduise, and Counsell, that you will

Sir, I ame, to praye your aduise, and Counsell, that you will aduertize mee. whether I may not depriue one that holdeth a Benefice of mee. that hath two wyves liuing. And whate is my best course, for the depriuing of him, being soe lewd a liuer as I ame enformed hee is. for willinglie I woulde not bestowe it soe baselie. vpon any of soe unhenest behauiour.

The rest of the letter concerns Mathew:

Also I ame further to desyre you, to send mee, the Exammacon which you tooke, at Winsor, touching the barbarous abvse, that was donne upon my Steward, by the procurement of Edmond Mathewe. which Examinacones you were determined to deliuer to the Lord President of the Marches of Wales. Good Sir, send them mee, by this bearer. for that I haue occasion to haue further vse for the same. So resting euer thankfull vnto you, for all your former kindesse. I bidd you farewell.

Your very assured frend.

M. Pembroke.[27]

Although Young suggests that her dispute with Mathew in the earlier letters was "concerned with a local administrative difficulty, presumably in Wiltshire," and Waller more accurately suggests that the administrative difficulty was in Wales,[28] it is clear from the tone of the newly discovered letters to Caesar that the problem quickly became far more grave. The Countess certainly believed that her honor was at stake. Her accusation had made it a case of Mathew's word against hers before the new king, and her obvious distress indicates that the court sided with Mathew; the king had never heard her side of the argument. If Caesar could not—or would not—present the "examination" to the king, she was determined to find another intermediary. Therefore she requested the original examination, since the copy Caesar had sent would not be admissible as legal evidence to present to the King. Once the official document was in his hands, James would presumably question Caesar about the matter, enabling him to speak for the Countess. (She has no doubt whatever that the examination will establish her case, despite Mathew's disingenuous report of a rumor to the contrary.) Unfortunately, this first examination never reached the king, nor is it preserved as part of the court records. If she retained both the copy and the original, they may well have been lost, like so many of the records of her life, in the disastrous fire at Wilton in 1647.

Although that original examination is not extant, we do know that this dispute with Edmund Mathew of Glamorganshire was one she had inherited from her husband. Edmund's older brother William Mathew of Radyr, Cardiff and Drury Lane, London, owned extensive lands around Cardiff. He had increased his status by marrying the sister of William Herbert, Pembroke's cousin; on the death of that William Herbert in 1577, William Mathew was elected to fill his position in Parliament. An unsavory character, Mathew used his position to enrich himself, even speculating in grain during the Cardiff famine of 1585. The following year, he infuriated Pembroke by using his position as piracy commissioner to cite the borough officials of Cardiff before the Privy Council on charges of collusion with pirates. Pembroke retaliated by charging William Mathew with collusion in a murder, essentially the same charge the Countess made nearly twenty years later against his brother Edmund. (It is quite possible both charges were true.) By pleading illness, William Mathew evaded the summons to appear before the Council in the Marches of Wales, of which Pembroke was President. Then he wrote denouncing Pembroke's government to Burghley:

> I never harde it thoughte agreable with the
> law of this, or of any countrey whatsoeuer . . . that
> such a one should heare . . . our Capital Cawses of
> whom (in a manner) all our landes especially within
> Monmouth and Glamorgan shieres are holden and vnto
> whom thes cheate of all that euer we have both
> landes and goodes doe fall and belong, wich this
> nobell man by his commision of oyer and terminer
> hath and may doe.[29]

William Mathew was understandably concerned about a conflict of interest when his judge was also his landlord—but in this case, his judge was also his relative and had sponsored his career in Parliament until he violated that trust. The Privy Council supported Pembroke and imprisoned William Mathew; he died in the summer of 1587, before his trial. Since his only legitimate son had died earlier, his estate went to his brothers Henry and then Edmund.[30] Edmund, the "vile Mathew" of the Countess's letters, undoubtedly blamed Pembroke for his brother's death in prison. Pembroke's legacy of animosity made it difficult for his widow to administer Cardiff, with the Mathews and others against her from the outset.

The primary issue was an attempt to break the seigneurial hold over Cardiff by the Earls of Pembroke; as soon as her husband died, the Countess was vulnerable to revolt against her authority, being but an English woman. Under her husband's will, the Countess had inherited the castle and borough of Cardiff in satisfaction of her dower, held in trust for her son William and his male heir. She took her administrative duties seriously. For example, in August of 1602 she had written a long letter to Sir Robert Cecil from Cardiff dealing with another problem. She thanked Cecil for his help, which had strengthened her position in Cardiff: "This frendly favore; the honor, queit & strengthe yow have giuen me . . . is of such auaile in consideration of the place and condission of this people as I had no reason to expect nor to hope after: so hath it coucht them all; your honorable address heerein, it is wonder to see the change." Apologizing for troubling him with "this too vnworthey ocation," she declares that his help has supplied "the want of thos frends of myne long since lost.[31]

Between 1586 and 1595 the Countess had lost, through death, her "frends" at court: her brothers Philip and Thomas; her parents; her powerful uncles the Earls of Leicester, Huntingdon, and Warwick; Francis Walsingham; and now, even her husband. Her brother Robert was still Governor in Flushing, a position which precluded any real influence at court, even though he had begged leave to return home because "my sister hath now no friend to rely upon, her son being under years, but myself."[32] Her sons, although they were to be greatly honored under James, were of no help in 1602; Philip was only 17, and William had recently been in the Fleet prison for impregnating and refusing to marry one of the Maids of Honor, Mary Fitton.[33] Well might Mary Sidney be grateful for Cecil's aid.

She particularly thanked Cecil for supporting her in a case involving an unnamed "sedisious beggerly wretche whom it pleasd yow to bring downe vnder my mercy & now seemes most penetent"; she asked that, given his "missiry" he be released from imprisonment. The second unnamed offender's "barbarus demeanur hath bin so odious & therein so obstenate as that this hand may in no reason consent to become any meane for his release till . . . others lykewise will be better tought by his smart."[34] A plausible explanation for this case appears in the record of "objections against Morgan Williams, one of the bailiffs, and Roger Spencer, Recorder of the Dowager Countess of Pembroke's Town of Cardiff." Morgan Williams, "a sworne Bayliff vnto her Ladyship," had set up a rival court and would not desist despite her orders and a letter from her son, the young Earl ("he obstinatelye hauinge receyued his Lordships letter, putt yt in his pockett, sawselye & vnreverentlye.") This was a direct challenge to the Pembroke authority to govern Cardiff. More personal insults followed: "by the ill example of thies two, beinge the had of ye rest and meanrer sorte, a turbelous and disordred people, her Ladyships walles fast under the Castle hath byn pulled downe . . . her Ladyships priuate walkes torne off in peeces and cast awaye. Her Ladyships men arrested at her Ladyships gates. Her Ladyships houwsehold & seruants neerlye attendinge her Ladyship threatened with vyle Lavgnage and Beten . . . sore wounded with the blood runninge about their eares."[35] Clearly order was disintegrating in Cardiff, as the officials flouted her authority. Perhaps they, like John Knox, resented the "monstrous regiment of women." In any case, the support of Cecil established her authority temporarily.

The ephemeral nature of this reasserted authority is demonstrated by her letters to Sir Julius Caesar in July and September of 1603. With a new monarch on the throne, Cecil was too concerned with his own position to worry about supporting her in Wales; she had to find a new friend at court. As we have seen, neither Wotton nor Caesar presented her case against "that bace Mathew" to King James; although her charge against Edmund Mathew was that he conspired to murder her servant, he somehow convinced the king that she was acting "maliciously against" him. His only grounds for such a complaint was that she had fired him. He had held the minor post of steward of Myskyn under the Earl, but the Countess dismissed him and gave the stewardship to Hugh Davyd. Mathew's animosity toward her was probably the cause, rather than the result, of his dismissal, but from her letters to Caesar we can deduce that the king took his part. (We do not know why James would agree to hear a Welsh Justice of the Peace and deny a countess—his notorious misogyny hardly seemed sufficient cause—nor do we know why the young Earl of Pembroke was not actively pleading his mother's cause, which was ultimately his own.) The Countess finally succeeded in bringing him to trial at the end of 1605, considerably after her impassioned letters to Caesar. As we have seen, Mathew successfully blocked her immediate efforts to bring him to account, the orginal examination was never given to the king, and James never listened to the witnesses she had brought from Cardiff at such expense. Therefore, she found a way to "worke otherwise," as she had promised Caesar.

Because of Mathew's own position as justice of the peace (her plea to Caesar on 8 July 1603 that he "may not . . . hold the place of a Iustice in the contrey" had gone unheeded), he was able to block discussion of her case in Wales, and her legal battle against him had to be rather convoluted. On 1 December, 2 James (1604), the Countess entered a complaint into Star Chamber against a number of citizens of Cardiff, including the same Morgan Williams and Roger Spencer who had pulled down parts of her castle and beaten her servants; although Mathew is not among the accused, he later does become implicated in the case. The Countess claimed that her late husband the earl had been "Seized in his demesne as of ffee of and in all that of the castle of Cardiffe . . . and in the town of Cardiffe."[36] The Countess herself now held the freehold of the town with remainder to William now Earl of Pembroke and his male heirs. Under her authority, a court of record was to be held on Thursday every fortnight in the presence of the mayor and bailiffs; but Robert Adams, alderman of Cardiff; Robert Thomas; Roger Spencer; Morgan Williams; Thomas Williams; Nicholas Hawkyn; Henry Ball; William Wells; John Nonney "with many others to the number of one hundred or thereabouts of the Burgesses of townsmen . . . seditiously combined together and practize by uniuste and unlawfull meanes to wronge and iniure [the Countess] in her Right and interest of the said court" and to disinherit William, Earl of Pembroke. What had happened is that Robert Adams, one of the bailiffs, had held a court at the Guildhall on 20 March to hear various cases himself. Neither the corporal nor the constable of the castle was present in accordance with the *Customes Libertes*, the book of regulations for town government. Furthermore, when town officials were elected at the Guildhall on 26 September before the mayor, Sir William Herbert, Robert Adams was elected but refused to take his oath of office. As a first step toward reasserting order and justice at Cardiff (not to mention her own authority) the Countess requested a *sub poena* summoning the townsmen to explain their behavior.

Each of the defendants denied all the charges. John Nonney conceded "that Henry late earl of Pembroke names in the said byll was sometime in his life seized in demesne of comen estate of inheritaunce of and in the castle of Cardyff" but hesitated to admit that the complainant also held the same rights in the town of Cardiff until so instructed by his counsel. Then he said that she "enjoys the profits and perquisities of the Town's courts."[37] He claimed to know nothing about the removal of the court records (presumably to Guild Hall) by Adams or anyone else. He was likewise ignorant of Adams's refusal to take the oath of office in the exchequer in the castle, according to custom. Morgan Williams, in a separate statement, contradicted Nonney's testimony by swearing that "Nonney was bailiff with Robert Adams when on 12 May 1 James Adams refused to take the bailiff's oath"; he described the occasion as "riotous," but supplied no details.[38] From these contradictions it appears that the Countess had legal justification for her suit. The town's resentment of Herbert authority, evident in William Mathew's complaint when Pembroke was appointed President of the Council in Wales, led to open revolt when they perceived weakness in their English rulers. With the death of Pembroke and then of the Queen, Mathew, Adams, and other Cardiff leaders saw their chance to break the seigneurial hold of the Herberts; unfortunately for Mary Sidney, she was the one obstacle in their path.

Approximately one year after that original Star Chamber suit, the Countess entered a second suit, specifically against Edmund Mathew. "The complaint of the Countess of Pembroke" begins by repeating substantially the same charges as the earlier complaint, charging that Adams had the support of numerous

townsmen and specifically of Edmund Mathew. More important is the second charge: Mathew had long "maligned the good
estate" of the Countess, "And for that cause Hugh Davyd gent
servante and steward of the household" to the Countess had been
approached by Mathew with gifts and money to bribe Davyd to
give him (Mathew) "underhand" some parcel (unspecified) of
her lands. When Davyd refused, Mathew conspired with Philip
Llen on 19 April 1603 to kill Davyd while Davyd was in Wales to
take the the Countess's "money, plate and jewels towards
London," where she was residing on account of the funeral of
Queen Elizabeth. Llen, armed with dagger, pistol, and cudgel,
attacked Davyd in New Park Wood and broke his skull in six
places with the cudgel. He then escaped with the Countess's
money, plate, and jewels on a horse from Mathew's stable.[39]
Davyd languished three months in great pain before dying,
which means he died just about the time the Countess went to
Windsor.

The questioning of Mathew begins with the lesser charge:
"Did you do encoreidge moue stirre or persuade Roger Jones
John Edward William Nayler the elder David Hloyd Richard
Carclesse or any of the [defendants]" or any other townsmen of
Cardiff "to stile the Courte there usually kept every forghtnighte
in any other name then the name of the complainantte had you
any talke or speech with them or any other to that end or purpose
where and when." In his reply to ten specific questions, Mathew
denied that Roger Jones and others conferred with him or asked
his assistance, or that he contributed to the cost of the court. He
said he did not remember if Robert Adams ever talked with him
about the court, nor could remember seeing the court records.
The last fourteen questions directed to Mathew involve the
charge that he was an accessory to murder. He said that a sale or
transfer of West Moores had been agreed (apparently with
Davyd) but could not remember the date or price. He denied
giving a horse to Philip Llen, could not remember what he had
heard concerning Hugh Davyd before 19 April, and did not even
know that Davyd had been beaten and killed by Llen. Although
Mathew admitted giving money to Philip Llen, he swore that he
was merely repaying a debt and that he never contributed to
Llen's legal defense. Mathew also testified that he never heard
Llen complain about Davyd's conduct as steward of Myskyn, did
not hide Llen at his house, nor did he tell William Gascoigne that

Llen had "hurt" that "baggage fellow Davyd" and that it would be good if he died.

When Philip Llen was questioned, he denied assaulting, wounding, and killing Hugh Davyd. Then, in a fine piece of doubletalk, he added that he had already been tried and convicted of the same crimes before the Council in the Marches: he had been fined 100 marks and bound over in good behavior for the year beginning 16 March 2 James, so he was invulnerable to further prosecution for the crimes he now said he did not commit.[40] Llen's answer certainly appears to corroborate the Countess's complaint that the murder of her servant had gone virtually unpunished. There is no way of proving that Mathew's influence on the Council had saved Llen, but it is a highly plausible explanation for his light sentence.

No further record of Mary Sidney's suit against Mathew is extant, but various legal documents provide evidence of her continued administrative problems in Cardiff. In November of 1607 a letter to the Bishop of Chichester, the King's Almoner, grants "the Countess Dowager, of Pembroke, a portion of the goods of a servant of hers, who committed suicide, to the amount that he had stolen from her."[41] In 1609 a bill of expenses was presented by Edward Jordan of Cardiff for his seizure of 398 Barbary hides, on behalf of the officers of customs, "being imprisoned for the same by the bailiffs of Cardiff, who claimed them as an escheat, to the use of Mary Countess Dowager of Pembroke."[42] The seizure (20 January 1608) probably resulted from problems with the same group of pirates whose ravages can be traced through the administrative papers of both Pembroke and his predecessor, Henry Sidney.

The fourth unpublished letter apparently refers to Edmund Mathew as well; although he is not mentioned by name, the letter was written between her two recorded attempts to bring him to trial. The letter is included in the Talbot papers purchased from the Royal College of Arms in July 1983 by the Library at Lambeth Palace. Dated 29 September 1604, it is addressed in the Countess's own hand "To the Right honorable my good Lord brother the Earle of Shrewsbury [Gilbert Talbot]. It still bears Mary Sidney's red wax seal, the Sidney pheon surmounted by a coronet and by the Sidney crest, the porcupine; she did not adopt the Herbert lions or griffin, choosing instead to emphasize her identity as a Sidney. This letter has been indexed as a compliment about her new daughter-in-law, Mary Talbot, which is what one would expect a few weeks prior to the wedding of her eldest son.[43] Indeed, the Countess does appear to begin in that conventional manner:

Noble Lord & Lady,

Such a testemony of your kind fauors & loue to me
how needless so euer tuching your dawghter &
myne, whose fortune you well may rest confident
in, as which will neuer, nor her selfe in any
sorte haue cawse to make any vse of me, or those
poore helpes that is in me to add therevnto: onely
my care & wellwisshing must euer be a part of me and
neuer to be wanted, as that which I do acknowlidly
owe to the uery worthey respect I haue fownd in her
honorable parents who hath iustly hethervnto
perchasd a greater interest in me, then it may
be, I shall haue means to make shew of, but such it
is in my vnfained regard.

So far the letter is merely complimentary, although the compliments are to the parents rather than the daughter. We might, however, detect some bitterness in the assurance that their daughter—who will soon supplant Mary herself as Countess of Pembroke and as mistress of Wilton, Ramsbury, Baynard's Castle, and of the various other Herbert estates—will never need her "poore helpes." Mary Talbot's state now is such that her parents need not fear for her welfare, nor need they entreat the Dowager to offer more of what little (comparatively) remained to her. But the rest of the letter may concern "that iniurious bace comepanion" Mathew again.

And so woold appeare if to speake plainely as I
loue to do (without disguise) & that now at first, as
last, and euer I say if bace instruments (with whom
I am in no sort to partisopate) stood not in my
way such a monster as hath deuided myne owne from
me he that was held the deerest part of me. Such a
one as beeing best knowne to me must if I liue be made
knowne by me. and receue his rights from me. in

the meane time not . . . spleene but trwe scorne of
so false so curupt & so vile a creture lett these
words from your sister & frend, both in affection,
remaine with you. which time will otherwise
conferme and make euen the best mynds know theire
owne errors by reposing trust there. And I will
wisshe the best both to you & yours acording to
that better knowlidg which may heereafter better
express me vnto you. So resting.

Yowrs uery affectionately,

Pembroke[44]

Inscribed by Mary Sidney, "in hast from the Savoy this Sunday
27th of September 1604," the letter does indeed betray haste.
Written in her own hand, it has four cross outs, two ink blots,
several additions above the line, one totally unsuccessful attempt
to erase and replace a word, and, presumably later, was water
stained so that some letters on the left margin have disappeared,
but the general content is quite clear: her case had not been given
fair trial, and the "monster's" reputation had gained—at the cost
of her own. Although there is no conclusive proof that this "so
false, so curupt, & so vile a creture" is Edmund Mathew, it was
written in the midst of her legal battles against him, and the tone
of her description certainly parallels her characterization of the
"bace Mathew," that "iniurious bace comepanion" she describes
to Caesar.

Together with the letters previously published by Young,
these legal records and the hitherto unpublished letters to Caesar
and to Shrewsbury clearly establish Mary Sidney's administrative duties in Cardiff, and the difficulties of the widow caught in
the town's struggle to abolish the seigneurial hold of the Earl of
Pembroke. The letter she wrote to Essex on behalf of her husband indicates that she may have been active in politics even
before Pembroke's death. Although she was eulogised primarily
as "Sidney's sister, Pembroke's mother,"[45] those roles were
more than they might appear. We have long known that as
Sidney's sister, she edited his work, completed his Psalm translation, and encouraged the hagiography which established him as a
Protestant martyr. We now know that as Pembroke's mother

she held the castle and borough of Cardiff until his majority, a position which involved this literary woman in struggles with determined advocates of self-rule, and with vandals, pirates, and murderers.

*Siena College*

## NOTES

1. Frances Berkeley Young, *Mary Sidney, Countess of Pembroke* (London: David Nutt, 1912), pp. 228-229 lists fourteen letters extant. Of these eleven are holograph or in a secretary's hand with holograph signature. Three other letters were printed in Sir Tobie Mathew's *A Collection of Letters*, ed. John Donne, 1660. Since they have not been found in holograph, these letters to Sir Tobie Mathew are considered doubtful.

Young's biography served as the foundation for later studies, works which focus on Mary Sidney's roles as writer and patron rather than on her life or correspondence. See, for example, J. C. A. Rathmell's introduction to *The Psalms of Sir Philip Sidney and the Countess of Pembroke* (Garden City, New York: Anchor Books, 1963); Mary E. Lamb, "The Countess of Pembroke's Patronage," *English Literary Renaissance,* 12 (1982), 162-179; M. E. Lamb, "The Myth of the Countess of Pembroke: The Dramatic Circle," *Yearbook of English Studies,* 11 (1981), 194-202; Pearl Hogrefe, *Women of Action in Tudor England* (Ames: Iowa State University Press, 1977), pp. 105-135; Gary Waller, ed. *The Triumph of Death and Other Unpublished and Uncollected Poems by Mary Sidney, Countess of Pembroke (1561-1621)*, Salzburg, Austria: Institut für Englische Sprache und Literatur Universität Salzburg, 1977); Gary Waller, *Mary Sidney, Countess of Pembroke* (Salzburg, 1979); Diane Bornstein, ed. *The Countess of Pembroke's Translation of Philippe de Mornay's Discours de la vie et de la mort* (Detroit: Michigan Consortium for Medieval and Early Modern Studies, 1983); three essays on Mary Sidney in *Silent but for the Word: Tudor Women as Translators, Patrons and Writers of Religious Works,* Margaret Hannay (Kent, Ohio: Kent State University Press, 1985). Four recent dissertations focus on the Countess: Janette Seaton Lewis, "'The Subject of All Verse': An Introduction to the Life and Work of Mary Sidney Herbert, The Countess of Pembroke" (UCLA, 1976); Mary Ellen Lamb, "The Countess of Pembroke's Patronage" (Columbia University, 1976); Sallye Jeannette Sheppeard, "The Forbidden Muse: Mary Sidney Herbert and Renaissance Poetic Theory and Practice" (Texas Woman's University, 1980); Beth Wynne, "The Education of Mary Sidney" (Rutgers University, 1983. For a complete annotated listing see Josephine A. Roberts, "Recent Studies in Women Writers of Tudor England. Part II: Mary Sidney, Countess of Pembroke," *English Literary Renaissance,* 14 (1984), 426-439.

In addition, almost every book on Sir Philip Sidney mentions the Countess, if only to praise or to berate her editorial judgment.

2. Pembroke's native language was Welsh. Because of his love for Welsh

society and language, Thomas Wiliems of Trefriw called him "llygad holl Cymru," or "the eye of all Wales." *Dictionary of Welsh Biography Down to 1940* (London: The Honorable Society of Cymmrodorion, 1959), p. 351.

3.   This previously unknown letter, owned by "a lady," was purchased from Sotheby's in the summer of 1983 by the Robert H. Taylor Collection at Princeton University Library. It is printed by permission of Robert H. Taylor. In this and the subsequent letters, the spelling and punctuation are Mary Sidney's except that I have expanded the following abbreviated words: Lord, Lords, Lordship, Lordships, Majesty, which, with, and your. See Figure 1.

4.   For details of these voyages, see R. Lacey, *Robert, Earl of Essex; An Elizabethan Icarus* (New York: Athenaeum, 1971); G. B. Harrison, *The Life and Death of Robert Devereux, Earl of Essex* (New York: Henry Holt and Company, 1937); Walter Bourchier Devere, *Lives and Letters of the Devereux, Earls of Essex, in the Reigns of Elizabeth, James I, and Charles I* (London: John Murray, 1853).

5.   Essex's mother, the famous beauty Lettice Devereux, became Mary Sidney's aunt when she married Mary's uncle Robert Dudley, Earl of Leicester. Essex's sister Penelope, Lady Rich, is famous as the Stella of Sir Philip Sidney's sonnets. Essex himself fought with Leicester at Zutphen, returning home with honors and with the sword given him by the dying Philip Sidney. His marriage to Frances Walsingham, Philip's widow, strengthened his alliance with the Sidneys, who continued to treat her as a sister after her remarriage. See below.

   Prior to the Norwood Park quarrel, Pembroke and Mary Sidney were also intimate friends of Essex and Frances. See, for example, the postscript in Robert Sidney's letter to his wife on 8 September 1594: "My Lady of Essex grows very big. My Lord of Pembroke is now fully recovered and retourned from [Essex]." De L'Isle Mss, U1475, C81/47. The letter, excluding the postscript, is printed in HMC De L'Isle, II, 155-156.

   For a detailed account of the factions in the Council, see Penry Williams, *The Council in the Marches of Wales under Elizabeth I* (Cardiff: University of Wales Press, 1958), pp. 287ff.

6.   Rowland Whyte's grandfather, John Whyte, served William, first earl of Pembroke; and his uncle, Harry Whyte, served Sir Henry Sidney. P. C. Croft, *The Poems of Robert Sidney* (Oxford: Clarendon Press, 1984), pp. xvi-xvii. Millicent Hay suggests that Robert Sidney's "most genuine, long-lasting friendship appears to have been with Roland Whyte," *The Life of Robert Sidney* (Washington, D. C.: Folger Books, 1984), p. 180. When Robert went to Christ Church College, Oxford, Whyte went to study with him; subsequently, they travelled together on the Continent. Philip wrote to Robert, "yow shall neuer have such a servant as he would proue," cited in Croft, p. xvii. Philip was correct: Whyte was devoted to the Sidneys. During Robert's long absences, Whyte represented him at court and sent regular reports on the political situation, using a numeric code for the various personages. Whyte also handled most of Sidney's finances, frequently lived at Penshurst, and was very close to the family, giving Robert regular reports about his wife, children, and about his sister Mary and her husband Pembroke. See De L'Isle Mss. U1475 C12/letters 1-289.

One of the most frustrating aspects of research on Renaissance women is that their letters were usually not thought worth saving. Barbara Sidney saved 323 letters from Robert; although she presumably wrote as often (since his letters refer to hers), he saved none of hers—yet he did save the 289 letters from Whyte. Croft speculates that she was nearly illiterate, that "we cannot know whether Barbara ever wrote to Robert with her own hand, but if so it would probably have been merely to add a few affectionate words to a letter whose 'business' part had been set down by an amanuensis," p. 77. The evidence does not necessitate this conclusion, since the absence of her letters proves nothing. Despite numerous contemporary references to letters written by the Countess of Pembroke to family members, we have only one, and that Barbara saved. British Library Additional Ms. 15232. Printed in Young, p. 54.

If Barbara did have trouble writing in English, it might have been because her native language, like Pembroke's, was Welsh.

7.   Mary Sidney often interceded for Robert. See Robert's letter to his wife, 24 May 1588, De L'Isle Mss. U1475 C81/3, for example. On 14 Jan 1597/8, Whyte wrote to Sidney, "The copies of her letter unto [my Lord Treasurer] she did vouchsafe to send unto me of her own hand writing. I neuer reade anything that could express an earnest desire like unto this." De L'Isle Mss. U1475 C12/121.

Whether or not Mary herself was involved in the attempt to give Pembroke's position to Robert is unclear, but William Lord Herbert was actively trying to persuade his dying father. See Whyte to Sidney, 29 Nov 1599, De L'Isle Mss. U1475 C12/188; and 22 Dec 1599, De L'Isle Mss. U1475 C12/198.

8.   Robert Sidney corresponded extensively with Essex from 1596 through 1598; their letters are printed in volumes VI-VIII of the *HMC Calendar of the Manuscripts of the Most Honorable the Marquesse of Salisbury* (London: His Majesty's Stationery Office, 1883-1923). Although Robert was giving official reports from Flushing, the letters include personal notes and shared jokes that evidence an easy friendship. See particularly VI, 452 and 464.

9.   Whyte to Robert Sidney, 8 December 1595, De L'Isle and Dudley Mss. U1475, C12/40. De L'Isle letters are published by permission of Viscount De L'Isle V. C., K. G., from his collection at Penshurst Place. The letter is summarized in the *Historical Manuscript Commission's Report of the DeLisle and Dudley Mss* (London: His Majesty's Stationery Office, 1925-1966), II, 196.

10.   Whyte to Sidney, 14 December 1595, De L'Isle Mss. U1475, C12/41.

11.   List of names of knights made at Cadiz, HMC Salisbury, XIII, 599. Although no first name is given, by process of elimination, this should be young William, who was consistently called "my Lord Herbert" by Whyte and others before he became Earl. Pembroke's brother Edward, Lord Herbert, had died in 1594/95. Edward's son William Herbert (1573-1656) would be the other most likely possibility, but he was not knighted until the coronation of James I; he subsequently represented Pembroke's interests in Parliament. Edward Herbert (1583-1648), brother of George Herbert, had not yet been created Lord Herbert of Cherbury. Brian O'Farrell, in his dissertation, "Politician, Patron, Poet: William Herbert, Third Earl of Pembroke, 1580-1630" (UCLA, 1966) states that "it is hardly likely that he went on the expedition," but

supplies no evidence for that assumption, p. 38, n29. Devere misidentifies this "Lord Herbert" as "Son of William, third Earl of Pembroke," clearly an impossibility since William was only sixteen and since he never had a son who lived past infancy.

O'Farrell believes that the Sir William Herbert involved in negotiations after a constableship in 1598 was probably the third Earl, p. 176, n5. But there are so many William Herberts active in Wales during this period—all closely related— that it is difficult to be certain of the identification. On the three major branches of the Welsh Herberts, see the introduction to W. J. Smith, ed. *Herbert Correspondence: the Sixteenth and Seventeenth Century Letters of the Herberts of Chirbury, Powis Castle and Dolguog* (Cardiff: University of Wales Press, 1963) and Tresam Lever, *The Herberts of Wilton* (London: John Murray, 1967).

An interesting reference occurs in John Udale's letter to Essex on 30 Oct 1598, recommending "this young Lord Herbert" to Essex. It was written from Wilton, suggesting that it was written on behalf of Pembroke or Mary Sidney herself. While Udale does establish that Essex knew William as "Lord Herbert," it would seem curious to recommend him if he had already served at Cadiz—unless he is to be reinstated in Essex's favor despite Pembroke's animosity toward Essex. HMC Salisbury, VIII, 415.

12.   William Lord Herbert to Essex, "Wilton, this Sunday night," no date, in HMC Salisbury, XIV, 164, The letter was written in the late 1590s, prior to Henry Herbert's death in January 1600/01, when William became the Earl of Pembroke.

13.   Robert Sidney wrote during the preparations for the July sailing. Sidney to Vere, 8 February 1596, De L'Isle Mss. U1475, C71/1; Sidney to Gilpin, 18 May 1596, De L'Isle Mss. U1475, C11/23.

14.   HMC Salisbury, VIII, 233.

15.   In 1594, Frances had been Barbara Sidney's "Goship" at the birth of her child, demonstrating a significant intimacy. See also the Countess of Essex's intercession for Mr. Harry Sydney of Norfolk, which begins, "I know he is very dear to my dearest brother Sir Robert Sidney," Frances Walsingham to Sir Robert Cecil, 24 Oct 1597, HMC Salisbury, VII, 442-443. Throughout 1599 and 1600 Lady Essex is constantly mentioned in the letters of Rowland Whyte to Robert Sidney; when Essex was in disgrace after his unauthorized truce with the Earl of Tyrone in Ireland, Whyte reported that Lady Essex "came to court all in black and all she wore was not valued at 5 pounds," 29 November 1599, De L'Isle Mss. U1475, C12/190.

Croft notes that both Lady Essex and Lady Rich showed considerable affection for Robert—and suggests that Lady Rich's support for Robert in 1597 "goes beyond what can reasonably be attributed to sisterly loyalty," p. 83.

16.   Whyte to Sidney, 12 April 1600, De L'Isle Mss. U1475, C12/233.

17.   Whyte to Sidney, 3 May 1600, De L'Isle Mss. U1475, C12/239.

18.   Account of Vincent Hussey, 11 Feb 1601 in *State Papers, Domestic* 12/278/49,50.

19.   Additional Ms. 12, 503. Letters printed with permission of the British Library.

20.   The first of these letters, f. 150, is identified in the British Museum Catalog as referring to [Edward] Mathew, although the inscription on the letter trails off into near illegibility. Young and other biographers were unable to identify him further. An earlier letter to Caesar, dated 1 June 1596 [British Library Additional Ms. 12, 506 f. 235], concerns a poor servant and is irrelevant to this series; it is printed, slightly inaccurately, in Young, p. 59.

21.   British Library Ms. 12, 503 f. 150. Printed accurately in Young, pp. 98-99, except that the name Mathew should be capitalized, and there are two minor errors in punctuation.

22.   John Nichols, *Progresses of James I* (London, 1828), I, 193-195.

23.   Note her earlier letter to Sir Edward, whom she addressed as "Cousin Wotton." She had lent him manuscripts which she asked him to return, promising "other things better worth your keeping." Lambeth Palace Bacon Papers, 650, f. 231, *ca.* 1594. Although he was not, strictly speaking, her cousin, Wotton had worked with Philip in Vienna in 1547-75 and later was sent on a mission to James in Scotland by Queen Elizabeth, under Philip's instruction in 1585. The following year, he was a pallbearer at Philip's funeral.

24.   British Library Additional Ms. 12, 503 ff. 151-152, Printed in Young p. 99-100. Young is accurate, although she does not adequately explain the change in hand and leaves out some minor punctuation.

25.   British Library Additional Ms. 12, 503 f. 35.

26.   12, 503 f. 38; the inscription is folio 41.

27.   12, 503 f. 42. Inscription is f. 45. Endorsed "the Countess of Pebroke touching the sending to her of the exammiation. . . . Mathew."

28.   Young, p. 98. Waller suggests that the Caesar letters printed in Young deal "with litigation over her lands in Wales," *Mary Sidney*, p. 26.

29.   William Mathew to Burghley, 28 April 1587, *State Papers, Domestic* 12/200/51. The context of the letter is described in Penry Williams, p. 276ff. William Mathew did receive a temporary stay, as Pembroke complains in his letter to Cecil, 23 July 1587, Harleian Ms. 6994, f. 82.

30.   P. W. Hasler, ed. *History of Parliament: The House of Commons 1558-1603* (London: H.M. Stationery Office, 1981), II, 35-36. For Pembroke's accusations and William Mathew's attempts to answer them (Sir Edward Stradling was accused jointly with Mathew), see their letters printed in *Stradling Correspondence: A Series of Letters written in the Reign of Queen Elizabeth*, ed. John Montgomery Traherne (London: Longman, Orme, Brown, Green and Longman, 1840), particularly pp. 91-93 and 291-296.

31.   Countess of Pembroke to Robert Cecil, 3 August 1602, Cecil Papers, 94, f. 106. Cecil Papers are quoted with permission of the Marquess of Salisbury.

32.   Robert Sidney to Robert Cecil, 26 April 1599, HMC Salisbury, IX, 141-142. Despite Robert's constant pleas for leave, Hay has calculated that of the 13 years he was Governor, he spent less than half that time in Flushing. See chart in Hay, p. 138. Robert missed his family desperately and occasionally sent for them to join him in Flushing, despite the expense and the danger of plague.

33. Tobie Mathew to Dudley Carleton, 25 March 1601, *State Papers, Domestic* 12/279/36.

34. Mary Sidney to Robert Cecil, 3 August 1602. Printed in Young, pp. 96-97.

35. Cecil Papers, Petition 2301. "Objections against Morgan Williams one of Bayliffs of her Ladyships Towne of Cardiff & Roger Spencer her Ladyships Recorder of the same towne."

36. Public Record Office, Star Chamber records, Stac. 8/183/35 m.5. The first record of the complaint (m.6) is dated 1 December 2 James; the improved copy is cited here.

37. Stac. 8/183/36 m.12 (13 May 3 James).

38. Stac. 8/183/35 m.4 (9 February 2 James).

39. Stac. 8/183/36 m.12 (no date; manuscript is damaged). The specific questions and Edward Mathew's answers are given on m.1—m.8 (15 November 3 James). Crown-copyright material in the Public Record Office is reproduced by permission of the Controller of Her Majesty's Stationery Office.

40. Stac. 8/183/35 m.9 (22 June 3 James)

41. November 1607, *State Papers, Domestic,* 14/28/32.

42. *State Papers, Domestic* 14/45/112.

43. This letter, overlooked by Young, is listed in the long unindexed section of unpublished papers in Edmund Lodge, ed. *Illustrations of British History, Biography, and Manners in the Reigns of Henry VIII, Edward VI, Mary, Elizabeth, and James I* (London: John Chidley, 1838), III, 115, where it is annotated as "Family affairs." The more recent HMC report lists it as compliments about her new daughter-in-law, Mary Talbot, daughter of the Earl of Shrewsbury. *A Calendar of the Shrewsbury and Talbot Papers in Lambeth Palace Library and the College of Arms,* ed. G. R. Batho (London: H. M. Stationery Office, 1971), II, 274.

The connection between the Herberts and the Talbots was long-standing. William Herbert, first Earl of Pembroke, married Lady Anne Talbot (date unrecorded); this marriage was childless although his previous marriage to Anne Parr had produced several children. In a double marriage on 17 February 1563, William Herbert's only daughter, Lady Anne Herbert, married Francis Lord Talbot, and his oldest son Henry married Lady Catherine Talbot. Lady Catherine also died childless; Henry married Mary Sidney in 1577. Their son William Herbert, third Earl of Pembroke, married Mary Talbot on 4 November 1604; that third marriage between an Earl of Pembroke and a Talbot once again failed to produce an heir.

44. *Talbot Papers,* M259, reclassified as Lambeth Palace Ms. 3202, f.259. Printed with permission of the Trustees of Lambeth Palace Library. After Mary Talbot married William Herbert, she began signing her letters "M. Pembroke"; Mary Sidney Herbert then changed her signature to "Pembroke" with an identifying design around her title.

45. William Browne, Lansdowne Ms. 777, British Library.

# Index

Achilles, 120, 124
Acteon, 36
*Actes and Monuments* (Foxe), 27 n.23
Adams, Hazard, 144 n.12
Adams, James, 180
Adams, Robert, 179, 180
Adonis, 120, 123, 124
Aeneas, 36
*Aeneid,* 35, 111 n.8, 132
Aeschylus, 16, 134
Agricola, Rudolphus, 112 n.18
Ainslie, Douglas, 143 n.4
Ainsworth, Henry, 50
Alençon, Duc d', 18, 24 n.4
Allen, D. C., 68 n.5
Allen, M. J. B., 68 n.5
Alpers, Paul J., 84, 93 n.3
Alva, Duke of, 18
*Anatomie of Abuses* (Stubbes), 10
Andrewes, Lancelot (Bishop of
    Chichester), 112 n.23, 182
Andrews, John F., 26 n.17
Angelica (*Orlando furioso*), 87
*Animadversions against Smectymnuus*
    (Milton), 31 n.58
*Annotations* (Ainsworth), 50
*Antiquitez* (Du Bellay), 78, 79, 81,
    82 n.7
Apollo, 122, 129, 133, 135
*Apologie for Poetrie, An* (Sidney), 12,
    129, 136, 137, 138, 140, 143–144
    n.5
Ariosto, Lodovico, 111 n.8
Aristophanes, 134
Aristotle, 116, 136
Armida (*Gerusalemme Liberata*), 100
*Arte of English Poesie, The*
    (Puttenham), 70 n.16
*Axiochus,* 95–113
Aylmer, John (Bishop of London),
    16, 17

Bacchus, 133, 135

Bahr, Howard W., 92 n.2, 94 n.16
Bale, John, 6, 7, 19, 20, 26 n.19, 78
Ball, Henry, 179
Batho, G. R., 190 n.43
Bayet, Jean, 68 n.4, 73 n.28
"Beaulah" (Blake), 111 n.8
Bede, the Venerable, 50
Bednarz, James P., 23 n.1, 29 n.41
Belprato, Don Giovanni Vincentio,
    112 n.18
Bembo, Pietro, 116, 117
Benson, Robert G., 72 n.27
Berger, Harry, Jr., 108, 109, 112
    n.30
Bernard, John D., 72 n.27, 74 n.38,
    88, 93 nn.11, 14
Berry, Lloyd E., 23 n.1, 30 nn.50, 56
Bevington, David, 25 n.8
Beza, Theodore, 20, 25 n.12
Bible, Books of
    Acts 3:15, 43, 56
    Acts 13:31-32, 43
    Acts 17:27, 46
    1 Corinthians 6:20, 43
    1 Corinthians 15:55, 56
    1 Corinthians 47:5, 43
    Ecclesiasticus 14-15, 46
    Ephesians 4:8, 43
    Ephesians 5:2, 43
    Ezekiel 17:24, 46
    Galatians 3:23, 45
    Galatians 6:2, 48
    Habbakuk 3:19, 68 n.4
    Isaiah, 57
    Isaiah 4, 57
    Isaiah 4:2, 46
    Isaiah 7, 53
    Isaiah 13:14, 73 n.28
    Isaiah 27:6, 46
    Isaiah 35:1, 46
    Isaiah 35:6, 73 n.28
    Isaiah 45:8, 53
    Jeremiah 2:13, 47

Job 39:4, 73 n.28
Joel 2:17, 54
John 10:1-16, 6
John 13:31-52, 43
John 15:12, 43
1 John 4:19, 43
Lamentations 1:6, 73 n.28
Luke 1, 53
Luke 8:5, 13
Luke 12:3, 45
Matthew 7:15, 6
Matthew 25:21, 44
Proverbs, 47
Proverbs 5:18, 47
Proverbs 5:18-19, 48
Proverbs 5:19, 48, 51, 61, 73 n.31
Proverbs 6:5, 73 n.28
Proverbs 14, 46
Psalm 1, 54
Psalm 16, 44
Psalm 18, 68 nn.3, 4
Psalm 21, 57
Psalm 22, 47, 49, 50, 51, 52, 54,
  61
Psalm 29, 73 n.28
Psalm 41, 55
Psalm 42, 33, 47, 51
Psalm 42:1, 46, 55
Psalm 47, 57
Psalm 47:5, 43
Psalm 51, 54, 75 n.41
Psalm 68, 43, 56
Psalm 104, 57, 68 nn.3, 4
Psalm 104:30, 46
Psalm 107, 43
Psalm 137, 79
Revelation, 87
Revelation 1, 75 n.39
Revelation 1:5, 43
Revelation 18:2, 78
Revelation 21:24, 45
Revelation 22:5, 45
Song of Songs, 41, 45, 47, 48,
  49, 51, 57, 75 n.44
Song of Songs 2:9, 73 n.29
Bible, Names
  Aaron, 16
  Adam, 137
  Christ, 41, 43, 44, 45, 46, 47, 48,

    49, 50, 52, 55, 57, 58, 61, 65
    nn.4, 5; 70 n.17, 72 n.27, 74
    n.33
  David, 49, 51, 68 n.4, 69 n.14,
    75 n.41, 120, 136
  Eve, 49
  Holy Spirit, 137
  Jesus, 137
  Moses, 16
  Noah, 53, 55
  Solomon, 61
Bieman, Elizabeth, 72 n.27
Blake, William, 111 n.8
Blissett, William 124, 127 n.16
Bolzani, G. P. V. (Valerianus), 49,
  73 n.32
Book of the Courtier, The
  (Castiglione), 117, 125 nn.5, 6
Book of Common Prayer, 9, 27 n.24,
  33, 53, 54, 56, 57, 59, 74 n.39, 75
  nn.44, 45
Book of Homilies, 8, 9
Book of Martyrs (Foxe), 1
Book of Sports, 9
Booty, John E., 27 n.24, 74 n.39
Bornstein, Diane, 185 n.1
Bottigheimer, Karl S., 162 n.4
Boyle, Elizabeth, 33, 58–59
Bromwich, Rachel, 69 n.9
Brown, James Neil, 71 n.21
Browne, William, 191 n.45
Bruno, Giordano, 69 n.10
Bryskett, Lodowick, 112 n.23, 125,
  127 n.17
Bucer, Martin, 4, 17
Bullinger, Heinrich, 4, 19, 25
  nn.11, 12
Burbie, Cuthbert, 95, 107, 109 n.1,
  110 n.3
Byrom, H. J., 29 n.49, 30 nn.50,
  53, 54, 56

Caesar, Julius, 35
Caesar, Sir Julius, 165, 169, 170,
  173, 178, 179, 184, 189 nn.20, 28
Calvin, Jean, 4, 20, 25 n.12, 50, 51,
  74 n.38
Canny, Nicholas, 162 n.4
Canterbury Tales, 13, 28 n.34

Carclesse, Richard, 181
Carleton, Dudley, 190 n.33
Cary, Henry, Lord Hunsdon, 18
Casady, Edwin, 68 n.3
Castiglione, Baldasarre, 117, 125
  nn.5, 6
Catullus, 76 n.45
Cecil, Robert, Earl of Salisbury,
  163 n.17, 177, 188 n.15, 189
  n.31, 190 nn.32, 34
Cecil, William, Lord Burghley, 2,
  17, 168, 176, 178, 189 n.29
Chambers, E. K., 28 n.32
*Chansons spirituelles* (Marguerite of
  Navarre), 37, 69 n.14
Charbonneau-Lassay, L., 71 n.70,
  73 n.28
Charlemagne, 35
Charlewood, John, 110 n.3
Chaucer, Geoffrey, 12, 13, 28 n.33,
  97, 99, 100, 101, 102, 131
Chester, A. G., 27 n.30
Chloe, 35
Chrysostom, John, 51, 74 n.36
Church, R. W., 24 n.3
Cicero, 130
Claudian, 97, 98, 99, 100, 101, 102
Clay, William C., 74 nn.34, 39
Clements, Robert J., 145 n.12
Cléonice, 72 n.23
Collinson, Patrick, 23 n.1, 25 n.12,
  26 nn.13, 14, 17; 29 nn.41, 45; 30
  n.52
*Commentaries* (Calvin), 50, 51
*Common Places* (Peter Martyr), 4,
  25–26 n.12
*Confession of Fayth . . . , A*
  (Bullinger), 25 n.11
Connell, Dorothy, 144 n.5, 145
  n.13
*Consensio mutua in re sacramentaria
  Ministrorum Tigurinae Ecclesiae*
  (Bullinger), 25 n.11
Cooper, Thomas, Bishop of
  Lincoln, 15, 29 n.41, 140
*Countrie Divinitie, The* (Gifford), 14
Coverdale, Miles, 20
Craig, D. H., 144 n.5
Craik, G. L., 24 n.3

Cranmer, Thomas, Archbishop of
  Canterbury, 8, 9, 10, 25 n.11, 27
  n.22, 52
Croce, Benedetto, 143 n.4
Croft, Sir James, 18
Croft, P. C., 186–187 n.6, 188 n.15
Crowley, Robert, 11, 50
Cullen, Patrick, 25 n.7, 111 n.8
Cummings, Peter M., 73 n.31
Cunliffe, J. W., 69 n.13
Curtius, Ernst Robert, 110–111 n.8
*Cyropaedia* (Xenophon), 139
Cyrus, 139

Daedalus, 138, 139, 141
David, Samuel, 69 n.11
Daphne, 86
Dasenbrock, R. W., 68 n.2
d'Aubigny, Duc, 29 n.41
David, Hugh, 179
Davies, Sir John, 160, 161, 163 n.17
Davies, Richard, Bishop of St.
  David's, 15
Davyd, Hugh, 181, 182
Day, John, 21
*Defense of Poesy, The* (Sidney), 117,
  118, 126 n.7
*Delia* (Daniel), 69 n.11
De L'Isle, Viscount, 187 n.9
De Neef, A. Leigh, 72 nn.25, 27,
  73 n.33
*De Non Plectendis morte adulteris
  Consultatio* (Foxe), 20
Dent, Arthur, 14, 15
*De rerum natura* (Lucretius), 111
  n.11
De Selincourt, E., 144 n.7
Desportes, Philippe, 57, 72 n.23
d'Estampes, Mme., 41
de Vere, Edward, Earl of Oxford,
  29 n.41, 110 n.3
Devere, Walter Bourchier, 186 n.4,
  188 n.11
Devereux, Lettice Knollys,
  Countess of Leicester, 186 n.5
Devereux, Penelope, Lady Rich,
  169, 186 n.5
Devereux, Robert, 2nd Earl of
  Essex, 165, 166, 167, 168, 169,

184, 187 n.8, 188 nn.11, 12, 15
*Dialogue between Custom and Veritie* . . . (Lovell), 10
Diana, 36
Dickens, A. G., 4
Dickinson, F. H., 74 n.39
Dido, 35, 36
*Difference of Hearers, The* (William Harrison), 14
*Discoverie of a Gaping Gulf Whereinto England Is Like To Be Swallowed by an other French mariage* (Stubbs), 19, 21, 30 nn.50, 56
*Discovery of the True Causes Why Ireland Was Never Entirely Subdued* (Davies), 163 n.11
*Discourse of Ciuill Life* (Bryskett), 125, 127 n.17
*Discourse of English Poetrie* (Webbe), 6
Dixon, John, 31 n.61
Dodge, R. E. N., 24 n.3
Dolet, Etienne, 104, 112 n.18
Don Antonio of Portugal, 166
Dottin, Georges, 69 n.14, 70 n.17
Drake, Sir Francis, 166
Drummond, William, of Hawthornden, 22
Du Bellay, Joachim, 18, 41, 57, 58, 59, 72 n.23, 76 n.47, 78, 79, 81, 82 n.7, 108
Dudley, Ambrose, Earl of Warwick, 177
Dudley, Robert, Earl of Leicester, 2, 4, 15, 18, 19, 25 n.11, 28 n.39, 29 n.41, 177, 186 n.5
Duff, E. Gordon, 30 n.50
Dunlop, Alexander, 71 n.21, 73 n.33, 75 n.41, 76 n.49
Dyer, Edward, 29 n.41

Ebreo, Leone, 11
Edward VI, 2, 4, 7, 8, 9, 10, 17, 20, 27 n.22, 31 n.67, 43, 49, 53, 56, 57, 74 n.39, 75 n.39
Edward, John, 181
E.K.,1, 3, 4, 6, 7, 8, 11, 12, 15, 16, 28 nn.39, 40; 29 n.41, 30 n.50,

110 n.3, 130, 131, 132, 133, 134, 135, 136, 137, 139, 142, 144 n.8
Elizabeth I, 2, 4, 8, 9, 16, 20, 22, 24 n.4, 29 n.41, 79, 147, 150, 151, 153, 154, 167, 169, 180, 189 n.23
Elliott, J. R., 72 n.27
Ellrodt, Robert, 144 n.5
Ennius, 134
*Epithalamium of Honorius and Maria* (Claudian), 99, 111 n.12
Erdman, David V., 110 n.5
Eros, 135
Estienne, Henri, 108, 109
Eucherius, 49, 73 n.32
Evans, Robert O., 93 n.11

*Faerie Leveller* . . . , *The* (Anon.), 31 n.62
*Fasti* (Ovid), 133
Ferguson, F. S., 30 n.51
Fichter, Andrew, 82 n.5
Ficino, Marsilio, 112 n.18, 116, 120, 125 n.3
Fitton, Mary, 178
Fletcher, Giles, 58, 59, 74 n.39
Fogel, Ephim G., 110 n.5
"Forty-two Articles," 9
Fowler, Alastair, 67 n.1, 71 n.21, 76 n.49, 92 n.2, 123, 127 n.15
Foxe, John, 1, 8, 20
François I, 41
Fraunce, Abraham, 23, 31 n.66
Freyd, Bernard, 95, 109 n.3, 110 n.3, 112 n.23, 25
Frye, Northrop, 111 n.8

Gannon, C. C., 69 n.10
*"Gaping Gulf" with Letters* . . . (Stubbs), 30 n.50
Gardiner, Stephen, Bishop of Winchester, 26 n.19, 27 n.20
Gascoigne, George, 37, 48, 69 n.13
Gascoigne, William, 181
*Gerusalemme Liberata* (Tasso), 100, 111 n.14
Gesner, Conrad, 47
Gesualdo, G. A., 34, 62 n.1
Giamatti, A. Bartlett, 93 n.15, 111

n.8

Gibbon, J. M., 70 n.17

Gifford, George, 14, 28 n.38

Gilbert, Sir Humphrey, 148, 149

Gilby, Anthony, 6, 7, 26 n.19

*Godly Dyalogue and Dysputacion* . . . (Anon.), 28 n.33

Goldberg, Jonathan, 162 nn.2, 5, 7

Golding, Arthur, 50

Gollancz, Israel, 28 n.40

Gorges, Sir Arthur, 69 n.11, 72 n.23

Gottfried, Rudolf, 95, 96, 107, 112 n.22

Gray of Reading, 71 n.17

Gray, J. C., 76 n.50

Greaves, Richard, 26 n.14

Greenblatt, Stephen, 31 n.66, 161

Greene, Thomas, 82 n.7

Greenlaw, Edwin A., 23 n.1, 24 n.3, 30 n.54, 68 n.2, 144 n.6, 162 n.10

Greg, W. W., 30 n.55

Greville, Fulke, 29 n.41

Grindal, Edmund, Archbishop of Canterbury, 2, 3, 5, 15, 16, 17, 29 n.41

*Gude and Godlie Balates* (Wedderburn), 70 n.17

Guild, Nicholas, 68 n.5, 69 n.9

Hamilton, A. C., 29 n.41, 88, 92 nn.2, 5, 10, 11, 13; 111 n.13, 124, 127 n.16, 144 n.5

*Handlyng Synne* (Mannyng), 10

Hannay, Margaret P., 70 n.15, 185 n.1

Hardin, Richard, 144 n.11

Hardison, O. B., Jr., 71 n.21, 144 n.5

Harrison, G. B., 186 n.4

Harrison, James (John Bale), 26 n.19

Harrison, John, the Younger, 21

Harrison, William, 14

Harrowing of Hell, 42, 43

Hartman, Geoffrey, 73 n.33

Harvey, Gabriel, 15, 22, 23, 28

n.40, 70 n.15, 131, 132

Hasler, P. W., 189 n.30

Hastings, Henry, 3rd Earl of Huntingdon, 177

Hawkyn, Nicholas, 179

Hay, Millicent, 186 n.6, 190 n.32

Helen of Troy, 92 n.2, 124

Henri IV, 166

Henry VIII, 7, 26 n.19, 31 n.67

*Heptaméron* (Marguerite of Navarre), 41, 70 n.15

Herbert, Lady Anne (only daughter to William Herbert, 1st Earl of Pembroke), 190 n.43

Herbert, Edward, Lord Herbert (brother of 2nd Earl of Pembroke; d. 1594/95), 187 n.11

Herbert, Edward, Lord Herbert of Cherbury (1583–1648), 187–188 n.11

Herbert, George (poet), 187 n.11

Herbert, Henry, 2nd Earl of Pembroke, 165, 166, 167, 168, 169, 176, 177, 180, 182, 186 nn.2, 5; 187 n.6, 188 nn.11, 12; 189 n.30, 190 n.43

Herbert, Mary Sidney, Countess of Pembroke (wife of Henry Herbert, 2nd Earl), 79, 165–191

Herbert, Mary Talbot, Countess of Pembroke (wife of William Herbert, 3rd Earl), 183, 190 n.43, 191 n.44

Herbert, Philip, Earl of Montgomery, 177

Herbert, William, 1st Earl of Pembroke, 186 n.6, 190 n.43

Herbert, Sir William, 3rd Earl of Pembroke, 168, 177, 179, 180, 187 nn.7, 11; 188 nn.11, 12; 190 n.43, 191 n.44

Herbert, William (1573–1656, son of Edward, Lord Herbert), 187 n.11

Herbert, William (cousin of Henry Herbert, 2nd Earl), 176

Herford, C. H., 24 n.3, 31 n.61

Hieatt, A. K. 71 n.21, 73 n.27, 76 n.49, 76 Ackn.

*Hieroglyphica* (Valerianus), 73 n.32
Higginson, J. J., 24 n.3
*History of Four-footed Beasts*
   (Topsell), 73 n.30
Himmelfarb, Anne, 76 Ackn.
Hloyd, David, 181
Hogrefe, Pearl, 185 n.1
Homer, 97, 98, 99, 100, 102, 111
   n.15. 136
Horace, 35, 37, 130, 134
Hugh of St. Victor, 47
Hughes, Merritt Y., 31 n.59
Hughes, Paul L., 30 n.50
Hulbert, Viola, 29 n.41
Hume, Anthea, 3, 23 n.2, 24 n.3,
   27 n.20, 29 n.41, 31 n.64, 72
   n.25, 92 n.1
*Hundred Sermons upon the Apocalipse,
A* (Bullinger), 19
Hunter, G. K., 71 n.21
*Hunting of the Fox and the Wolfe,
The* (Gilby), 26 n.19
*Huntyng and Fyndyng Out of the
Romishe Fox* (Turner), 26 n.19
*Huntyng of the Romyshe Vuolfe, The*
   (Turner), 26 n.19
Hussey, Vincent, 189 n.18

Icarus, 138, 141, 169
*Image of Both Churches* (Bale), 19
*In Apocalypsim Iesu Christi*
   (Bullinger), 19
*In priores quinquaginta Psalmos*
   (Sampson), 50
*Institutes* (Calvin), 4, 25 n.12
*Ion* (Plato), 130, 143 n.2
Isabella (*Orlando furioso*), 91

Jackson, William A., 30 n.51, 110
   n.3
James VI and I, 9, 29 n.41, 159,
   160, 171, 175, 178, 179, 187
   n.11, 189 n.23
Jayne, Sears, 125 n.3
*John Bon and Mast[er] Person*
   (Sheperd), 28 n.33
Johnson, L. Staley, 29 n.41
Johnson, William, 53, 54
Johnson, William C., 69 n.12, 71

n.21, 72 n.26, 74 nn.38, 39; 75
   nn.39, 40, 41, 42; 76 n.45

Jones, Roger, 181
Jonson, Ben, 22
Jordan, Edward, 182
Jortin, John, 97, 98, 99
Judson, Alexander C., 28 n.40, 112
   nn.23, 29

Kane, Sean, 119, 124, 127 n.9
Kaske, Carol, 71 n.21, 72 n.22, 73
   n.33
Kelly, Robert, 28 n.36
Kennedy, J. M., 81 n.1, 93 n.11
King, John N., 26 n.12, 27 nn.20,
   22; 28 nn.35, 37; 29 n.48, 31 n.67
Kingston, John, 26 n.12
Knappen, M. M., 4
Knight, Edward, 110 n.3
Knox, John, 20, 178
Kolb, Herbert, 73 n.28
Kostić, Veselin, 68 n.2
Lacey, R., 186 n.4
Lake, Peter, 5, 7, 26 nn.13, 16
Lamb, Mary Ellen, 185 n.1
Lamb, W. R. M., 143 n.2
Langer, Susanne K., 145 n.16
Langland, Robert, 12
Langland, William, 12, 13, 28 n.36
Lantier, Raymond, 73 n.28
Larkin, James F., 30 n.50
Latimer, Hugh, 11, 13, 14, 28 n.36
*Laws* (Plato), 132
Le Comte, Edward, 68 n.5
"Legend of Holiness, The"
   (Harvey), 23
Legg, J. W., 74 n.39
Lever, Tresam, 188 n.11
Levin, Harry, 111 n.8
Lewalski, Barbara K., 25 n.10
Lewis, C. S., 92 n.2
Lewis, Janette Seaton, 185 n.1
*Little Catechism* (Beza), 20
Llen, Philip, 181, 182
*Loci Communes* (Peter Martyr), 26
   n.12
Lodge, Edmund, 190 n.43
Lodge, Thomas, 37

Lombard, Peter, 68 n.4
Loomis, Roger S., 28 n.33
Lotspeich, H. G., 68 n.2
Lovell, Thomas, 10
Lowell, James Russell, 24 n.3
Lownes, Mathewe, 147
Luborsky, Ruth S., 30 n.57, 144
    n.8
Lucretia, 140, 141
Lucretius, 97, 98, 99, 100, 102, 136
Luther, Martin, 20, 73 n.29, 74
    n.37
Lycidas (Milton), 22

MacCaffrey, Isabel, 85, 93 n.8
MacGregor, Duncan, 76 n.45
MacLachlan, Hugh, 27 n.22
MacLure, Millar, 77, 78, 82 n.2
McLane, Hugh, 29 n.41
McLane, Paul, 24 n.4
McNeir, Waldo F., 111 n.8
Maier, Bruno, 67 n.2, 111 n.14
Mannyng, Robert, of Brunne, 10
Marguerite of Navarre, 38, 41, 42,
    43, 44, 45, 46, 47, 49, 55, 57, 61,
    62, 69 n.14, 70 nn.15, 17; 71
    nn.17, 18; 72 n.25
Marlowe, Christopher, 23, 31 n.66
Marot, Clément, 108
Marotti, Arthur F., 72 n.25, 73
    n.31
Marten, Anthonie, 26 n.12
Martyr, Peter, 25–26 n.12
Mary I, 7, 20, 26 n.19, 79
Massinger, Arthur, 167
Mathew, [Edward], 189 nn.20, 21;
    190 n.39
Mathew, Edmund, 165, 169, 170,
    174, 175, 176, 177, 179, 180, 181,
    182, 183, 184, 189 n.27
Mathew, Henry, 177
Mathew, Sir Tobie, 185 n.1, 190
    n.33
Mathew, William, 176, 177, 189
    nn.29, 30
Menelaus, 98
Milton, John, 21, 22, 145 n.17
Milward, Peter, 27 n.27
Miner, Earl, 68 n.5, 69 n.9, 143 n.4

Minturno, Antonio Sebastiano, 130,
    145 n.17
Miola, Robert S., 72 n.25
Miroir de l'âme pécheresse
    (Marguerite of Navarre), 41
Modest Enquiry . . . A(Henry
    More), 31 n.60
Monroe, Robert D., 112 n.18
Montylard, Jean de, 73 n.32
More, Henry, 22
Morley, Henry, 163 n.17
Mornay, Phillippe de, 108, 112
    n.18, 140
Munday, Anthony, 95, 105, 107,
    109–110 n.3
Murtaugh, Daniel M., 93 n.7
Musculus of Bern, 25 n.12
Myrrha, 86

"Naive und Sentimentalische
    Dictung" (Schiller), 143 n.3
Narcissus, 120, 124
Nashe, Thomas, 14
Nayler, William, the Elder, 181
Neely, Carol T., 73 n.33
Nelson, William, 25 n.7
Neuse, Richard, 76 n.48
Newman, John Henry, 4
Nichols, John, 171, 189 n.22
Nietzsche, Friedrich W., 143 n.4
Noble art of venerie (Gascoigne), 48,
    69 n.13
Noble, James, 75 n.44
Nohrnberg, James, 123, 124, 127
    nn.8, 14
Nonney, John, 179
Noot, Jan van der, 18, 19
Norbrook, David, 23 n.2, 25 n.6,
    27 nn.20, 28
Northbrooke, John, 10

Oakeshott, Walter, 31 n.61
Odes (Horace), 35, 68 n.6
Odyssey, 97
    IV, 566–568, 111 n.10
    VI, 43–45, 111 n.9
Oecolampadius, Johannes, 20
O'Farrell, Brian, 188 n.11
Olive (Du Bellay), 58

Orgel, Stephen, 73 n.32
Origen, 48, 74 n.35
Orlando furioso (Ariosto), 87, 91, 93
    n.12
Orpheus, 120, 127 n.11, 131, 136
Osborne, Thomas, 109 n.2
Osgood, C. G., 23 n.1, 68 n.2, 106
Oswald, Hilton C., 73 n.29
Ovid, 86, 88, 133

Padelford, F. M., 23 n.1, 24 n.3,
    95, 96, 102, 105, 107, 108, 109,
    109 n.2, 110 nn.3, 4, 6; 111
    nn.16, 17; 112 nn.18, 19, 21, 22,
    24, 25, 27, 28; 144 n.12
Page, William, 21
Pageant of Popes, A (Studley, trans.
    Bale), 82 n.6
Panofsky, Erwin, 116, 117, 125
    nn.2, 4
Pantzer, Katherine F., 30 n.51
Parker, Kenneth, 27 n.26
Parker, Matthew, 50
Parlement of Foules (Chaucer), 100,
    101
Parr, Anne (first wife to William
    Herbert, 1st Earl of Pembroke),
    190 n.43
Parr, Queen Catherine, 17
Patterson, Annabel, 163 n.16
Pearson, A. F. Scott, 29 n.49
Penthouse, 119
Petrarch, 18, 33, 34, 35, 61, 62 n.1,
    85, 118
Pfaff, Richard, 75 n.44
Phoebus, 133
Phoenix Nest, The, 69 n.12
Pierce Penilesse His Supplication to the
    Divell (Nashe), 14
Piers, John, Bishop of Salisbury, 16
Piers Plowman, 12, 13, 16
Pindar, 145 n.17
Pineas, Rainer, 27 n.20
Plaine Mans Path-way to
    Heaven . . . (Dent), 14
Plato, 116, 125 n.3, 130, 131, 132,
    142, 143 n.2, 145 n.13
Pleasaunt Dialogue . . . (Gilby), 28
    n.33

Pliny, 47
Plowman's Tale, The (Chaucer),
    13–14
Pocock, J. G. A., 163 n.15
Poetices liber septem (Scaliger), 134
Poinssot, Louis, 73 n.28
Pollard, A. W., 30 n.51
Ponsonby, William, 42
Prescott, Anne Lake, 70 n.15, 74
    n.39, 76 n.48
Prestwich, Menna, 25 n.12
proceeding in the harmonie of King
    Davids harpe, A (Strigelius), 52
Procopius, 49
Provost, G. Foster, 111 n.8
Psyche, 92 n.2
Puech, Henri-Charles, 73 n.28, 75
    n.43
Puttenham, George, 41

Quinn, David B., 162 n.3
Quitslund, Jon A., 67 n.1

Raban Maur, 74 n.35
Ralegh, Carew, 31 n.61
Ralegh, Sir Walter, 22, 31 n.61
Rasmussen, Carl J., 29 n.48, 77, 78,
    82 n.4
Rathmell, J. C. A., 82 n.8, 185 n.1
Redgrave, G. R., 30 n.51
Regius, Urbanus, 20
Reither, James A., 81 n.1, 93 n.11
Renwick, W. L, 24 n.3, 29 n.49,
    162 n.1
Rescuynge of the Romishe
    Foxe . . . (Turner), 26 n.19
Richmond, Duchess of, 20
Ricks, Don, 72 n.25
Ringler, William A., Jr., 27 n.29,
    28 n.39, 30 n.50
Roberts, Josephine A., 185 n.1
Robinson, F. N., 28 n.34, 111 n.13
Robinson, Forrest G., 140 143 n.1,
    144 n.5, 145 nn.14, 15
Robinson, R., 52
Roche, Thomas P., Jr., 85, 92 n.2,
    93 nn.6, 15; 94 n.17, 122, 124,
    125 n.1, 127 n.13
Roland, 35

Rollins, Hyder E., 69 n.12

St. Ambrose, 74 n.35
St. Augustine, 48, 51, 68 n.4
St. Eustace, 35
St. George, 75 n.41
St. Jerome, 50, 51
Salisbury, Marquess of, 189 n.31
Sampson, Richard, Bishop of
    Chichester, 50
Sandison, Helen E., 66 n.11
Sarum Missal, 33, 43, 49, 53–57,
    60, 74 n.39, 75 nn.41, 44, 45; 76
    n.45
Sasso, Pamfilo, 36
Saulnier, V.-L., 76 n.47
Scaliger, Julius Caesar, 130, 131,
    134, 135, 136, 137, 142, 144-145
    n.12, 145 n.17
Schilders, Richard, 19
Schiller, Friedrich von, 130, 143 n.3
Schless, Edmeé de M., 76 Ackn.
Schoeck, Richard, 28 n.34
Scott, Janet C., 68 n.2
Second Helvetic Confession
    (Bullinger), 25 n.11
"Sermon on the Plowers"
    (Latimer), 13
Sermon upon the Parable of the Sower
    (Gifford), 14
Seymour, Edward, Duke of
    Somerset, 17, 20
Shakespeare, William, 44
Shepherd, Geoffrey, 143 n.5
Shepherd, Luke, 28 n.33
Sheppeard, Sallye Jeannette, 185 n.1
short yet sound commentary, A
    . . . (Wilcox), 49, 73 n.32
Sidney, Lady Barbara (wife to Sir
    Robert), 169, 187 n.6, 188 n.15
Sidney, Sir Henry, 172, 182, 186
    n.6
Sidney, Sir Philip, 2, 12, 14, 15, 18,
    25 n.11, 28 n.39, 77, 79–81, 126
    n.7, 129, 130, 135, 136, 137, 138,
    139, 140, 141, 142, 143, 143
    nn.1, 5; 145 nn.13, 17; 184, 189
    n.23
Sidney, Sir Robert, 167, 168, 169,

177, 186–187 n.6, 187 nn.8, 9,
    10; 188 nn.15, 16, 17; 190 n.32
Siegenthaler, David, 27 n.24
Silvia, 36
Simpson, Evelyn, 31 n.61
Simpson, Percy, 31 n.61
Sims, Dwight J., 92 n.2
Sinfield, Alan, 24 n.2, 25 n.10
Singleton, Charles S., 125 n.5
Singleton, Hugh, 18, 19, 20, 21, 29
    n.49, 30 n.51, 31 n.57
Smith, G. G., 26 n.18, 70 n.16
Smith, J. C., 144 n.7
Smith, W. J., 188 n.11
Socrates, 96
Spencer, Roger, 178, 179, 190 n.35
Spenser (characters)
    Acrasia's bower, 96, 101, 108
    Aemylia, 119
    Agape, 123, 124
    Algrind, 10, 15, 16, 17, 29 n.41
    Amoret, 35, 36, 119, 122, 123
    Arthegall, 85, 119
    Arthur, 83, 84, 85, 116, 118, 119
    Ate, 119
    Bellona, 133
    Blatant Beast, 125
    Bower of Bliss, 34, 99, 100, 108,
        111 n.8
    Britomart, 85, 90, 93 n.7, 94
        n.17, 118, 119, 120, 122, 123
    Busyrane, 35, 123
    Calidore, 125
    Cambella, 116, 123
    Canacee, 123
    Colin Clout, 15, 77–78, 80, 125,
        131, 133
    Cuddie, 22, 23, 131, 132, 133,
        134, 135, 144 n.11
    Cupid, Temple of, 36
    Cymodoce, 116, 122, 123, 124
    Diggon Davie, 6, 10, 11, 13, 15
    Eudoxus, 154, 155, 157, 158,
        159, 161
    False Florimell, 119
    Fame, 77
    Fisherman, the, 84, 87–88, 89–90,
        91, 93 n.11, 94 n.16
    Florimell, 83–94, 115–127

Garden of Adonis, 111 n.8
Guyon, 71 n.21, 83, 84, 116
Hobbinol, 11, 15
House of Mammon, 71 n.21
House of Pride, 77
Irenius, 152, 154, 155, 157, 158,
    159, 161
Malbecco, 85, 86, 93 n.7
Marinell, 85, 89–90, 91, 92, 93
    nn.7, 15; 115–127
Morrell, 17
Neptune, 122
Orgoglio, 83, 91
Orgueil, 42, 71 n.19
Palinode, 9, 11
Palmer, 84
Paridell, 118
Piers, 1, 9, 10, 11, 12, 13, 15–16,
    22, 23, 131, 133, 135
Poena, 118, 119
Proserpina, 124
Proteus, 84, 89–90, 91, 92 n.2, 93
    nn.11,15; 94 n.16, 115–116,
    118, 120, 121, 122, 123
Redcross Knight, 83, 84, 91
Roffy, 6, 11, 15
Rumour, 77
Sansloy, 87
Satyrane, 94 n.17, 119
Sclaunder, 119
Scudamor, 36, 69 n.11, 118, 123
Serena, 85, 93 n.7
Sir Burbon, 41
Squire of Dames, 118
Thames and Medway, 120
Thomalin, 6, 13, 15, 16, 29 n.41
Timias, 118
Triamond, 116, 123, 124
Tryphan, 120
Una, 83, 84, 87, 88, 89, 91
Venus, 118, 120
Venus, Temple of, 118
Whore of Babylon, 77
Verlame, 77–78, 80, 81
Witel's son, 118
Spenser, Edmund
    Amoretti, 3, 75 n.39
        35, 76 n.49
        44, 127 n.11

        64, 75 n.44
        67–70, 33–76
        78, 35
        88, 73 n.33
        89, 73 n.33
    Astrophel and Stella, 117, 118
    Epithalamion, 41, 51, 56, 59, 60,
        75 n.45
    Faerie Queene, 22, 23, 27 n.22
        I.5, 87
        II, 35, 107–108
        II.3.13, 43
        II.7.62, 43
        III, 83–94
        III.12.38, 35
        III.12.44, 36
        IV.6.19–22, 119
        IV.10.55, 36
        IV.12, 115–127
        V.2.29–54, 22
        VII.7.35:9, 31 n.63
    Hymn of Beavtie, 119
    Hymn of Love, 119
    Mother Hubberds Tale, 7
    Mutabilitie Cantos, 22
    Prothalamion, 81
    Ruines of Rome, The, 44
    Ruines of Time, The, 77–82
    Shepheardes Calender, The, 1, 2, 3,
        6, 7, 8, 15, 18, 19–20, 21, 22,
        23, 25 n.5, 28 n.40, 130–136
    View of the Present State of Ireland,
        A, 147–163
Spenser, "Edw.", 95, 109 n.1
Spiritus est vicarius Christi in tera
    (Northbrooke), 27 n.31
Spyrytuall and Moost Precyouse
    Pearle, A (Werdmueller), 20
Starnes, De Witt T., 112–113 n.31
Steadman, John M., 145 n.17
Stein, Harold, 27 n.20
Stewart, Stanley, 111 n.8
Stockwood, John, 10
Stradling, Sir Edward, 189 n.30
Strigelius, Victorinus, 52
Stuart, Prince Henry, 171
Stubbes, Philip, 10, 30 nn.50, 56
Stubbs, John, 19, 21, 30 n.50
Studley, John, 77

Sutherland, Duke of, 27 n.25
Svensson, Lars-Håken, 69 n.11
Swan, Marshall W. S., 95, 107, 110
  n.3, 112 n.26
Sydney, Harry (of Norfolk), 188
  n.15
*Symposium* (Plato), 116

Talbert, Ernest William, 113 n.31
Talbot, Lady Anne (wife of William
  Herbert, 1st Earl of Pembroke),
  190 n.43
Talbot, Lady Catherine (wife of
  Henry Herbert, 2nd Earl of
  Pembroke), 190 n.43
Talbot, Francis, Lord Talbot, 190
  n.43
Talbot, Gilbert, Earl of
  Shrewsbury, 165, 170, 182, 184,
  190 n.43
*Tamburlaine the Great,* Part 2
  (Marlowe), 31 n.66
Tasso, Torquato, 33, 34, 35, 37,
  61, 67 n.2, 68 nn.2, 4; 97, 100,
  101, 102, 111 nn.8, 14
Tayler, Edward W., 76 Ackn.
Taylor, Jerome, 28 n.34
Taylor, Robert H., 186 n.3
*Theatre for Worldlings* (Van der
  Noot), 18
*Thesaurus* (Cooper), 140
*Thesaurus graecae linguae* (Estienne),
  108
Thiebaux, Marcelle, 68 nn.5, 7; 69
  nn.9, 13; 73 n.28
Thomas, Robert, 179
Thompson, Charlotte, 71 n.21
*Three proper wittie familiar Letters*
  (Spenser and Harvey) 22, 144 n.8
Titian, 116, 117
Tolman, A. H., 24 n.3
Topsell, Edward, 73 n.30
Tottel, Richard, 21
Traherne, John Montgomery, 189
  n.30
*Traveiler of Jerome Turler, The,* 28
  n.40
*Trewnesse of the Christian Religion*

(Mornay), 140
Turberville, George, 69 n.13
Turner, William, 6, 7, 26 n.19, 27
  n.20
Tyrone, Earl of, 188 n.15

Udale, John, 188 n.11
Uhlig, Claus, 68 n.5
Upton, John, 97

Valerianus (G. P. V. Balzani), 49,
  73 n.32
Van der Noot, Jan, 29 n.48
Van Dorsten, Jan, 29 n.48
Vellutello, Alessandro, 34, 62 n.1
Venus, 116, 117, 124
Vergil, 35, 111 n.8, 132
Vermigli, Pietro Martire (Peter
  Martyr), 4

Waldegrave, Robert, 19
Wall, John N., Jr., 27 nn.22, 24
Wallace, Dewey D., Jr., 25 n.10, 28
  n.38
Waller, Gary, 175, 185 n.1, 189
  n.28
Walsingham, Frances, Countess of
  Essex (widow of Sir Philip
  Sidney), 169, 186 n.5, 188 n.15
Walsingham, Sir Francis, 4, 18, 19,
  177
Warton, Thomas, 22, 97
Warwick, Lady, 167
Weatherby, Harold, 74 nn.36, 39;
  75 n.41
Webbe, William, 6
Wedderburn, John, 70 n.17
Weiner, Andrew D., 25 n.11, 29
  nn.44, 46, 47; 137, 144 n.5, 145
  n.13
Wells, William, 31 n.66, 179
Welsdalius, Rayanus, 102, 103, 104,
  105, 106, 107, 108, 109
Werdmueller, Otto, 20
Whitaker, Virgil, 3, 24 n.3, 25 n.10
Whitgift, John, Archbishop of
  Canterbury, 5, 16
Whyte, Harry, 186 n.6
Whyte, John, 186 n.6

Whyte, Rowland, 167, 169, 186
n.6, 187 nn.9, 10, 11; 188 nn.15,
16, 17
Wilcox, Thomas, 49, 73 n.32
Wiliems, Thomas, of Trefriw, 186
n.2
Williams, Kathleen, 89, 92 n.2
Williams, Morgan, 178, 179, 190
n.35
Williams, Penry, 186 n.5, 189 n.29
Williams, Thomas, 179
Wilson, J. Dover, 30 n.52
Winstanley, W., 24 n.3
Wittreich, Joseph A., Jr., 31 n.59
Wolfe, Don M., 31 n.58
*Works* (Gorges), 72 n.23
Wotton, Sir Edward (Lord
Wotton), 171, 174, 178, 189 n.23
Wraghton, William, 26 n.19

Wright, Celeste Turner, 95, 96,
107, 110 n.3, 112 n.26
Wyatt, Sir Thomas, 33, 34, 62 n.1
Wynne, Beth, 185 n.1

Xenophon, 139

Yeats, W. B., 149, 153
*Yet a Course at the Romyshe Foxe*
(Bale), 26 n.19
Young, Frances, 165, 170, 175, 184,
185 n.1, 189 nn.20, 21 24, 28;
190 n.43
Young, John, Bishop of Rochester,
2, 3, 15, 28 n.40, 29 n.44

Zwingli, Ulrich, 4, 25 n.11

# Contents of Previous Volumes

## VOLUME I (1980)

"Quietnesse of Minde":
*A Theatre for Worldlings* as a Protestant Poetics
CARL J. RASMUSSEN

The Allusive Presentation of *The Shepheardes Calender*
RUTH SAMSON LUBORSKY

On Reading *The Shepheardes Calender*
BRUCE R. SMITH

The Final Emblem of *The Shepheardes Calender*
JUDITH M. KENNEDY

The Drama of *Amoretti*
ALEXANDER DUNLOP

Babbling Will in *Shake-speares Sonnets* 127 to 154
MARGRETA DE GRAZIA

The "carelesse heauens":
A Study of Revenge and Atonement in *The Faerie Queene*
HUGH MacLACHLAN

The Art of Veiling in the Bower of Bliss
ANTOINETTE B. DAUBER

Canto Structure in Tasso and Spenser
MAREN-SOFIE RØSTVIG

## VOLUME II (1981)

The Illustrations to *The Shepheardes Calender*
RUTH SAMSON LUBORSKY

Supplantation in the Elizabethan Court:
The Theme of Spenser's February Eclogue
RONALD B. BOND

Interpreting Spenser's February Eclogue:
Some Contexts and Implications
LOUIS ADRIAN MONTROSE

Elizabeth, Bride and Queen: A Study of Spenser's April Eclogue
and the Metaphors of English Protestantism
L. STALEY JOHNSON

The Medieval Sources of Spenser's Occasion Episode
DAVID W. BURCHMORE

The Houses of Mortality in Book II of *The Faerie Queene*
WALTER R. DAVIS

*Daphnaida* and Spenser's Later Poetry
WILLIAM A. ORAM

"How Weak Be the Passions of Woefulness":
Spenser's *Ruines of Time*
CARL J. RASMUSSEN

"And nought of *Rome* in *Rome* perceiu'st at all":
Spenser's *Ruines of Rome*
ANDREW FICHTER

"Un certo amoroso martire": Shakespeare's "The Phoenix
and the Turtle" and Giordano Bruno's *De gli eroici furori*
ROY T. ERIKSEN

"Some Other Figure":
The Vision of Change in *Flowres of Sion*, 1623
SIBYL LUTZ SEVERANCE

"The Onely Perfect Vertue":
Constancy in Mary Wroth's *Pamphilia to Amphilanthus*
ELAINE V. BEILIN


**VOLUME III (1982)**


Spenser's Study of English Syllables
and Its Completion by Thomas Campion
SETH WEINER

The Georgics in *The Faerie Queene*
ANDREW V. ETTIN

"Pourd out in Loosnesse"
HAROLD L. WEATHERBY

Isis Versus Mercilla: The Allegorical Shrines in
Spenser's Legend of Justice
DONALD V. STUMP

Language and Politics: A Note on Some Metaphors
in Spenser's *A View of the Present State of Ireland*
EAMON GRENNAN

Tarquin, Juliet, and other *Romei*
DONALD CHENEY

Philisides and Mira:
Autobiographical Allegory in the *Old Arcadia*
DENNIS MOORE

*Astrophil and Stella:* A Radical Reading
THOMAS P. ROCHE, JR.

Observations on a Select Party
JOHN HOLLANDER


**VOLUME IV (1983)**

Spenser's Fortieth Birthday and Related Fictions
DONALD CHENEY

Elizabethan Fact and Spenserian Fiction
WILLIAM A. ORAM

Ralegh in Spenser's Historical Allegory
JAMES P. BEDNARZ

The Menace of Despair and Arthur's Vision, *Faerie Queene* I.9
THOMAS P. ROCHE, JR.

The Death of Guyon and the *Elizabethan Book of Homilies*
HUGH MacLACHLAN

"Fixt in heauens hight":
Spenser, Astronomy, and the Date of the *Cantos of Mutabilitie*
RUSSELL J. MEYER

"Sometimes I . . . mask in myrth lyke to a Comedy":
Spenser's *Amoretti*
ELIZABETH BIEMAN

*Fowre Hymnes:* Spenser's Retractations of Paradise
MARY I. OATES

206 SPENSER STUDIES

## VOLUME V (1984)

Abessa and the Lion: *The Faerie Queene,* I.3. 1–12
KATHRYN WALLS

The Status of Faeryland: Spenser's 'Vniust Possession'
JACQUELINE T. MILLER

Triamond, Agape, and the Fates: Neoplatonic Cosmology in
Spenser's Legend of Friendship
DAVID W. BURCHMORE

'Deuicefull Sights': Spenser's Emblematic Practice
in *The Faerie Queene,* V. 1-3
R. J. MANNING

Minims and Grace Notes: Spenser's Acidalian Vision
and Sixteenth-Century Music
SETH WEINER

The Old Theology: Spenser's Dame Nature
and the Transfiguration
HAROLD L. WEATHERBY

Politics, Precedence, and the Order of the Dedicatory
Sonnets in *The Faerie Queene*
CAROL A. STILLMAN

'Vnto My Selfe Alone': Spenser's Plenary Epithalamion
DOUGLAS ANDERSON

The Rhetoric of Fame: Stephen Hawes's Aureate Diction
SETH LERER

Spenser's 'Emblematic' Imagery: A Study of Emblematics
MASON TUNG

Autobiographical Elements in Sidney's *Astrophil and Stella*
THOMAS P. ROCHE, JR.

Sidney's Portrayal of Mounted Combat with Lances
E. MALCOLM PARKINSON

'The Gardin of Proserpina This Hight': Ruskin's
Application of Spenser and Horizons of Reception
JEFFREY L. SPEAR

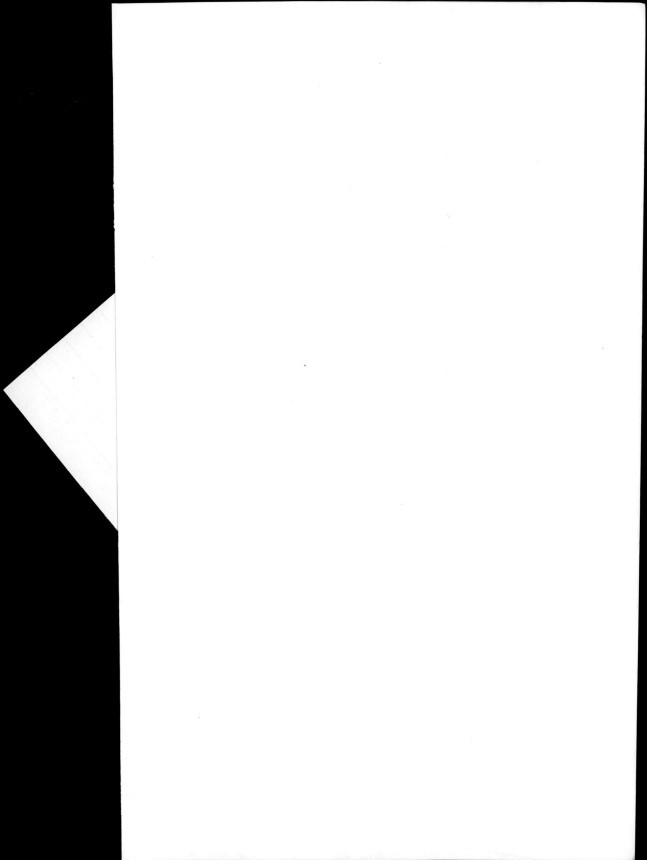

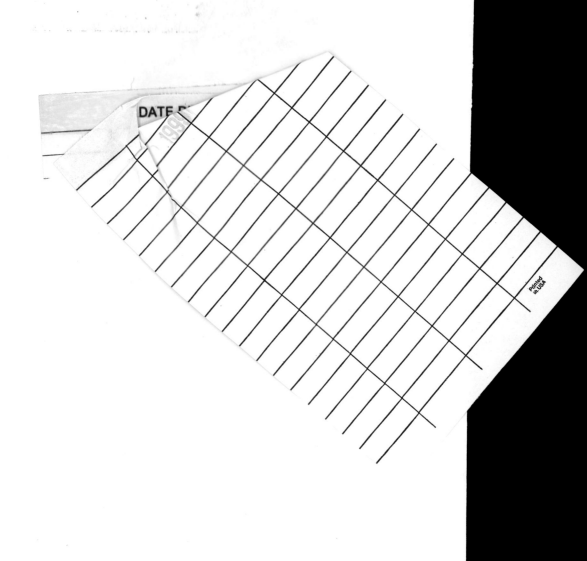

DATE

Printed
in USA